Instructor's Manual
for

Nietzel • Speltz • McCauley • Bernstein

ABNORMAL PSYCHOLOGY

Instructor's Manual
for

Nietzel • Speltz • McCauley • Bernstein

ABNORMAL PSYCHOLOGY

Prepared by

Peggy Nash
Broward Community College

Allyn and Bacon
Boston · London · Toronto · Sydney · Tokyo · Singapore

Copyright © 1998 by Allyn and Bacon
A Viacom Company
160 Gould Street
Needham Heights, Massachusetts 02194

Internet: www.abacon.com
America Online: Keyword: College Online

All rights reserved. The contents, or parts thereof, may be reproduced for use with *Abnormal Psychology* by Michael T. Nietzel, Matthew L. Speltz, Elizabeth A. McCauley and Douglas A. Bernstein, provided such reproductions bear copyright notice, but may not be reproduced in any form for any other purpose without written permission from the copyright owner.

ISBN 0-205-26281-3

Printed in the United States of America

10 9 8 7 6 5 4 3 2 1   01 00 99 98 97

Table of Contents

Chapter 1. Abnormal Behavior: Past and Present Perspectives...................1

Chapter 2. Assessment and Diagnosis...................16

Chapter 3. Disorders of Infancy, Childhood, and Adolescence...................33

Chapter 4. Developmental Disorders and Learning Disabilities...................45

Chapter 5. Stress, Sleep, and Adjustment Disorders...................54

Chapter 6. Psychological Factors and Health...................64

Chapter 7. Anxiety Disorders...................76

Chapter 8. Dissociative and Somatoform Disorders...................94

Chapter 9. Mood Disorders and Suicide...................107

Chapter 10. Schizophrenia...................131

Chapter 11. Cognitive Disorders...................146

Chapter 12. Personality Disorders...................162

Chapter 13. Substance-Related Disorders...................180

Chapter 14. Sexual and Gender Identity Disorders...................211

Chapter 15. Biological Treatment of Mental Disorders...................228

Chapter 16. Psychotherapy...................243

Chapter 17. Alternatives to Individual Psychotherapy...................265

Chapter 18. Legal and Ethical Issues in Mental Disorders...................277

PREFACE

Welcome to the resource manual to accompany *ABNORMAL PSYCHOLOGY* by Nietzel, Speltz, McCauley and Bernstein.

This manual is prepared as a tool for classroom excitement. Each chapter begins with a meaty outline of the material. Suggestions for lecture activities called Lecture Makers, follows the outline. Videos, websites, organizations, and transparencies are listed to complete the resources section.

This resource manual has been designed with the newer instructor in mind. Your knowledge base, the text, and this reference could put a dynamic course into action immediately. The material here is "pick and choose" to fit your needs. The chapter summaries can suffice as lecture notes. The Lecture Makers can serve as hands-on integration of the material, and a high point for discussion. From the Resource Section you can draw from a wealth of possible support material—including how to contact Schizophrenics Anonymous or have an E-mail chat with Albert Ellis.

The instructor having weathered many seasons of teaching abnormal psychology may not reference the chapter summaries so much, but should have fun exercising with the Lecture Makers and Resource listings.

Chapter Summary. This outline could serve as a complete set of lecture notes for class. It organizes text material into key information for handy access.

Lecture Makers. These are suggestions for activities and demonstrations that enliven concepts in each chapter. They also provide students with the opportunity to work with and apply new concepts.

Resources. This diverse section includes listings of videos, transparencies, educational films, and contacts. The contacts include address/phone/fax/e-mail for agencies, organizations or resource people that specialize in the chapter topics.

I hope you enjoy using this instructor's manual and that it is useful to you. Having taught abnormal psychology for many years, I have included the best from my experience. In here are the "never-failed-yet" exercises and resources. Any feedback or suggestions are always welcome. Enjoy!

Peggy Nash

Peggy Nash

Coconut Creek, Florida

1   Abnormal Behavior: Past and Present Perspectives

CHAPTER OUTLINE

I. Making Sense of Abnormality: A Brief History (pp. 5-11)
    A. Faraway Places, Ancient Times, and Supernatural Forces
        1. No written records prior to Egyptian and Mesopotamian cultures
            a. Archeological discoveries and interpretation of myths
            b. Trephining done to allow evil spirits to escape
        2. Ancient Chinese, Egyptian and Hebrew civilizations
            a. Blamed abnormal behavior on evil spirits and demons
            b. Divine punishment for disobedience or other misbehavior
        3. Treatment of abnormal behavior
            a. Prayer and faith healing timed with movements of planets or stars
            b. Exorcism rituals and correction of biological processes
    B. The Birth of the Medical Tradition: The Classical Period
        1. Development of formal philosophy by Greeks (600-500 B.C.E.)
            a. Belief that humans capable of understanding and controlling selves
            b. Critical analysis and observation refined (Plato and Aristotle)
            c. Plato: humans gained knowledge rationally
            d. Aristotle: analyzing *perceived* events leads to empirical method
            e. Hippocrates, "the father of medicine": restore balance
            f. Galen: refined humoral theory; prescribed *medicine*
        2. Chinese culture and philosophy of *Taoism*
            a. Proper balance between *yin* and *yang*
            b. Goal is to unify the two.
        3. Epictetus: "Men are disturbed not by *things*, but by the *view of things*
        4. Marcus Aurelius, in *Meditations*: *Opinions* lead to unhappiness
        5. Classical Period thinkers emphasize natural over supernatural causes
        6. Idea: medical doctors are experts in mental disorders leads to psychiatry
    C. From Demons to Instincts: The European Tradition
        1. Early Middle Ages: Fall of Roman Empire in A.D. 476
            a. Period of great political and economic upheaval
            b. Empiricism replaced by belief that God would reveal divine truths
            c. Contemporary mental health fields from Western European origins
            d. Middle East and Africa
                (1) Folk healers—magic, herbal medicines, and common sense
                (2) Both cultures stressed value of local community
        2. Middle Ages and the Return of Demons
            a. Christian theology grew; science less important
            b. Supernatural forces once again responsible for abnormal behavior
            c. Treatments returned to exorcisms and religious rituals

3. Greek and Roman traditions still influence
   a. Islamic physician, Avicenna, wrote *The Canon of Medicine*
      (1) Philosophical traditions—Aristotle;
      (2) Medical practices—Galen
      (3) Islamic physicians pioneered use of hospitals
   b. In Europe, monasteries served as sanctuaries
4. Late Middle Ages: A New Era
   a. Influence of Christian Church began to weaken
      (1) Church intensified search for suspected heretics and witches
      (2) Thousands tortured and burned at stake
      (3) *Malleus Maleficarum* or *Witches Hammer* published
5. Renaissance and Rise of Humanism
   a. Marked by fall of Constantinople ending the Byzantine Empire
   b. Secularization of life and values known as *humanism*
   c. Facilitated by advent of printing press
   d. *Psychological* concerns equaled or surpassed theological issues
   e. Physicians again view human body as biological machine
      (1) Descartes: explains mental activity in physical terms
      (2) Peracelsus and Weyer: naturalistic explanation of disorders
      (3) Weyer often considered first psychiatrist
         (a) Convinced brain influenced by moon
         (b) Treatment required "therapeutic relationship"
         (c) Ridiculed beliefs in witches
         (d) Condemned brutal treatment
   f. Treatment: confinement in hospitals and asylums
      (1) Not much better than Middle Ages
      (2) "Insane" treated like prisoners; abominable conditions
6. The Enlightenment and the Rise of Science
   a. Late 1800's: psychology to become a scientific discipline
   b. Chiarugi, Tuke, Rush ushered in *moral treatment era*
   c. Dorothea Dix and Clifford Beers started *moral hygiene movement*
   d. Psychiatrists believe biological disorders required medical treatment
   e. 1825: Deteriorative brain syndrome termed *general paresis*
   f. General paresis caused by syphilitic infection of brain
   g. Search to find links between mental disorders and physical causes
7. The Psychoanalytic Revolution
   a. Hypnotism (mesmerism) best remembered
      (1) Hypnotic anesthesia during surgery
      (2) Helpful in treatment of hysteria
      (3) Reawakened idea mental disorders might be psychological

    b. Sigmund Freud, Viennese neurologist
     (1) Successfully used hypnotism
     (2) Abnormal behavior caused by unconscious mental struggles
     (3) Theory of *how* and *why* these create disordered behavior
     (4) Applied theory of abnormality in *psychoanalysis*
    c. New mental health profession: *clinical psychology*
     (1) Devoted to scientifically studying mental disorders
     (2) Assessing, diagnosing, and treating them
  D. Contemporary Approaches to Abnormality
   1. Models of abnormality—how and why behavior develops
   2. Which aspects most important to study—overt behavior or thoughts
   3. Treatment methods most likely to succeed—exorcism, drugs, talking
   4. Western culture—biological, physiological, sociocultural, diathesis-stress
II. The Biological Model (pp.11-18)
  A. The Nervous System and Abnormality
   1. *Biological Model*
    a. *Nervous system* controls all thought and behavior
    b. Changes in neural functioning triggered by *biological* factors
    c. Biological treatments (drugs) change patient's physical condition
   2. *Medical model*
    a. Involves *symptoms—etiological factors*
    b. Symptoms form pattern known as *syndrome*
    c. Medical model seeks biochemical or physical cause of syndrome
    d. Expanded greatly due to research in *neuroscience*
   3. *Central nervous system(CNS)*—brain (hind-mid-fore) and spinal cord
   4. *Peripheral nervous system(PNS)*—somatic and autonomic
   5. *Somatic(SNS)*—voluntary control of muscles
   6. *Autonomic nervous system*—motivational, emotional, and physical
   7. *ANS*—sympathetic and parasympathetic
    a. *Sympathetic nervous system*—fight or flight response
    b. *Parasympathetic nervous system*—decreases arousal
   8. Spinal cord links parasympathetic nervous system with brain
    a. *Hindbrain*—medulla, reticular formation, cerebellum
    b. *Midbrain*—coordinates head and eye movements, responses stimuli
    c. *Forebrain*—thalamus hypothalamus(of *limbic system*), cerebrum
    d. *Hypothalamus* responds to *hormones* from *endocrine system*
    e. Hypothalamus connects to *pituitary gland* (key elements in stress)
    f. *Cerebrum* and outer covering, *cerebral cortex (*divided into *lobes)*
    g. *CAT* scans, *MRI* scans, *PET* scans—ways of watching brain work
   9. *Neurotransmitters* carry messages between *neurons* (nerve cells)
    a. Neurotransmitters from *axon*, across *synapse*, contact *dendrites*
    b. Neurotransmitter *acetylcholine*—learning, memory, and sleep
    c. Neurotransmitter *norepinephrine*—increase heart rate, respiration

B. Genetic Influences and Abnormality
1. *Gene*—basic unit of heredity—strands of *deoxyribonucleic acid (DNA)*
   a. At conception 23 pairs *chromosomes*—half father's, half mother's
   b. Each gene rests at *locus*
   c. DNA—*nucleotides*—sugar, phosphate, base containing nitrogen
2. At locus, alternative forms—*alleles* (one father's, one mother's) inherited
   a. If alleles alike—person *homozygous* for that gene
   b. If alleles different—person *heterozygous* for that gene
   c. *Recessive* alleles—only when paired—similar alleles both parents
   d. *Dominant* alleles—expressed whenever present
3. *Polygenic inheritance*—involving multiple, interacting genes
4. *Penetrance*—degree predisposition is expressed
5. *Phenylketonuria (PKU)* disorder caused by malfunction of single gene
6. *Genotype*—genetic makeup   *Phenotype*—characteristics displayed
7. *Nature*—genetic endowment   *Nurture*—environmental factors
8. *Behavior Genetics*—study of genetic influences on behavior
   a. *Family studies*—pattern of disorder in members of same family
   b. *Monozygotic twins* share 100% genes—*dizygotic twins* only 50%
9. *Huntington's disease* caused by single dominant gene
10. *Kuru* thought to be genetic but is not
11. *Adoption* studies—traits more like biological parents
12. *Twin studies*
    a. Similar traits in identical twins reared apart
    b. Evidence in children's temperament and personality

III. Psychological and Sociocultural Models (pp. 18-29)
A. Psychodynamic Theories
1. Freud's *psychoanalysis*—behaviors influenced by *unconscious forces*
2. Sexual or aggressive instincts at war with moral demands of society
3. Freudian Personality Structures
   a. *Id*—most basic, unconscious instincts (food, water)
      (1) Provides energy called *libido*
      (2) Operates on *pleasure principle*
   b. *Ego*—self develops in response to cultural limits
      (1) Ego operates on *reality principle*
      (2) Ego seeks rational compromises between Id and culture
   c. *Superego*—insists on socially acceptable behavior
4. Constant conflicts among the id, ego, and superego cause guilt, anxiety, etc
   a. Ego employs *defense mechanisms*
      (1) *Repression*—motivated forgetting
      (2) *Regression*—retreat to primitive behavior

5. Stages of Psychosexual Development
    a. *Oral stage*—first year
        (1) Eating, sucking, biting main source of pleasure
        (2) Oral needs neglected or overindulged, can become *fixated*
    b. *Anal stage*—second year
        (1) Elimination and retention of feces focus of pleasure
        (2) Toilet training critical feature
    c. *Phallic stage*—third or fourth year
        (1) Genitals focus of pleasure
        (2) *Oedipus complex* from Greek tragedy *Oedipus Rex*
        (3) *Identification* (boys) *Penis Envy* (girls) resolves
    d. *Latency period*—fifth or sixth year
        (1) Oedipus complex resolved
        (2) Focus on academic skills and same-sex friends
    e. *Genital stage*—adolescence
        (1) Not selfishness of phallic stage
        (2) Love and long-term relationships
6. Contemporary Psychodynamic Theories
    a. Theorists suggested revisions to Freud's theories
    b. Carl Jung altered or rejected principles
    c. Alfred Adler—*style of life*—child pursues superiority
    d. Adaptive lifestyles characterized by *social interest*
    e. Erik Erikson—eight stages of *psychosocial development*
    f. *Object relations theory*—failure to achieve adequate separation leads to personality problems in adulthood
7. Psychoanalytic Treatment
    a. Goal—insight into unconscious origins of behavior
    b. *Free association*—say whatever comes into mind
    c. *Interpretation of* dreams, slips of tongue, and mistakes
    d. *Transference*—reliving of emotional reactions
    e. *Ego analysts*—people more capable of controlling behavior
    f. *Object relations therapists*—therapeutic relationships repair

B. Behavioral Theories
    1. Also called *learning theories*—how people *learn* to behave
    2. *Operant* theorists—rewards and punishment
    3. *Respondent*—stimuli and responses
    4. *Cognitive-behavioral:* consequences and expectations acquired
    5. Operant Conditioning
    6. Thorndike—learning follows *law of effect*
        a. Skinner—*antecedent conditions and consequences*
        b. Behavior strengthened through *reinforcement*
        c. Being paid to work—*positive reinforcement*
        d. Take aspirin, get rid of headache—*negative reinforcement*

          e.   *Punishment*—negative consequences
          f.   *Extinction*—absence of any notable consequences
          g.   *Schedules of reinforcement*—key to understanding behavior
     7.   Classical Conditioning
          a.   Pavlov—behavior based on reflexes
          b.   *Unconditioned stimulus*—food;—neutral stimulus—tone
          c.   *Unconditioned response*—salivation;—neutral stimulus—tone
          d.   Eventually—*conditioned stimulus; conditioned response*
          e.   "Little Albert"—learned fear
     8.   Behavioral Treatment
          a.   Also known as *behavior therapy* or *behavior modification*
          b.   Focus is on here and now
          c.   Interventions aimed at measurable changes
C.   Cognitive Theories
     1.   Observers say operant or classical conditioning ignores what one *thinks*
     2.   Cognitive or social learning theories developed (cognitive revolution) 60's
     3.   Theories include operant, classical *plus* perceptions, thoughts, memories
     4.   Important Cognitive Processes:
          a.   Bandura emphasizes *observational learning*, from *models*
          b.   Rouse: new responses, inhibit, disinhibit already learned responses
          c.   Rotter: (expectancies), probability behavior will occur depends on
                (1)   What person has learned to expect
                (2)   Value person places on outcome
                (3)   *Self-efficacy*, belief one can successfully perform behavior
          d.   *Appraisals*—evaluations of one's own and others' behavior
          e.   *Attributions*—explanations for behavior
                (1)   *Internality*—is it about ourselves or the environment?
                (2)   *Stability*—is the cause enduring or temporary?
                (3)   *Globalness*—is it specific to situation or all situations?
          f.   Ellis—role of *irrational beliefs* associated with "should" statements
     5.   Cognitive and Social-Learning Therapies
          a.   Give new information, correct misconceptions
          b.   Change the way they think about themselves, people, world
          c.   Ellis—*rational-emotive therapy*
D.   Phenomenological Theories
     1.   Also known as *humanistic model*
          a.   Behavior determined by person's *perceptions*
          b.   Perceptions allow emotionally effective life
          c.   Perceptions create excessive desire to meet others' expectations
     2.   Carl Rogers' Self Theory
          a.   People have innate drive for *self-actualization*
          b.   All experiences are positive or negative from that outlook
          c.   In childhood, *conditions of worth*—only if behavior is approved

    3. Abraham Maslow and Humanistic Psychology
      a. Failure for full potential is caused by unmet needs
      b. Lower levels of needs met before self-actualization
    4. Phenomenological Therapies
      a. Create a context in which clients feel free to explore potential
      b. Help client express full range of emotions
  E. Interpersonal Theory
    1. Sullivan—interaction styles so rigid they become maladaptive
    2. Relationships so disturbed, interactions impossible
    3. *Interpersonal*, rather than psychosexual stages
    4. Rule of *reciprocity*
    5. Accounts well for *personality disorders*
  F. The Sociocultural Model
    1. Also known as *ecological model*
    2. Emphasizes *external* not internal factors
    3. Harmful environments, social policies, cultural traditions, powerlessness
    4. *Epidemiological studies*—patterns and frequency of disorders related
    5. Social Causation *(theory)*—stress, poverty, racism, inferior education, unemployment, and social changes as risk factors
    6. Social Drift *(social selection hypothesis)*—higher rates of disorders in lower socioeconomic groups due to the disorders
    7. Social Relativism— standards of abnormal do not apply in all cultures
      a. *Koro*— Southeast Asia—penis will enter stomach and kill man
      b. *Windigo*—North American Indians—monsters make them cannibals
      c. *Anorexia nervosa*—Western societies—thinness as beauty criterion
    8. Social Labeling
      a. Szasz—mental illness is a myth created by medical professionals
      b. People just have " problems in living"
      c. Labels produce prejudice and discrimination
      d. *Community psychology* studies interventions
      e. *Preventing* abnormal behavior is preferable to *treating* it
IV. The Diathesis-Stress Model (pp. 29-31)
  A. Behavior disorder results from two influences
    1. *Diathesis*—a *predisposition* for that disorder
    2. *Stressor*—any event that causes a person to adjust to it
  B. Stressors are the triggers to convert predisposition to actual disorder
  C. Does not assume only one cause per disorder; factors from all fields can contribute
  D. May be impossible to say *exactly* what causes some behavior disorders
  E. *Developmental psychopathology*—problems in childhood linked to disorders later
  F. Advocates suggest treatment must include combination of techniques
    1. Psychotherapy and medication for anxiety and depression
    2. Medication and community support programs for schizophrenics
    3. Implications for how best to *prevent* disorder

V. Scientific Methods and Models of Abnormality (pp. 31-34)
    A. *Hypothesis*—propositions describing how two or more variables are connected
    B. *Theory*—propositions to predict and explain certain phenomena
    C. *Operational definition*—equates a concept with method used to measure it
    D. *Correlational Research*
        1. Correlation—measure of degree to which one variable is related to another
        2. *Positively correlated*—variables change together in the same direction
        3. *Negatively correlated*—variables move in opposite directions
        4. If correlation is large, knowing one variable allows for predictions of other
        5. Correlations cannot inform *why* two variables correlated
        6. Cannot establish one variable *caused* the other
    E. Experiments
        1. Researcher manipulates one variable; measures effect on second variable
            a. *Independent variable*—variable that is manipulated
            b. *Dependent variable*—variable that is observed
            c. People in *experimental group* receive treatment
            d. People in *control group* receive no treatment
            e. *Random assignment* of subjects is vital
            f. *Confounding variables* act to confuse or distort results
            g. Was difference due to treatment or *expectations?*
            h. *Experimenter's* expectations may give motivation to improve
            i. Expectations causing improvement—*placebo effect*
            j. *Placebo control group* gets phony treatment
            k. *Double-blind study*—only director knows who is placebo group
    F. Quasi-Experiments
        1. Study that resembles a true experiment
        2. Lacks one or more of the elements of a true experiment
        3. Subjects not randomly assigned or variables not manipulated or no control
        4. If subject to replication—researcher gains confidence in results
    G. Human Diversity and Research Methods
        1. Replication of results is important
            a. How well do results represent people in general?
            b. Apply to men and women; Black and White and Asian ?
        2. *Sampling* is important
            a. Methods used for selecting research participants
            b. Ideal—utterly random sampling from all people of earth
            c. *Representative samples* represent all levels of variables
                (1) Age
                (2) Gender
                (3) Ethnicity
    H. Resolving Controversy Through Scientific Methods
        1. Each study provides part of an answer
        2. Studies raise new questions and controversies
        3. Theories constantly being tested, revised, abandoned, and refined
        4. Field without uncertainty and controversy; field without progress

1   Abnormal Behavior: Past and Present Perspectives

LECTURE MAKER 1.1

Purpose   To provide historical accounts of acceptable and unacceptable behavior (pp. 3-7)

Resource   The Bible. Leviticus
Bring the book to class. Bookmark your resource with notes for smooth transitions.

Lecture Introduction   Review the history of abnormal behavior from Chapter 1, noting the theological interpretations and the idea of demons and the devil.

Demonstration   1. Definition of who is unacceptable, unclean, or repulsive to God:

         A.   A man with a discharge from his body (Lev: 15)

         B.   A woman with a discharge from her body, including her menstrual cycle

         C.   To cleanse these impurities, the afflicted must wait seven days, wash and bring a ritual sacrifice for a burnt offering to God.

    2. Definition of impure houses and clothes (Lev: 14)

         A.   A house with mildew/fungus is unclean and must be left for seven days. If it is still unclean the walls must be torn out and replastered. If the mildew re-appears, the house must be destroyed

         B.   Clothing with mildew is also unclean, ultimately to be burned. (Lev: 13)

    3. Definition of how to purify after soiling act of childbirth (Lev: 12)

         A.   The mother is unclean for seven days after the birth of a boy, waits 33 days and then brings a one-year-old lamb for purification through burnt sacrifice

         B.   The mother is unclean for 2 weeks after the birth of a girl, waits 66 days to begin purification ceremony

4. Definition of foods that are to be eaten or not eaten. Foods eaten determine acceptability

   A. It is acceptable to eat animals with a completely divided split hoof that chews cud. It is against God's will to eat other land animal including the camel, pig, or rabbit. From the sea, it is God's will to eat that with fins and scales only.

   B. Unclean foods make the individual unclean, unacceptable to God

5. Definition of standards of living and unlawful sexual relations (Lev: 18)

   A. Sex with animals is prohibited

   B. Homosexuality is abhorrent to God

   C. It is sinful to mate different species of animals; plant a field with two kinds of seed, or wear clothing from two types of material (Lev: 19)

   D. It is wrong to eat the fruit from any planted tree for the first four years. (Lev: 19)

   E. It is impure to eat any meat with blood still in it (Lev: 19)

   F. It is wrong to cut or mark (tattoo) the body (Lev: 19)

6. Punishment for those disobedient to God's will is ugly (Lev: 26) and includes terror, disease, fever, blindness, crop failure, destruction of flocks and herds, children taken away, and plagues.

Lecture Capsule

These examples and quotes should stimulate a great deal of discussion regarding the relative nature of normal/abnormal and acceptable/unacceptable. This is *NOT* a theological discussion, it is a historical and colorful one that students generally have some familiarity with, regardless of their personal beliefs.

LECTURE MAKER 1.2

Purpose To bring ideologies about abnormal behavior into the 1900s (pp. 5-11)

Resources An old medical text, autobiography, or nonfiction piece will be colorful. Example: Wllman, Reinhold, M.D. *Married Life: A Family Handbook* J.S. Hyland & Co. Chicago, Illinois, 1917

Lecture Introduction The transition from demonology to scientific questioning has been a bumpy one. Students often think that the level of scientific sophistication from the 1900s on has been fairly even. Introduce the scientific beginnings of psychopathology.

Demonstration Read or summarize from the turn of the century authors. Ask the students what member of their family would have been alive in 1900-1930. When a student can place the lecture information into their personal family time line, the transition in ideas and knowledge across this century becomes very impressive.

Dr. Willman's book includes:

1. The notion of "neurosis of the ovaries" caused by sexual dysfunction

2. The insistence that frigid women should not marry

3. Assurance that hysteria is caused by an over-indulgent husband

4. That nervousness is caused by unsatisfactory sexual relations

5. Treatment of depression includes ragtime music

6. Masturbation is abhorrent

7. Nature has rules for who should marry whom; they are listed

Lecture Capsule This type of "read aloud" illustration placed in a recognizable time line for students tends to provide perspective. It is also effective, at the end of the discussion, to ask, "What do you think our DSM-IV, textbooks, and journals will look like to college students 100 years from today?" There is an excellent chronological layout in the Case Study Book entitled *Major Historical Developments Related to Mental Disorder*. (introduction)

LECTURE MAKER 1.3

Purpose To highlight rational emotive therapy and provide students with the opportunity to interact with Albert Ellis (pp. 24-25)

Lecture Introduction Outline the essentials of RET, comparing irrational thoughts with rational alternative thoughts. Define catastrophizing, minimizing, globalizing, internalizing, and stabilizing. Summarize the ABCs.

      A= Activating event
      B= Beliefs
      C= Client feelings

Demonstration Present a series of irrational statements, have the students identify the type of thought process and create a rational alternative.
For example:

Irrational Thought	Type	Rational Alternative
This is the worst!	Catastrophizing	It may be bad, it could be worse, it can get better
I can't do it!	Minimizing Internalizing Globalizing	I may not be perfect but I can try. I can do other things very well.

Lecture Capsule Albert Ellis founded the Albert Ellis Institute in 1968. It is educational and not-for-profit. The institute offers referral, self-help training, and workshops. This information is free. Contact:
Albert Ellis Institute http://www.REBT.org
1-800-323-4738
Dr Ellis will also personally respond on-line to one question per month. You can review previous question/answers and submit questions from your students. This is a rare opportunity to interact with a legend.

Dr. Ellis has copyrighted a number of Rational Humorous Songs including those on the following page.

Reprinted from *A Garland of Rational Songs* with the permission of Albert Ellis Institute, 45 E. 65th Street, N.Y., N.Y. 10021

LOVE ME, LOVE ME, ONLY ME
(Tune: Yankee Doodle Dandy)
Love me, love me, only me
Or I'll die without you!
Make your love a guarantee,
So I can never doubt you!
Love me, love me totally—
really, really try, dear,
But if you demand love too,
I'll hate you til I die, dear!

Love me, love me all the time,
Thoroughly, and wholly!
Life turns into slushy slime
'Less you love me solely!
Love me with great tenderness,
With no ifs or buts, dear.
If you love me somewhat less,
I'll hate your goddamned guts, dear!

GLORY, GLORY HALLELUJAH!
(Tune: Battle Hymn of the Republic)
Mine eyes have seen the glory of
 relationships that glow
And then falter by the wayside as
 love passions come-and go!

I've heard of great romances where
There is no slightest lull—
But I am skeptical!
Glory, glory hallelujah!
People love ya till they screw ya!
If you'd cushion how they'd do ya,
Then don't expect they won't!
Glory, glory hallelujah!
People cheer ya—then pooh-pooh ya!
If you'd soften how they screw ya!
Then don't expect they won't!

I WISH I WERE NOT CRAZY
(Tune: Dixie, by Dan Emmett)
Oh, I wish I were really put together—
Smooth and fine as patent leather!
Oh, how great to be rated innately sedate!
But I'm afraid that I was fated
To be rather aberrated—
Oh, how sad to be mad
as my Mom and my Dad!

Oh, I wish I were not crazy!
Hooray, Hooray!
I wish my mind were less inclined
To be the kind that's hazy!
I could agree to really be
less crazy,
But I, alas, am just too
goddamned lazy!

WHINE, WHINE, WHINE!
(Tune: Yale Whiffnepoof Song,
 by Guy Scull- A Harvard Man!)
I cannot have all of my wishes filled—
Whine, whine, whine!
I cannot have every frustration stilled—
Whine, whine, whine!
Life really owes me the things that I miss,
Fate has to grant me eternal bliss!
And since I must settle for less than this,
Whine, whine, whine!

RESOURCES

Media *Albert Ellis: A Demonstration With a Young Divorced Woman* (1 RL, 30 min.)
Ellis' rational emotive therapy helping a woman deal with her guilt.

Three Approaches to Psychotherapy (PF1, 50 min.)
Gestalt client-centered and rational-emotive therapies are presented.

Abnormal Behavior (CRM, 26 min.)
Freud, Rogers, Maslow, and Fromm discussed as well as stress, range of abnormal behavior, and interviews with psychiatric patients.

Abnormal Behavior: A Mental Hospital (McG, 28 min.)
Documentary of a day in a psychiatric hospital.

Madness and Medicine (CRM, 49 min.)
Documentary about mental institutions, ECS, and psychosurgery.

Mental Health: New Frontiers of Sanity (EMC, 22 min.)
History of therapy and mental disorders.

Nietzel et al., *Abnormal Psychology*, Transparencies

Chapter One

		Text Figure Number	Text Page Number
1.	Organization of the Nervous System	1.1	11
2.	The Human Brain	1.2	12
3.	Major Glands in the Endocrine System	1.3	13
4.	The Synapse	1.4	15
5.	Communication Between Neurons	1.4	15
6.	The Structure of DNA	1.5	16
7.	Genes and Their Function	1.6	17
8.	Freud's View of the Human Mind: The Mental Iceberg		19
9.	Freud's Psychosexual Stages of Development		20
10.	Some Mechanisms of Behavior Change		22
11.	Pavlovian Conditioning	1.8	23
12.	The Diathesis-Stress Model of Abnormality	1.9	30
13.	The Role of Theory and Empirical Research in the Scientific Method	1.10	33

2 Assessment and Diagnosis

CHAPTER OUTLINE

I. Identifying Mental Disorders: Some Basic Issues (pp. 44-49)
   A. What Is a Mental Disorder?
      1. Past terms used—mental illness, deviant behavior, psychopathology, psychological abnormality, psychiatric illness, mental disorder
      2. This chapter and rest of book, term that mental health professionals today employ most often: *mental disorder*
      3. Mental disorder defined throughout history
         a. As a deviation from social expectations
         b. As what mental health professionals treat
         c. As subjective distress
         d. As a label for disliked actions
         e. As a dysfunction that causes harm
      4. Defining "normal" just as complicated; not a solution
      5. Disorder as Deviation from Social Expectations
         a. Deviation is in negative direction from expectations
         b. Definition ignores characteristics that are rare but a problem
         c. How rare? Schizophrenia 1% of American adults
         d. Conformity to expectations means mental health—no, not always
      6. Disorder as What Clinicians Treat
         a. Definition occasionally used in epidemiology
         b. Not everyone who consults clinician is suffering symptoms
         c. Assumes all equally likely to seek treatment—poor least likely
      7. Disorder as Subjective Distress or Unhappiness
         a. Distress alone cannot define disorder
         b. Does not distinguish between temporary and intense, unrelated
         c. Some disorders cause distress only for people *around* person
      8. Disorder as a Label
         a. Some say only labels bestowed by mental health professionals
         b. Szasz argued should be only ones traceable to organic causes
         c. Some have problems with no biological malfunction
         d. Problems often improve with treatment
      9. Disorder as Dysfunction That Causes Harm
         a. Similar to definition in DSM-IV
         b. *Dysfunction*—failure of a mechanism to operate as it should
         c. Breakdown in the way person thinks, feels, or perceives world
         d. Concept of harm refers to negative consequences
         e. This definition most workable, least arbitrary
   B. Assessment and Classification
      1. Clinical *assessment*: foundation of accurate *diagnosis* of mental disorders
      2. Three steps of assessment:
         a. Clinicians gather assessment information

    b. Organize and process information into description of person
    c. Compare description with what is known of disorders—get diagnosis
   3. Last step—*nosology*—a classification system
   4. *Diagnostic and Statistical Manual of Mental Disorders (DSM-IV)*
   5. World Health Organization's *ICD-10* for other parts of world
   6. Reliability and Validity
    a. *Reliability*—consistency or agreement among assessment data
    b. *Test-retest reliability*—many times with same results
    c. *Internal consistency*—information similar on other parts of test
    d. *Interrater reliability*—different clinicians reach same diagnosis
    e. *Validity*—degree instrument measures what it is supposed to
    f. *Content validity*—tool measures all aspects of a domain
    g. *Predictive validity*—assessment procedure accurately forecasts
    h. *Concurrent validity*—result of one procedure agrees with another
    i. *Construct validity*—results coincide with what theory predicts
    j. Reliability and validity are expressed as *correlation coefficients*
   7. Diagnostic Errors
    a. Validity of clinician's judgement is crucial.
    b. Two kinds of correct diagnostic conclusions
     (1) *True positive*—correctly concludes disorder is present
     (2) *True negative*—correctly concludes there is no disorder
    c. *Sensitivity*— person with disorder will be diagnosed as such
    d. *Specificity*—person without disorder is correctly diagnosed
    e. *False positive*—mental disorder diagnosed—there is none
    f. *False negative*—No disorder diagnosed—there is one
    g. Both errors can have severe consequences
     (1) False positive—unnecessary labeling
     (2) False negative—keep troubled people from getting help
II. Assessment Tools (pp. 49-60)
  A. Life records
    a. School grades, court records, police reports, and medical records
    b. Determine whether, when, and how often problem has occurred
  B. Interviews
    a. Personality Disorder Interview-IV
    b. *Mental Status Examination* (MSE)
  C. Psychological Tests
   1. *Psychological test*— procedure of observing and describing behavior
   2. *Standardization*—uniform procedures for all respondents
   3. Responses then compared to *norms*
   4. Tests grouped into one of five categories
    a. Achievement and aptitude—educational or training experiences
    b. Attitude and interest—preferences and values
    c. Intelligence tests—measure general mental ability

        d.   Neuropsychological—deficits in behavior, cognition, emotion
        e.   Personality—predominant personality traits and characteristics
            (1)   *Objective* tests require answers to specific questions
            (2)   *Projective* tests—person responds to stimuli

    D.   Observations
        1.   *Naturalistic*—behavior as it occurs spontaneously
        2.   *Controlled*—reactions to controlled events
        3.   *Participant*—observer may interact with clients
        4.   *Nonparticipant*—observers not in the same room
        5.   *Self-monitoring*—clients record their own behaviors
        6.   Observations highly valid if
            a.   Observed behavior must provide satisfactory example
            b.   Format must fairly represent observed behaviors
            c.   Fair representation of behavior when not observed

    E.   Biological Measures
        1.   Allow observation of changes not visible to the naked eye
        2.   Important because biological factors may explain mental disorders
        3.   *Biological markers*
            a.   Counting fat cells associated with obesity
            b.   Liver enzymes or blood cell size to detect alcoholism
            c.   Changes in immune system following stressors
            d.   Neurochemical and endocrinological changes in depression
        4.   Useful for assessing anxiety, mood, sexual, and other disorders
        5.   Most widely used study—brain and its functions
            a.   *Computerized tomography* (CT scan)
            b.   *Positron emission tomography* (PET scan)
            c.   *Single photon emission computed tomography* (SPECT)
            d.   *Magnetic resonance imaging* (MRI)
            e.   *Magnetic resonance spectroscopy* (MRS)

III.   Diagnostic Classification (pp. 60-71)
    A.   A Brief History
        1.   Emil Kraepelin, German psychiatrist-mental patients fit in three categories
            a.   *Dementia praecox* (now called schizophrenia)
            b.   *Manic-depressive psychosis* (now called bipolar disorder)
            c.   *Organic brain disorders* (dementia, delirium, amnestic, etc)
        2.   1948: World Health Organization published ICD-6
        3.   1952: American Psychiatric Association published first edition DSM-I
        4.   1968: ICD-8
        5.   1968: DSM-II
        6.   Early DSM systems did not predict as a valid classification should
        7.   1980: DSM-III, a radically revised edition
        8.   1987: DSM-III-R
            a.   Specific, clearly defined criteria
            b.   Greatly improved the reliability of diagnoses by clinicians
            c.   *Multiaxial classification*—person described along many dimensions

9. APA formed a task force to develop the DSM-IV one year later
   a. WHO was ready to publish ICD-10
   b. U.S. under treaty to maintain sytems consistent with WHO
   c. Desire to build a better empirical foundation
   d. Did not clearly document empirical support for diagnostic criteria
   e. 13 groups of researchers and clinicians studied disorders
   f. *Field trials*— research study in natural environment
   g. 6,000 subjects at 70 locations throughout U.S.A.
   h. Decisions of each group reviewed by 100 advisors
   i. Documentation of activity in *DSM-IV Sourcebook*

B. Diagnoses with the DSM-IV
   1. DSM-IV used in U.S. and Canada
   2. Rest of world officially uses ICD-10
   3. Axis I
      a. Disorders first diagnosed in infancy, childhood, or adolescence
      b. Delirium, dementia, amnestic, and other cognitive disorders
      c. Mental disorders due to general medical condition
      d. Substance-related disorders
      e. Schizophrenia and other psychotic disorders
      f. Mood disorders
      g. Anxiety disorders
      h. Somatoform disorders
      i. Factitious disorders
      j. Dissociative disorders
      k. Sexual and gender identity disorders
      l. Eating disorders
      m. Sleep disorders
      n. Impulse-control disorders not elsewhere classified
      o. Adjustment disorders
      p. Other conditions that may be a focus of clinical attention
   4. Axis II
      a. Mental retardation
      b. 10 personality disorders
      c. Diagnoses continue mostly because of custom
   5. Axis III: General medical conditions relevant to treatment
   6. Axis IV
      a. Acute problem, chronic strain, lack of social support
      b. General focus on stressors present during prior year
   7. Axis V
      a. Scale on which clinician rates functioning at time of evaluation
      b. Summary assessment of clinical status and gauges response
   8. Criteria for Diagnosis
      a. *Polythetic approach*—person must meet particular number of criteria

        b.   Create *heterogeneous* categories (similar but not identical)
        c.   *Classical method*—every disorder is assumed to be distinct
        d.   Yields *homogeneous* categories (appear very similar)
        e.   *Comorbidity*—mental disorders likely to coexist
        f.   Increasing interest in biological, cultural, and social context

C.   Criticisms of DSM Diagnoses
    1.   Labeling produces stereotypes, prejudice, and harm
        a.   Labeling applies to disorders; not individuals
        b.   Labeling can cause discrimination and rejection
        c.   Study done by Rosenhan—8 normal people admitted to hospitals
        d.   Labels lead to *self-fulfilling prophecy*, particularly in childhood
    2.   Mental disorders occur on a continuum, not in discrete categories
        a.   All-or-none approach has been challenged by professionals
        b.   *Dimensional approach* (personality) offered as alternative
            (1)   Extroversion
            (2)   Openness to different kinds of experiences
            (3)   Conscientiousness
            (4)   Emotional stability
            (5)   Scores on each of above produce a profile
        c.   Categorical approach has remained dominant
            (1)   Medical tradition of diagnosis emphasizes discrete illnesses
            (2)   Clinicians find it easier to use categorical systems
            (3)   Disagreement on nature and number of dimensions needed
    3.   DSM-IV: Too much attention to reliability; not enough to validity
    4.   DSM diagnoses imply disorder result of internal, not external causal factors
        a.   Critics believe this one of the most harmful effects of medical model
        b.   Blames victims of poverty, discrimination, unemployment, abuse
        c.   Practices that ignore these do a disservice to persons and society

D.   Diagnosis in the Real World
    1.   Money, Privacy, and Diagnoses
        a.   Money
            (1)   May be *financial* incentive to diagnose disorder
            (2)   Insurance-covered disorder if Axis I
        b.   Privacy
            (1)   Diagnosis not kept confidential by insurance company
            (2)   Fear of dismissal from job
        c.   Diagnoses
            (1)   Clinicians specialize and find ways to get favored diagnosis
            (2)   Primary care physicians underdiagnose mental disorders
    2.   Diversity and Assessment Measures
        a.   Most psychological test developed on European Americans
        b.   Are these measures biased against ethnic minorities?
            (1)   Certain ethnic groups do poorly on some tests
            (2)   Reasons have nothing to do with what is being measured
            (3)   Scores on tests valid for one ethnic group but not another

3. Diversity and Definitions of Mental Disorders
   a. Ethnic or cultural factors distort diagnoses when not understood
   b. Example: Asian-Americans tend to use *somaticizing*
   c. DSM-IV includes glossary of *culture-bound syndromes* (koro)
4. Diversity and Interactions between Clients and Clinicians
   a. Difficulty understanding language leads to problems
   b. Cultural values affect willingness to disclose problems
   c. Hispanic Americans use professional services less than any
   d. *Overpathologizing*—behavior is desirable in client's culture
   e. *Underpathologizing*—dismiss bizarre behavior as cultural; it is not

IV. The Frequency of Mental Disorders (pp. 71-72)
   A. How many people currently suffer or have suffered mental disorders?
      1. *Prevalence*—total of people who suffer in a specific population
      2. *Lifetime prevalence*—at any time in their lives
      3. *Incidence*—a disorder in specific time (6 or 12 months)
   B. Most comprehensive study in the United States
      1. Epidemiologic Catchment Area (ECA) Project
      2. Sponsored by National Institute of Mental Health
      3. Used the Diagnostic Interview Schedule
      4. Information about 30 major mental disorders
      5. Los Angeles, St. Louis, New Haven, Baltimore, Durham
      6. 20,000 subjects—community residents, prisons, nursing homes, etc
   C. Most important findings
      1. Lifetime prevalence of any of 30 disorders was 32%
      2. One in five people had an active disorder in prior year
      3. Lifetime prevalence frequently related to demographic or social
      4. Higher rates associated with being poor; not finishing high school
      5. Rates—41% in Baltimore; 28% in New Haven
      6. Most common are phobias and alcohol abuse
      7. 38% of people with history were in *remission*
      8. ½ drug abuse, anxiety, alcohol, antisocial free of symptoms prior year
      9. Remission rates far exceeded percent of people seeking treatment
      10. Children, elderly, minorities, poor, physical abilities likely *underserved*
      11. Comorbidity of mental disorders common
      12. Major burden concentrated in comorbid (less than 1/6 of population)
      13. Average age of first symptoms—16
      14. Need for preventive programs focusing on children and adolescents

2   Assessment and Diagnosis

LECTURE MAKER 2.1

Purpose To demonstrate the implicit nature of social norms and sanctions against abnormal/deviant behavior (pp. 44-49)

Lecture Introduction Present current definitions of abnormal behavior. Elaborate the ideas from the text (p 44) regarding expectations for behavior and deviations from what is socially accepted. Explain the cultural bias inherent in norms and mores.

Demonstration Ask for a student volunteer from the class and assure him or her that there is no harm in this exercise. Have the volunteer join you at the front of the class, extend your hand and introduce yourself to the student. Explain that you wish the student to stay while you explain a concept. As you explain the concept, subtly move closer the student. Keep talking and inching toward the student. Generally, as you inch closer, the student will inch away from you as you "violate their personal space." If you have a "non-moving student, inch closer (do not touch) and finally turn to face them instead of the class. If you are a foot or two from their face as you speak, even the most immovable student will back up a bit. Thank the student and ask the class for feedback on what happened and why.

Lecture Capsule Norms are often not verbally articulated by a social group, but are acted upon. Provide examples of mild cultural norms like elevator-riding protocol. Extra credit can be offered to students to experience this phenomenon. Have them select a norm and break it, then write about the experience. Ground rules include *NO* unlawful, harmful, or obscene behavior to be used. This experience prototype is often emotionally revealing for the students.

LECTURE MAKER 2.2

Purpose To illustrate potential biases in diagnosis and treatment based on gender (pp. 68-70)

Lecture Introduction Discuss the concepts of bias and cultural disparity. Introduce the DSM-IV as a tool for diagnosis, its strengths and weaknesses. Outline the diagnostic axes of the DSM-IV

Demonstration Make copies of the following case study. For half of your students, present the case as a female, the other half as a male. Have them read the case and briefly fill in the axes from the information provided. This is done anonymously. Collect the diagnoses, separate them into M/F Case studies. Inform the students of the difference in the case (half male, half female). For this class simply read aloud the GAF for males, then for females and see if there are obvious differences or not. For the next class, survey your data to see if there is any indication of gender bias in diagnosis

Lecture Capsule

Emphasize the subtlety of bias. Gender bias is committed by even the most conscientious professionals. Why might this be the case?

Profiles

The client is a 38 year old married female with two young children. She has held a steady job for the past 10 years. Although she has no physical abnormality, the client complains of tension and anxiety. From self-report, the client is currently given to outbursts of verbal and physical rage in the home. She is able to handle the work situation fairly well with only momentary lapses in concentration. However, these lapses are becoming more intense with her employer threatening her with a possible layoff if no improvement is made in the near future. In family life, she is unable to be a loving companion and spouse. She is anxious about the lack of affection and warmth she exhibits in interacting with her family. She complains of sleeplessness and nightmares. She has been questioning the value of life and her own adequacy as a woman.

The client is a 38 year old married male with two young children. He has held a steady job for the past 10 years. Although he has no physical abnormality, the client complains of tension and anxiety. From self-report, the client is currently given to outbursts of verbal and physical rage in the home. He is able to handle the work situation fairly well with only momentary lapses in concentration. However, these lapses are becoming more intense with his employer threatening him with a possible layoff if no improvement is made in the near future. In family life, he is unable to be a loving companion and spouse. He is anxious about the lack of affection and warmth he exhibits in interacting with his family. He complains of sleeplessness and nightmares. He has been questioning the value of life and his own adequacy as a man.

Adapted from: Trudy Soloman, *The Impact of Training on Clinical Decision-Making*, (Unpublished Masters Thesis, 1976)

LECTURE MAKER 2.3

Student Assignment

Discuss self-efficacy and the ability to see oneself as integrated and sufficient. Expectations each individual has on behavior or feelings is often more rigorous than what friends, family or the culture

Purpose

To introduce the concept of self-acceptance and to assess and evaluate personal levels among students. (pp. 44-49)

Lecture Introduction	Reproduce copies of the "Self-Acceptance Scale" and scoring/interpretation guide for the students to individually complete and score. They should *not* return their scores, just the scale to you, giving them assured anonymity.
Demonstration	With the students referring to the evaluation instrument, discuss the interpretation and indications of score ranges. Students seem to enjoy self diagnostics and can relate concepts better when they are actively involved in the process.
Lecture Capsule	Review the limits of questionnaire style testing. Speculate on: Axis I symptoms might be present for low scorers

LECTURE MAKER 2.4

Student Assignment	Reproduce copies of the "Fear of Appearing Incompetent Scale" and scoring/interpretation guide for students to individually and anonymously complete and score. Do not collect scores.
Purpose	To enhance awareness about self comparisons and evaluations as a component of personality. The idea of competency can be illustrated as a socioculturally relative phenomenon. (pp. 55-57)
Lecture Introduction	Discuss cultural expectations on performance and the rewards for outstanding performance, the sanctions for poor performance. Develop the concept of competence as culturally relative.
Demonstration	With the students referring to the evaluation instrument, discuss the interpretation and indications of score ranges. Students find this inventory revealing but not threatening and can get a sense of the etiology of self-efficacy.
Lecture Capsule	Review the limits of questionnaire style testing. Speculate on: Axis I symptoms might be present for low scorers.

SELF-ACCEPTANCE SCALE 2.3
by Emanuel M. Berger

On the next page are a series of statements that ask about personal feelings. Read each one carefully and decide how true or false that statement is for you. Using the scale provided below, mark your answer on the answer sheet in the next column.

1 = Completely true
2 = Mostly true
3 = Half true, half false
4 = Mostly false
5 = Completely false

1. _____
2. _____
3. _____
4. _____
5. _____
6. _____
7. _____
8. _____
9. _____
10. _____
11. _____
12. _____
13. _____
14. _____
15. _____
16. _____
17. _____
18. _____
19. _____
20. _____
21. _____
22. _____
23. _____
24. _____
25. _____
26. _____
27. _____
28. _____
29. _____
30. _____
31. _____
32. _____
33. _____
34. _____
35. _____
36. _____

© Emanuel M. Berger, University of Minneapolis, Minnesota.
Reprinted with permission.

SELF ACCEPTANCE SCALE 2.3

1. I would like it if I could find someone who would tell me how to solve my personal problems.
2. I don't question my worth as a person, even if I think others do.
3. When people say nice things about me, I find it difficult to believe they really mean it. I think maybe they're kidding me or just aren't being sincere.
4. If there is any criticism or anyone says anything about me, I just can't take it.
5. I don't say much at social affairs because I'm afraid that people will criticize me or laugh if I say the wrong thing.
6. I realize that I'm not living very effectively, but I just don't believe I've got it in me to use my energies in better ways.
7. I look on most of the feelings and impulses I have toward people as being quite natural and acceptable.
8. Something inside me just won't let me be satisfied with any job I've done—if it turns out well, I get a very smug feeling that this is beneath me, I shouldn't be satisfied with this, this isn't a fair test.
9. I feel different from other people. I'd like to have the feeling of security that comes from knowing I'm not too different from others.
10. I'm afraid for people that I like to find out what I'm really like, for fear they'd be disappointed in me.
11. I am frequently bothered by feelings of inferiority.
12. Because of other people, I haven't been able to achieve as much as I should have.
13. I am quite shy and self-conscious in social situations.
14. In order to get along and be liked, I tend to be what people expect me to be rather than anything else.
15. I seem to have a real inner strength in handling things. I'm on a pretty solid foundation and it makes me pretty sure of myself.
16. I feel self-conscious when I'm with people who have a superior position to mine in business or at school.
17. I think I'm neurotic or something.
18. Very often, I don't try to be friendly with people because I think they won't like me.
19. I feel that I'm a person of worth, on an equal plane with others.
20. I can't avoid feeling guilty about the way I feel toward certain people in my life.
21. I'm not afraid of meeting new people. I feel that I'm a worthwhile person and there's no reason why they should dislike me.
22. I sort of only half believe in myself.
23. I'm very sensitive. People say things and I have a tendency to think they're criticizing me or insulting me in some way and later when I think of it, they may not have meant anything like that at all.
24. I think I have certain abilities and other people say so too. I wonder if I'm not giving them an importance way beyond what they deserve.
25. I feel confident that I can do something about the problems that may arise in the future.
26. I guess I put on a show to impress people. I know I'm not the person I pretend to be.
27. I do not worry or condemn myself if other people pass judgment against me.
28. I don't feel very normal, but I want to be normal.
29. When I'm in a group, I usually don't say much for fear of saying the wrong thing.
30. I have a tendency to sidestep my problems.
31. Even when people do think well of me, I feel sort of guilty because I know I must be fooling them—that if I were really to be myself, they wouldn't think well of me.
32. I feel that I'm on the same level as other people and that helps to establish good relations with them.
33. I feel that people are apt to react differently to me than they would normally react to other people.
34. I live too much by other people's standards.
35. When I have to address a group, I get self-conscious and have difficulty saying things well.
36. If I didn't always have such hard luck, I'd accomplish more than I have.

SCORING KEY

	A	B
1.	____	
2. Reverse		____
3.	____	
4.	____	
5.	____	
6.	____	
7. Reverse		____
8.	____	
9.	____	
10.	____	
11.	____	
12.	____	
13.	____	
14.	____	
15. Reverse		____
16.	____	
17.	____	
18.	____	
19. Reverse		____
20.	____	
21. Reverse		____
22.	____	
23.	____	
24.	____	
25. Reverse		____
26.	____	
27. Reverse		____
28.	____	
29.	____	
30.	____	
31.	____	
32. Reverse		____
33.	____	
34.	____	
35.	____	
36.	____	

☐

TOTAL SCORE

SCORING THE SCALE

To score the scale, fold back along the dotted line to line up your answers with the scoring key.
First, transfer your answers into the spaces in column A for items 1, 3, 4, 5, etc.
Next, in column B, reverse the numerical value of your answers for items 2, 8, 15, 19, etc

For example:
In Column B, an answer of
1 earns 5 points
2 earns 4 points
3 earns 3 points
4 earns 2 points
5 earns 1 point

To find your final score, add together totals of column A and B and record in the box marked "total score."

SELF-ACCEPTANCE SCALE 2.3

SELF-ACCEPTANCE SCALE 2.3
INTERPRETING YOUR SCORE

- *Low Scorers (0-110)*—If you scored here, look at where you scored within this range. It will be difficult for you to share life with others until you can feel more accepting of yourself.
- *Average Scorers* (111-150)—It is not easy to interpret a normal or average level of self-acceptance because such acceptance varies with your roles in life. This means that you may confront a situation one day in which you bubble with confidence, and yet feel that could have done much better in a different situation the next day. This level of self-acceptance describes the way most of us are, praising ourselves one moment, condemning ourselves the next. For most of us, this is an accurate reflection of our skills and our striving to do better. The important part of such a view is that we have accurate perceptions of when we are doing well and when we could have done better. Goals that are set unreasonably high (for whatever reasons) reduce the positive feelings that our behavior may really deserve.
- *High Scorers* (151-180)—If you are a high scorer, your level of self-acceptance is such that this scale can't tell you anything new. You are stating on this scale that you consider yourself a confident and worthy individual. Others probably find you easy to talk to, since you report that you accept both praise and criticism from others in an objective fashion. In addition you are likely to base your behavior on internalized values and accept the responsibility for whatever the consequences of your behavior may be. You feel comfortable about your ability to handle any problem or challenges that arise.

Fear of Appearing Incompetent Scale 2.4
by Lawrence R. Good
and Katherine C. Good

T or F

1. _____
2. _____
3. _____
4. _____
5. _____
6. _____
7. _____
8. _____
9. _____
10. _____
11. _____
12. _____
13. _____
14. _____
15. _____
16. _____
17. _____
18. _____
19. _____
20. _____
21. _____
22. _____
23. _____
24. _____
25. _____
26. _____
27. _____
28. _____
29. _____
30. _____
31. _____
32. _____
33. _____
34. _____
35. _____
36. _____

The thirty-six statements on the next page refer to feelings that all of us share to varying degrees. Read each one and decide if the statement is true (T) or false (F) as it pertains to you personally. Though some may be difficult to answer, do answer each one. Record your answers on the answer sheet in the next column.

© Reprinted with permission of author and publisher from Good, L. R. and Good K.C. An objective measure of the motive to avoid appearing incompetent. *Psychological Reports*, 1973, 32, Table1, 1077

FEAR OF APPEARING INCOMPETENT 2.4

1. I would never worry about the possibility of being judged a fool in some activities.
2. I would very much like to be less apprehensive about my capabilities.
3. I would not be prone to worry about my supervisory abilities if I were in a supervisory position.
4. I tend to be concerned about not being effective enough in my dealings with others.
5. After having had a conversation with someone, I have a tendency to worry about having said something that was inappropriate.
6. I am not prone to be apprehensive or worried about my ability to do a task well.
7. I am prone to worry sometimes that others may think I am not intelligent enough for my job.
8. I am frequently prone to take actions to counteract previous bad impressions which I believe I have made.
9. I would never be at all apprehensive or worried about my adequacy in handling business transactions.
10. After completing an assignment or task, I am prone to have doubts about whether I did it right.
11. I am never concerned about the possibility that others may regard me as being somewhat odd or strange.
12. I rarely worry about being considered by others to be misinformed or ignorant about certain things.
13. I am occasionally concerned about the possibility of being considered to have inappropriate friendships.
14. I have a tendency to worry that others will consider my behavior in some activities to be inappropriate or tactless.
15. I am almost never concerned about the possibility of being regarded as spastic or clumsy around others.
16. I have a tendency to worry that others may regard me as not knowing what is really going on in the immediate social situation.
17. I tend to worry about the possibility of displaying inappropriate etiquette at a formal social event.
18. I would never worry about my adequacy in sexual relationships.
19. I would never worry about the possibility of failing to meet the work standards at my place of employment.
20. I might be inclined to avoid criticizing someone else's judgment for fear of appearing wrong.
21. I tend to worry that others will think I am not keeping up with my work.
22. I am rarely concerned about my adequacy in physical or athletic events.
23. If I were functioning in a professional field, I would not worry about my relationships with fellow professionals.
24. I am prone to worry that others may regard my beliefs and opinions as incorrect or funny.
25. I tend to worry that others may think that I am not keeping well enough informed about the developments in my field.
26. I am prone to worry about my adequacy in classroom work or activities.
27. I would never worry about the possibility of saying something inappropriate in a new social situation.
28. I tend to worry that others may think I don't know what I'm doing.
29. I have a tendency to worry that others will laugh at my ideas.
30. I am rarely concerned about whether others will take me seriously enough.
31. I am prone to worry that my parents or friends will regard me as irresponsible or undependable.
32. If I were functioning as a salesperson, I would not worry about the possibility of appearing to be clumsy in my handling of clients or customers.
33. I tend to fear that others may see me as not sufficiently self-disciplined.
34. I tend to worry that others may think I am not devoting enough energy or enthusiasm to my work.
35. I would never worry about the possibility that others might feel I have poor judgment in some situations.
36. I would never worry about appearing to be in over my head or beyond my capabilities in my line of work or my course of study.

SCORING KEY

☐

TOTAL SCORE

1. F _____
2. T _____
3. F _____
4. T _____
5. T _____
6. F _____
7. T _____
8. T _____
9. F _____
10. T _____
11. F _____
12. F _____
13. T _____
14. T _____
15. F _____
16. T _____
17. T _____
18. F _____
19. F _____
20. T _____
21. T _____
22. F _____
23. F _____
24. T _____
25. T _____
26. T _____
27. F _____
28. T _____
29. T _____
30. F _____
31. T _____
32. F _____
33. T _____
34. T _____
35. F _____
36. F _____

SCORING THE SCALE
FEAR OF APPEARING INCOMPETENT SCALE 2.4

To find your score, fold this page back along the dotted line and compare your answers on the previous page to those on the Scoring Key. Give yourself one point for each match. Your total score equals the total number of agreements.

INTERPRETING YOUR SCORE

Low scorers (0-12)—Low scorers are reporting little worry about feeling incompetent in their interpersonal behavior If you are a low scorer, you are likely seen by others as confident in your work and social activities. You are stating on this scale that you have a low need to maintain face and do not go into activities worried that you that you will look foolish. Such personal feelings suggest that you also know your own strengths and are accepting of your deficiencies. The psychological term that is often used to describe such a self-directed individual is "self-actualized," suggesting someone with a high level of self-acceptance and self-esteem

Average Scorers (13-22)—If you scored in this range, You are in the company of most people. Scores here suggest a normal combination of self-confidence and apprehension involving your perception of how you will perform in various situations. Your life is likely to be a mix of times when you feel as confident as a superhero and other times when you feel more like Bozo the Clown. Most people have gotten used to this combination of feelings and regard them as "just the way they are." Some, however, are not willing to accept the uncomfortable times, yet cannot specify their concerns enough to work on reducing them. If this last statement describes you, a combination of self-examination and the information from some of the other tests in this book will help.

High Scorers— Most high scorers spend considerable energy worrying about appearing incompetent regardless of the situation. Although such fears may be strongest in one particular type of activity, your score here suggests a general lack of self-acceptance and a fear that others will find you unacceptable as well. Scores near the bottom of this range may be those of a typically average scorer involved in a stress which has temporarily increased self-doubt. In that case, the interpretation for average scorers may be more accurate for you.

RESOURCES

Media   *Keltie's Beard: A Woman's Story* (FML, 9 min)
A heavily bearded woman makes a case for what is normal

Individual Differences (CRM, 16 min)
Looks at what is "normal."

King of Hearts (VA, 105 min)
Long but poignant film questioning what is normal.

Nietzel et al., *Abnormal Psychology*, Transparencies

Chapter Two

	Text Figure Number	Text Page Number
14. Correlations Showing Different Relationships Between Two Variables	2.1	47
15. Outline for a Mental Status Examination		50
16. Rorschach Inkblot		54
17. Computerized Axial Tomography (CAT Scan)		59

3 Disorders of Infancy, Childhood, and Adolescence

CHAPTER OUTLINE

I. A Developmental Perspective (pp.78-81)
   A. Prospective, Longitudinal Studies
      1. Investigators assess same people at different ages (months or years)
      2. New discipline, *developmental psychopathology*, emerged
      3. One investigation shows 90% adult disorders started in childhood
      4. Alan Sroufe, Michael Rutter—basic propositions—developmental tasks
         a. Tasks described by Erikson, Piaget, Bowlby, and Kohlberg
         b. Effective *attachment relationship* with parent (infancy)
         c. Attaining *empathy and self-reliance* (preschool years)
         d. Developing *academic competence* (middle school years)
         e. *Emancipating* (separating) from family (later adolescence)
   B. Developmental Tasks and Psychopathology
      1. Major link between developmental tasks and psychopathology:
         a. Child's failure to effectively handle an early developmental task will impair the capacity to handle later tasks successfully
         b. Early problems increase likelihood, do not guarantee it
         c. Infants learn to avoid or minimize contact with abusive parent
         d. Long-term—child loses adult as secure base for emotional support
         e. Cripples child's ability to become close to others
      2. Probability a preschooler will develop conduct problems later
         a. Predicted by quality of attachment to parent; degree of self-reliance
         b. Not by child's compliance with parental directions
   C. Analyzing Development: The Example of Attachment
      1. Reliable methods for studying performance on these tasks
         a. *Strange Situation*: 20-minute laboratory assessment
         b. Studies infant-parent attachment
         c. How infant responds to separation from parent, usually mother
         d. Parent repeatedly leaves infant and returns
         e. Researchers use responses to describe attachment patterns
         f. *Secure attachment*—moderate separation distress, strong reunion
         g. *Insecure attachment*—Three patterns
            (1) Minimal separation distress; reunion avoidance
            (2) Excessive and unrelenting separation distress not relieved when parent returns
            (3) Contradictory, undirected, or confused behaviors during reunion
         h. Children of secure attachment function better in later life
      2. Clinicians convinced attachment difficulties major role in development of child psychopathology
      3. Suomi studies done on rhesus monkeys with similar results

II. Classification and Diagnosis of Children's Disorders (pp. 81-83)
    A. *Categorical Approach*
        1. Assumes clear boundaries between normal and abnormal
        2. Disorders are like "boxes" into which one is placed
        3. DSM-IV most widely used approach to disorders
        4. "Disorders first diagnosed in infancy, childhood, adolescence"
        5. Clinician forms hypothesis; interviews child, parents, others
    B. *Dimensional Approach*
        1. Not categorically different from normal
        2. Psychopathology described along continuous dimensions
        3. Clinicians assess by acquiring behavior checklists
        4. Resulting data subjected to *factor analysis*
        5. Method uses *statistical criteria* to group maladaptive behaviors
    C. *Externalizing problems* (undercontrolled behaviors)
        1. Excess of undesirable behavior
        2. Disruptive behaviors—nuisance, aggression, hyperactivity, etc
        3. Two scales: aggressive and delinquent
    D. *Internalizing problems* (overcontrolled behaviors)
        1. Deficits in behavior accompanied by subjective distress in the child
        2. Example: failing to interact with peers; avoiding school due to anxiety
        3. Three scales: withdrawn; somatic complaints; anxious/depressed
    E. Three scales do correlate highly enough for internalizing or externalizing
        1. Attention problems—daydreaming and inability to concentrate
        2. Thought problems—seeing or hearing things; harboring strange ideas
        3. Social problems—being teased often and not being liked by peers

III. Disruptive Behavior and Attention-Deficit Disorders (pp. 83-98)
    A. Oppositional Defiant Disorder (ODD): disobedient; antisocial; defiant
        1. Usually diagnosed in children 3 to 7
        2. Poor control of emotions
        3. Extremely noncompliant and argumentative with parents and teachers
        4. Repeated conflicts with peers as result of hostile interactions
        5. Blame other people for their mistakes—have chip on their shoulders
        6. High need for control of social interaction—MY WAY
        7. Parents usually "walking on eggs"
        8. Early pattern will persist and increase over time
        9. Continuing problems more likely when
            a. Problems in more than one setting (school and home)
            b. Aggression and hyperactivity co-occur with core ODD features
            c. Covert behaviors— lying and stealing
            d. Overt behaviors—excessive arguing and aggression
            e. High level of stress in family
    B. Conduct Disorder (CD)—antisocial with aggression
        1. Requires more serious antisocial behaviors
        2. Vandalism, truancy, physically aggressive action
        3. Taking advantage of others for personal gain

4. Infringing on rights of others and violating community rules
5. Exhibit behaviors potentially harmful to the child or others or property
6. Diagnosis requires 3 symptoms previous 12 months; 1 previous 6 months
7. Some clinicians identify subtypes
    a. Aggressive or nonaggressive
    b. Antisocial behavior alone or in peer groups
8. Longitudinal Course
    a. Adolescent onset (after age 10) more likely to dissipate
    b. Childhood onset (before age 10) more likely to have adult problems
    c. Diagnosed antisocial personality disorder as adults
    d. Higher risk for substance abuse and emotional disorders
    e. Associated with divorce, joblessness, abusive parenting
9. Causes of Conduct Disorder: Biological Factors
    a. Possible genetic basis—children of alcoholics or criminals
    b. Boys show higher incidence than girls
    c. Correlation between aggression and *testosterone*
    d. Aggression related to *neurotransmitters*
    e. Low levels of *serotonin* associated with high levels of aggression
    f. Physiological arousal—lower arousal rates; less fear of risk
10. Causes of Conduct Disorder: Cognitive and Psychosocial Factors
    a. Deficits in neuropsychological abilities
    b. Deficiencies in *executive functioning*
    c. Parenting skills—*coercive cycles*—exchange of negative behavior
    d. Parental interaction styles the *result* of having a difficult child
    e. Positive, warm bond associated with greater child compliance
    f. 80 % preschool boys referred for ODD show insecure attachment
    g. Researcher use *family adversity index*-number of negative factors
        (1) Severe marital discord
        (2) Low socioeconomic class
        (3) Large family size
        (4) Criminality by the father
        (5) Mental disorder in the mother
        (6) Placement of the child in foster care
    h. Higher the index—more likelihood of antisocial behavior in child
    i. Child's *social-cognitive skills*
        (1) Trouble thinking of nonaggressive ways of solving problems
        (2) Accidental physical contact seen as deliberate aggression
        (3) Poor at communicating their sides of issue in conflict
        (4) Two or more factors usually at work
    j. Arise from combination—biological, psychological, and social factors

C. Treatment of Disruptive Behavior Disorders
1. Most widely used—improve specific parenting skills
   a. Use praise
   b. Reinforce child's prosocial behavior
   c. Reserve use of negative consequences only for serious problems
   d. Give clear, simple instructions
   e. Talk to children without nagging them
   f. Discipline without losing tempers
2. Problems limit long-term utility of parent training
   a. Interventions fail to produce behavior changes outside home
   b. Work less well with parents poorly educated, stressed, isolated
   c. Not shown long-term effects on "early starting" children
3. Cognitive-behavioral programs
   a. Attempt to change child's perceptual inaccuracies
   b. Monitor their emotions
   c. Use specific problem-solving steps
   d. Avoid physical confrontations

D. Attention-Deficit/Hyperactivity Disorder (ADHD)
1. Disruptive but not antisocial
2. Marked by inattention, impulsivity, or high motor activity
3. DSM-IV:
   a. Symptoms must produce problems in two settings
   b. "Clinically significant impairment" in day-to-day functioning
   c. Behavior must be primary cause of functional problems
4. Three subtypes of ADHD
   a. ADHD primarily characterized by *inattention*
   b. ADHD primarily marked by *hyperactivity* or *impulsivity*
   c. ADHD in which all are *combined*
   d. All share academic underachievement
5. Children with ADHD with hyperactivity
   a. Externalizing behavior problems (non-compliance, aggression)
   b. Low popularity among peers
   c. Comorbid conduct disorder
6. Children with ADHD without hyperactivity
   (1) Internalizing behavior problems (anxiety, depression)
   (2) A slow pace of solving problems
   (3) Comorbid sensory-motor problems and learning disorders
7. Longitudinal Course
   a. Primary symptoms are highly persistent over time
   b. ADHD children risk for antisocial personality disorder as adults
   c. Children higher-than-average risk for substance abuse as adults
8. Causes of ADHD: Biological Factors
   a. Infants with low birth weight (primarily with premature birth)
   b. Prolonged oxygen deprivation at birth
   c. Maternal alcohol consumption during pregnancy

d. Deficit of neurotransmitters (dopamine; norepinephrine)
e. May be genetically predisposed to develop
f. Low *reticular activating system* (RAS) activity
g. Deficits in the *frontal lobe*
    (1) Children do not perform well on neuropsychological tests
    (2) MRI shows frontal lobe smaller than in normal children
9. Causes of ADHD: Psychological Factors
    a. Diathesis-stress model
    b. Neurobiological vulnerability aggravated by psychosocial risk factors
10. Treatment of ADHD
    a. One of three types of stimulant medications
        (1) *Methylphenidate* (MPH) sold as Ritalin
        (2) *Dextroamphetamine* sold as Dexedrine
        (3) *Pemoline* sold as Cylert
    b. Facilitates the release and blocks the reuptake of norepinephrine and dopamine
    c. Children better able to focus on relevant stimuli
    d. Medication normalizes a child's attention and academic efficiency
    e. Psychological treatments similar to those for disruptive behaviors
        (1) Behavior management procedures
        (2) Cognitive-behavioral training
    f. Combination of behavior management and medication

E. Anxiety and Mood Disorders of Childhood and Adolescence
1. Anxiety Disorders
    a. Must be persistent (lasting weeks or months)
    b. Must interfere significantly with responsibilities or tasks
    c. Observable behaviors such as trembling and avoidance
    d. Physiological arousal, such as upset stomach or sweating
2. Types of Anxiety Disorder
    a. *Generalized Anxiety Disorder*
    b. *Panic attacks*
    c. *Obsessive-Compulsive Disorder*
    d. *Separation Anxiety Disorder*
        (1) Inappropriate fear of separation from home or parents
        (2) Clingy and dependent on adults
        (3) Worry about parents getting sick or injured
        (4) Often have nightmares
    e. *Social phobia*—fear of social contact and scrutiny by others
    f. *Specific phobia*—fear of specific object or circumstance
3. Longitudinal Course of Childhood Anxiety Disorders
    a. *Behavioral inhibition:* in toddlers—shy, quiet, withdrawn
    b. *Inhibited* toddlers more likely to develop phobias

4. Causes of Childhood Anxiety Disorders
    a. Relationship between theses disorders and inhibition
    b. Inhibited children show heightened physiological arousal
    c. Biological diathesis depends on
        (1) Frequency and type of stressors child encounters
        (2) Degree of "goodness of fit"
        (3) Social relationships that reinforce fearful behavior
    d. Cognitive factors
        (1) They expect that bad things will happen
        (2) Blame themselves for misfortunes
        (3) Lack self-confidence
        (4) Criticize their past performances excessively
        (5) Express pessimism about the future
5. Treatment of Children's Anxiety Disorders
    a. *Systematic desensitization*
        (1) Client learns to use an anxiety-inhibiting technique
        (2) Used in conjunction with learning-based methods
    b. Desensitization in conjunction with cognitive-behavioral treatment
        (1) *Cognitive restructuring*—distorted thoughts replaced
        (2) *Coping skills training*—control negative emotion
        (3) *Self-reinforcement*—positive self-evaluative statements
    c. Medications
        (1) Antidepressants
        (2) Antianxiety drugs
        (3) Neuroleptics
        (4) Antihistamines and stimulants

F. Depression in Childhood and Adolescence
    1. Symptoms of Depression
        a. DSM-IV descriptions use adult criteria
        b. Specific symptoms common in depressed children
            (1) Mixture of strong negative emotions
            (2) Irritability, sadness, hopelessness, and guilt
            (3) Physical ailments such as stomach pains and headache
            (4) Low self-esteem
            (5) Not maintaining friendships and academic difficulties
            (6) Self-destructive (substance abuse, reckless driving, etc)
            (7) More serious—suicidal thoughts and suicide attempts

G. Causes of Children's Depression
    1. *Cerebral asymmetry*—decreased activity in left frontal region of brain
    2. Genetic transmission
    3. Family environment
    4. Poor *affect regulation*

H. Treatment of Childhood Depression
    1. Drugs—*tricyclic antidepressants* (imipramine or Tofranil)
    2. Cognitive-behavioral treatments and group therapy

IV. Other Disorders of Childhood and Adolescence (pp. 98-106)
    A. Feeding and Eating Disorders
        1. Anorexia Nervosa (unreasonable fear of gaining weight)
        2. Causes-pathogenic family interactions and dysfunction of hypothalamus
            a. Consequences: severe malnutrition, skin disease, death
            b. *Restricting type*—extreme dieting, fasting, excessive exercise
            c. *Binge-eating/purging*—vomiting, laxatives, diuretics
        3. Bulimia Nervosa (recurrent binge eating)
        4. Causes-pathogenic family interactions and dysfunction of hypothalamus
            a. *Purging subtype*—people induce vomiting or use laxatives
            b. *Nonpurging subtype*—use fasts or stringent exercise
            c. Tend to be of normal weight or overweight
    B. Longitudinal Course of Eating Disorders
        1. Have been found in children as young as 8
        2. Plague individuals throughout most of their adult lives
        3. Onset of eating problems preceded by stressful event
        4. Bulimia related to childhood *pica* (eating nonfood substances)
        5. Anorexia related to picky eating and digestive problems
    C. Treatment of Eating Disorders
        1. Anorexia
            a. Drugs with *appetite-enhancing* characteristics
            b. Antidepressants; desensitization
            c. Self-administered reward (effective) and punishment (not effective)
        2. Buliminia
            a. Group psychotherapy was superior to antidepressants
            b. Drug *fluoxetine* (Prosac)
            c. Cognitive-behavioral therapy most successful
        3. Improved communication thought to make disordered eating unnecessary
    D. Elimination Disorders
        1. Enuresis: release of urine into bedding or clothes
            a. Theories
                (1) Lack of normal coordination of bladder muscles
                (2) Deficiency in which *arginine vasopressin* is released
            b. Treatment—*Dry bed training* (alarms can also be used)
                (1) Child practices getting up from bed and using toilet
                (2) Receives reinforcement from parents
                (3) Must remake the bed and change clothing following accident
        2. Encopresis: passage of feces in inappropriate places
            a. Theories
                (1) Dysfunctional family relationships
                (2) Excessive parental control
                (3) Children's anger or stress
            b. Treatment
                (1) *Biofeedback training*
                (2) parental reinforcement of appropriate toileting

3   Disorders of Infancy, Childhood, and Adolescence

LECTURE MAKER 3.1

Purpose   To introduce culturally accepted fairy tales that may enhance the development of anxiety in some children (pp. 98-101)

Lecture Introduction   I always ask, "So what do children have to worry about? They don't work, have their primary needs for food/clothing/shelter met by someone else. What do you think?" When stated so blatantly, my students rise to the occasion! Explore possible sources of children's anxiety and cognitive skill to accommodate this.

Demonstration   Select a children's fairy tale or two, such as Cinderella, Little Red Riding Hood, Hansel and Gretel, The Three Little Pigs, or Snow White. Read a few passages, pre-selected and book marked. These stories are replete with anxiety messages, fear images, and terror.

Variations on The Theme

1. Select a few children's songs or games and follow the same anxiety analysis.

    Example: Rock-a-bye Baby (Song)
    London Bridge   (Game)

2. Select a child's prayer from different religious primers and follow the guilt/anxiety analysis.

    Example: Now I lay me down to sleep,
    I pray Thee, Lord, my soul to keep.
    If I should die before I wake
    I pray Thee, Lord, my soul to take.

3. Select a few Saturday morning cartoons and videotape a few minutes from each that show vivid examples of anxiety-producing situations.

Lecture Capsule   Students are generally animated in this discussion, as they readily see anxiety issues laced in childhood! Review the criteria for anxiety and mood disorders in children from the DSM-IV.

LECTURE MAKER 3.2

Purpose To sensitize student to "body image" messages around them and the pressure to conform to accepted body types. (pp. 106-110)

Lecture Introduction Introduce anorexia and bulimia. Discuss features of the disorders, treatment and mortality. Trace history of preferred body types changing from full bodied to thin for women.

Demonstration
1. Collect body images used in popular magazines to sell products. Discuss the "look" and the intention of the ad.
2. Review the feature article titles in five or so popular women's and men's magazines. Compare and contrast the assumed interests of males versus females.
3. Bring in a Barbie type doll (large bust, small waist) and GI Joe type figure. What are the messages to males and females?
4. Select a few cartoons that depict males and females. Focus on children's cartoons and the roles played by males versus females and the messages conveyed.
5. Have the students read about Karen Carpenter in the case study book p 158.

Lecture Capsule Relate and contrast anxiety and mood disorders in childhood to anorexia and bulimia. Identify the symptoms and review potential causes of these disorders.

LECTURE MAKER 3.3

Purpose To examine and assess personal levels of hostility. (pp. 84-87)

Lecture Introduction Introduce the concepts of conduct disorder and oppositional defiant disorder. Discuss the general characteristics and diagnostic criteria for evaluation.

Demonstration Reproduce copies of The Annoyance List and scoring/interpretation guide for the students to individually and anonymously complete and score. With the student referring to the evaluation instrument, discuss the interpretation and indications of score ranges. Students find this an interesting inventory and can more readily conceptualize anger/hostility/irritability/defiance.

Lecture Capsule Review the limits of questionnaire type testing. Discuss theoretical positions regarding etiology of oppositional defiant disorder and conduct disorders. Follow with treatment alternatives.

The Annoyance List 3.3

Below is a list containing types of people and various daily occurrences. If the situation or person described is annoying to you, place a check next to the statement

 1. A person telling me how to drive
 2. A person acting in an affected manner.
 3. Getting a telephone busy signal.
 4. To see reckless driving.
 5. To hear a loud talker.
 6. To see an adult picking his nose.
 7. A person telling me to do something when I am just about to do it.
 8. A person continually criticizing something.
 9. A person being sarcastic.
 10. To wait for someone to come to the phone.
 11. To know a person is staring at me.
 12. To have my thoughts interrupted.
 13. A person putting his hands on me unnecessarily.
 14. A person adjusting my TV set.
 15. A person giving me a weak handshake.
 16. A person picking his teeth.
 17. A person who "can't leave the party."
 18. A person continually trying to be funny.
 19. Being asked constantly to do something.
 20. To be evaluated critically by a relative stranger.
 21. To hear a person use "shock words."
 22. To have to walk on slippery sidewalks.
 23. To listen to politicians make promises.
 24. To hear a person talking during a musical number.
 25. To hear "loud" music.
 26. To be unable to find a bus seat.
 27. A person watching me work.
 28. To hear a person swear.
 29. To see overaffectionate demonstration between members of the same sex.
 30. To hear disparaging remarks about a member of a minority group.
 31. A man frequently referring to his girlfriends.
 32. A woman frequently referring to her boyfriends.
 33. Too much discussion of sex on a date.
 34. To have to kiss an unattractive relative.
 35. To see public lovemaking.
 36. A person talking a great deal and not saying anything very important.
 37. To listen to a sales pitch.
 38. To have "too many" TV commercials.
 39. A person interrupting me when I am talking.
 40. To see a person spit.
 41. To have a hostess repeatedly urging me to take some food I do not want.
 42. Not being able to find the rattle in the car.
 43. To discover that the library book is not there.
 44. To see colors that clash.
 45. To see an untidy room.
 46. To find a hair in my food.
 47. To have a hole in my stocking or sock.
 48. The classmate who talks too much.
 49. Not to be listened to.
 50. To be given impractical instructions.

Adapted from Instructor's Manual to accompany
Psychology
B. Von Haller Gilmer, Harper & Row, 1973

TOTAL SCORE

SCORING AND INTERPRETATION

The Annoyance List 3.3

There are no score ranges or specific cutoff points for this list; it is just that—a list of types of people and situations. Some research has suggested that most people find approximately 15 to 20 of these items annoying, but its main use is that of providing you with information about how you, personally, feel about these daily situations. The information is here for you to use in furthering your self-understanding and in deciding whether or not you need to change your level of frustration and stress.

RESOURCES

Media

Bulimia (CRM, 12 min)
Description, motivation, and treatment

I Don't Have to Hide (FNL, 28 min)
Bulimia and anorexia examined

Anorexia and Bulimia (FHS, 19 min)
Etiology and damage of eating disorders

Portraits of Anorexia (MINN 28 min)
Seven anorexics interviewed

The Waist Land: Eating Disorders (MINN, 23 min)
You can never be too thin is an obsession resulting in eating disorders.

Nietzel et al., *Abnormal Psychology,* Transparencies

Chapter Three

	Text Figure Number	Text Page Number

18. Prevalence of Childhood Disorders..82

19. Externalizing Disorders and Their Prevalence...................................3.2.................84

20. Criteria for Conduct Disorder..86

21. Multiple Factors in the Causes of Conduct Disorder...............................3.4..................89

22. Criteria for ADHD..93

23. Diathesis-Stress Model of Childhood Anxiety Disorders.....................3.6.................101

24. Common Signs of Depression in Children and Adolescents...103

25. Criteria for Anorexia Nervosa..107

26. Criteria for Bulimia Nervosa..107

4 Developmental Disorders and Learning Disabilities

CHAPTER OUTLINE

I. Domains of Development (pp. 119-121)
    A. Motor Skills
        1. *Gross motor skills*— controlling large movements and posture
        2. *Fine motor skills*— upper extremity and hand and finger movements
        3. *Visual motor skills*— eye-hand coordination
    B. Language Development
        1. *Expressive language*—use of language to communicate one's thoughts
        2. *Receptive language*—the understanding of language
    C. Cognition
        1. Capacity to learn
        2. Retain acquired information
        3. Use information to solve problems
        4. Essentially what we mean by *intelligence*
    D. Assessment of Skills
        1. *Habituation speed*—time it takes infant to lose interest in stimulus
        2. After age 3
            a. Stanford-Binet Intelligence Scale
            b. Weschler Intelligence Scale for Children
            c. Norms allow computation of individual's *mental age*
            d. Today—intelligence tests use *deviation IQ scores*
    E. Adaptive Behaviors
        1. Enable individual to meet cultural expectations for independent functioning
        2. Intellectually skilled does not mean "common sense" of everyday life
    F. Measurement of Adaptive Behavior
        1. Vineland Adaptive Behavior Scales
        2. American Association of Mental Retardation Adaptive Behavior Scale

II. Mental Retardation (pp. 121-135)
    A. Significantly Subaverage Intellectual Functioning Before Age 18
        1. American Association on Mental Retardation—IQ score 70-75
        2. DSM-IV and ICD-10 retain IQ cutoff score of 70
        3. AAMR, DSM-IV, ICD-10 definitions list specific areas:
            a. Skills in communication
            b. Self-care
            c. Home living
            d. Health
            e. Safety
        4. Impairment in two areas for diagnosis of mental retardation
    B. A Classification
        1. Mild Mental Retardation
            a. Subtle deficits in adaptive behavior and IQ of 50-70
            b. 85% of all mentally retarded in this category
            c. Delayed in acquisition of basic language and cognitive abilities

    d. Middle childhood-limitations become more obvious
    e. As adults—hold semiskilled jobs and get married
    f. Parenting skills and ability to care for self suffer under stress
    g. At increased risk of psychopathology
      (1) Attention deficit disorders
      (2) Disruptive behavior disorders
      (3) Substance abuse
    h. *Dual diagnosis*—mental retardation and other psychiatric disorder
  2. Moderate Mental Retardation
    a. Significantly limited adaptive behavior and IQ 35-55
    b. 10% of mentally retarded in this range
    c. Early childhood—significant delays language, cognitive, motor skills
    d. Can learn to read and write; do simple addition and subtraction
    e. As adults—unskilled jobs in supervised settings
    f. Most live in supervised group homes
    g. Few marry; fewer have children
  3. Severe Mental Retardation
    a. Severe impairment indicated by IQ of 20-40
    b. 3-4 % of mentally retarded in this range
    c. Early childhood—verbal communication limited
    d. Most do not learn to read
    e. Motor deficits common—may limit capabilities for self-care
    f. Vocational opportunities limited to sheltered workshops
  4. Profound Mental Retardation
    a. IQ's below 20 or 25
    b. 1 to 2% of mentally retarded in this range
    c. Pervasive neurological damage present
    d. Has significant adverse effects on all developmental domains
    e. Many wheelchair bound; constant supervision; self-care impossible
    f. Do not usually acquire speech
  5. Variation in Motor Development
    a. Lower the IQ—more likely significant motor dysfunction
    b. Many *cerebral palsy*—motor disorders from cerebral insult, injury
      (1) *hemiplegic spasticity*—arm and leg on one side of body
      (2) *quadriplegia*—affects all four extremities
      (3) mental retardation in 60% of cerebral palsy cases
C. Causes of Mental Retardation
  1. Organic
    a. 300 known biological causes
    b. Genetic disorders
    c. Prenatal problems
    d. Vast array perinatal and postnatal diseases and injuries
    e. Genetic errors
      (1) Abnormalities in how chromosomes are paired
      (2) Deletions or additions of genes to chromosomes

(3) Mutations in genes
2. Chromosomal Abnormalities—Down Syndrome
   a. Fetus receives too few or too many chromosomes
   b. 21st pair chromosomes fail to separate during maturation of egg
   c. Egg fertilized—contains three chromosomes (not usual two)
   d. Down Syndrome also known as *trisomy 21*
   e. Extra chromosome disrupts cell metabolism
   f. Error in reproductive process—not inherited
   g. Adults show pattern of brain cell deterioration
3. Genetic Additions or Deletions—Fragile X and Williams Syndromes
   a. Fragile X Syndrome
      (1) Involves chromosome 23—*sex-linked chromosome*
      (2) Duplicate in the female (xx) male normally (xy)
      (3) Excess of genetic material on one tip of x makes "fragile"
      (4) Heritable—worsens as passed one generation to another
      (5) Retardation less in females because of the two x's
   b. Williams Syndrome
      (1) Deleted gene on chromosome 7
      (2) Demonstrate vocabulary and grammar skills
      (3) Fascinated with sounds, hearing extremely good
      (4) Severely limited spatial ability, including drawing
      (5) Described "language in the relative absence of thought"
      (6) All have heart defects; smaller-than-normal cerebral cortex
4. Genetic Mutations: PKU
   a. *Phenylketonuria*—abnormality in protein metabolism
   b. Carried by recessive gene
   c. Infant poisoned by *phenylalanine* in foods (meat and cow's milk)
   d. Enzyme required for conversion of phenylalanine to tyrosine is missing; converted instead to *phenylpyruvic acid*
   e. Phenylpyruvic acid toxic to central nervous system, thus retardation
   f. Newborns now routinely screened for condition
5. Environmental Damage to the Central Nervous System
   a. Viral and bacterial infections that cross the placenta
   b. *Rubella* causes mental retardation, deafness, etc
   c. Herpes virus in mother—mental retardation in child
   d. *Teratogens*—cocaine, tobacco, marijuana, alcohol
   e. Two drinks of alcohol can result in IQ drop of 7 points
   f. Five or more drinks associated with *fetal alcohol syndrome* (FAS)
   g. Premature birth and low birth weight cause slower development
   h. Head injuries, brain tumors, and infectious diseases (encephalitis)
6. Psychosocial Adversity
   a. *Cultural-familial*—retardation with no known organic cause
   b. Due to psychosocial disadvantage
   c. Linked to greater number of adversities in lower socioeconomic
   d. Parents with limited skills more critical; less attentive

    e. Form of *environmental deprivation*
  D. Detecting and Preventing Mental Retardation
   1. Prenatal Detection and Prevention
    a. Parents complete detailed interview of family's history
    b. Submit to blood analysis of their chromosomes
   2. *Amniocentesis*—samples of blood or amniotic fluid
    a. Good physical and psychological health in mother
    b. T.V. ads and warnings on bottles to increase awareness
   3. Postnatal Detection and Early Childhood Education
    a. Prevention by early detection as in PKU
    b. Controlling diets of infants with lactose or fructose intolerance
    c. Nursery or preschool programs with intellectually enriched environment
    d. Head Start programs for children and parents
  E. Treatment of Mental Retardation
   1. Treatment techniques
    a. *Applied behavior analysis*—complex broken down to smaller units
    b. *Target behaviors* followed by positive consequences
    c. Formal applications—*behavior modification programs*
    d. Used to teach self-care skills (washing, dressing, eating, toileting)
    e. Self-instruction—repeat instructions aloud or use pictures
   2. Special Problems in the Treatment of Self-Injury
    a. Abnormal regulation of *endogenous opiates*—retarded have excess
    b. *Naltrexone* (keeps opiates from reaching receptors)
    c. "Escape from task demands" powerful reinforcer of self-injury
    d. Aversive consequences not well taken by some experts
   3. Institutionalization and Normalization
    a. Prior to 70's children institutionalized
    b. Residential program, staffed professionals: better care, education
    c. Parents protected from psychological distress
    d. In the 70s— *Normalization* Movement
    e. "Norms and patterns of the mainstream society" in everyday life
    f. Emphasis on family care; education in public schools; community
    g. Severe, profoundly retarded: supervised apt. dwelling, foster homes
   4. Special Education and Mainstreaming
    a. 1975 Individuals with Disabilities Act—special education mandatory
    b. *Individualized education program*—formal record goals, strategies
    c. Partially served in regular classrooms—*mainstreaming*
    d. *Inclusion*—teachers move one class to another; extra help to needy
III. Autistic Disorders (pp. 135-143)
  A. Autism Derived From Greek (*Autos*)
   1. Literal preoccupation with the self
   2. Incapable of relating to parents or to other people
   3. More interest in objects than people
  B. Kanner's contemporary guidelines

     1. Severe deficits in establishing *reciprocal* social relationships
     2. Nonexistent or poor language skills
   C. Typical Autism
     1. DSM-IV—problems must be present before age 3
     2. Autism described as *Spectrum Disorder*
     3. Social Relationship Problems
       a. Gross and sustained impairment in reciprocal social interaction
       b. Unaware of others or view them as objects
     4. Expressive Language Deficits
       a. Spoken language absent or minimal in 50% autistic
       b. In other 50%, pragmatic use of language extremely limited
     5. Stereotypic Behavior
       a. Inflexible adherence to a specific routine
       b. *Insistence on sameness* in physical and psychological environment
       c. Stereotyped body movements; some self-injurious
     6. Distinguishing Autism from Mental Retardation
       a. Mentally retarded engage others socially; use language to interact
       b. Autistic near average in nonverbal intellectual skills
   D. Causes of Autistic Disorder
     1. Biological factors
       a. Genetic basis for autism suggested by twin studies
       b. Complications of pregnancy and birth
       c. Cerebellum and frontal lobes less well developed than normal
       d. Serotonin levels significantly higher
     2. Psychological Factors
       a. Deficit in understanding or expression of emotional states
       b. Cognitive and social disabilities
       c. Cannot assign meaning to social stimuli—as mother's face
       d. Deficit in *theory of mind*
       e. Do very poorly on *executive functioning* tests
   E. Other Pervasive Developmental Disorders (Atypical Autistic Disorders)
     1. Rett's disorder
     2. Child disintegrative disorder
     3. Asperger's disorder (autistic psychopathy)
     4. Pervasive developmental disorder not otherwise specified
   F. Treatment of Pervasive Developmental Disorders
     1. Behavior modification
     2. Education
     3. Medication—the antipsychotic *haloperidol*
IV. Learning Disabilities (pp. 143-149)
   A. Defining and Identifying Learning Disabilities
     1. Defining
       a. Underachieving children who do *not* have mental retardation
       b. *Not* emotionally disturbed; *not* culturally deprived
       c. No specific cause received empirical support
       d. DSM-IV—achievement in reading, writing, mathematics is below

       that expected for age, schooling, and level of intelligence
    e. Discrepancy of 2 or more standard deviations between achievement and IQ
    f. Differentiates by area of academic deficit; specify reading, writing, and written expression; overlap in reading and writing
    g. *Nonverbal* type—relatively normal reading and spelling, but difficulties in visual-motor skills, math, and social skills

B. Reading Disabilities
 1. *Dyslexia* most frequent learning problem
 2. Poor readers *do not* perceive letters and words as reversed
 3. Do not make abnormal eye movements; do not benefit from glasses
 4. Most consistent differences are *linguistic*
 5. Poor readers have more difficulty remembering verbal information
 6. Problems in *phonetic decoding* (phonemes smallest sound unit)

C. Causes of Reading Disability
 1. Genetic and Neurological Factors
  a. Reading problems run in families
  b. Fathers and sons (poor-reading families) show similar patterns
  c. Higher concordance in monozygotic twins
  d. Location of genes by *linkage analysis*
  e. Genes on chromosomes 1, 6, and 15 may be involved with reading
  f. Normal adults—*planum temporale* larger, longer on the left side
  g. Note—left temporal lobe specialized to handle language
  h. Poor readers show symmetry
  i. Poor readers smaller neurons on the left side
 2. The Role of Schooling and Parenting
  a. Failures in how reading is taught
  b. Poor readers given fewer opportunities to read orally
  c. Reading curricula not matched to individual needs
  d. Parents affect *learning readiness*
  e. Factors—self-efficacy, persistence, emotional responses to feedback
  f. Children who succeed reinforced, buffered from stress, secure
  g. *Compensatory strategies* could lessen impact biological problems

D. Prevention and Treatment of Learning Disabilities
 1. Ideal Program for Prevention
  a. Screen children for deficits in phonetic decoding
  b. Give individual intensive training to segment words
 2. Treatment
  a. Only treatment with clear positive effects—educational intervention
   Two methods of reading instruction
   (1) *whole language*— teaches child to recognize whole word
   (2) *sound-based*—teaches phonetic decoding word recognition

4 Developmental Disorders and Learning Disabilities

LECTURE MAKER 4.1

Purpose To introduce developmental concept and differences among children with art work. (pp. 122-123)

Lecture Introduction Discuss criteria related to a mental retardation diagnosis. Explain limitations of skills acquisition and cognitive functioning for development disorders. Review cultural-familial retardation. Explain the Draw-a-Person test as a diagnostic tool used with children.

Demonstration With permission and protection of the children's anonymity, have elementary school children "draw their family." Out of every thirty drawings or so, one will usually be odd. Twenty-nine drawings will have a sun, smiling faces and a pet (the "normal") and one will be crudely drawn, have angry faces or other unusual features. Showing the children's drawings to your class impresses them with the developmental consistency of ability and the obvious inconsistency with the "odd" picture. (Your students can collect these samples for extra credit.)

Variations on The Theme
1. Invite an Exceptional Education teacher to speak to your class.
2. Invite a speaker from Child Protective Services
3. Videotape a few minutes from Sesame Street. This is one of the few shows that includes exceptional children in the cast.

Lecture Capsule Students normally shy away from these discussions due to the emotional concern and uncertainty for their own future children.

LECTURE MAKER 4.2

Purpose To dramatically present seriously disturbed children in a language acquisition program. (pp. 137-138)

Resource Behavior Modification: Teaching Language to Psychotic Children (EMC, 43min)

Lecture Introduction Research from Lovaas using an operant conditioning paradigm. Review the principles of operant conditioning as a therapeutic technique. Lovaas termed these children as "psychotic." Would there be a more fitting DSM-IV diagnosis today? Define self-abusive behavior and controlling techniques. Describe the criteria for autistic disorder.

Demonstration This is a vivid video, and has been the focus of some controversy. Prepare your students for the possible emotional stirrings brought about by this video. Play the tape for the class.

Lecture Capsule This video engenders a wide ranging discussion. Remind students of ethics in research, the probability of lifetime institutionalization for these children, and the training necessary to implement a program like this. From the casebook, weave in the story of Delano, his experiences with having an EEG, and the information received from it into your discussion.

Resources

Associations Organizations
The Arc, a national organization on mental retardation
You can join The Arc, or get the location of our chapter in your area by contacting:
The Arc of the United States
500 East Border Street
Arlington, Texas 76010
(817) 261-6003 (Voice)
(817) 277-3491 (FAX)
(817) 277-0553 (TDD)

Children and Adults with Attention Deficit Disorder
C.H.A.D.D.
499 Northwest 70th Avenue
Suite 101
Plantation, Florida 33317
(800) 233-4050
WEBMASTER @ CHADD.ORG

THE LEARNING CENTER is a professional clinic-school directed by Dr. Gerald Deskin, Ph. D. Since 1967 for children, adolescents and adults with learning disabilities. It is operated by the non-profit, Learning Center Foundation and is located at 16944 Ventura Blvd. Encino, Ca. 91316
Phone: (818) 783-6633   E-Mail: Dr. Gerald Deskin

Learning Disabilities Association
4156 Library Road
Pittsburgh, PA 15234-1349
(412) 341-1515 (Voice)
(412) 344-0224 (FAX)
E-Mail LDANATL@USAOR.NET

Media

Autism's Lonely Children
 (PCR, 20 min)
Excellent depiction of childhood disorders

Behavior Modification: Teaching Language to Psychotic Children
 (EMC, 43 min)
Lovaas Operant Conditioning of speech with severely disturbed children

Behavior Therapy with an Autistic Child
(USPHS, 40 min)
Operant conditioning with an autistic child

Harry: Behavioral Treatment of Self-Abuse
(RP, 38 min)
Harry is mentally retarded and behavior modification is used

Learning Disabilities
(FHS, 19 min)
Case study of a 9-year-old

Learning Disability: A Family Crisis
(MVP, 41 min)
An 8-year-old with a learning disability is diagnosed.

Case Video to accompany Nietzel et al.,
Abnormal Psychology Features Devon, an autistic boy, whose mother is interviewed by pediatric psychologist, Sandra D'Angelo

Nietzel et al., *Abnormal Psychology*, Transparencies

Chapter Four

	Text Figure Number	Text Page Number
27. Criteria for Mental Retardation		122
28. Diathesis-Stress Model of Mild Mental Retardation	4.2	129
29. Criteria for Autistic Disorder		136
30. Multiple Factors in the Etiology of Autistic Disorder	4.4	140

5 Stress, Sleep, and Adjustment Disorders

CHAPTER OUTLINE

I. What Is Stress? (pp. 154-159)
   A. Stress
      1. Process occurs when environmental or social threats (called *stressors*) place demands on individuals
      2. Way an individual experiences depends on
         a. The nature and timing of the stressors
         b. Person's psychological characteristics and social situation
         c. Biochemical variables that influence stress responses
   B. Types of Stressors
      1. Unpredictable traumas
         a. Earthquakes, floods, natural disasters, serious accidents
         b. Violent encounters with other persons
         c. Four major crimes
            (1) Rape
            (2) Other sexual assault
            (3) Assault with weapon
            (4) Killing of a family member
         d. Even if only one in lifetime—leaves lasting psychological scars
         e. Sample of adolescents' trauma
            (1) 18% of boys age 10-16 victim of assault with weapon or that resulted in physical injury
            (2) 15% of girls victims of sexual assault
            (3) 6% children victims of attempted kidnappings
      2. Predictable Stressors
         a. Getting married, having children, starting college, new job
         b. Academic setbacks, financial losses, occupational failures
         c. Marital difficulties, unemployment, illness or death of loved one
      3. Occupational Stressors
         a. Air-traffic controllers—life and death decisions
         b. Waitresses—always urged to hurry
         c. Miners—constant danger of cave-in
         d. Jobs that make many demands—allow little or no control
   C. Individual Differences and Potential Stressors
      1. Exposure to Stressors—Individual and Cultural Differences
         a. People differ in responses due to meaning each gives event
         b. Certain people more likely to experience stressful events
         c. Possibly poor social skill or long-term psychological handicaps unintentionally bring them about
         d. Repeated financial or interpersonal setbacks lead to more stress
         e. Severe stressors cause change in brain chemistry
         f. Ethnic differences, gender and age affect frequency and types

2. Reactions to Stressors—Individual and Cultural Differences
    a. *Subjectively perceived* stress correlated with later adjustment problems more than frequency of negative life events
    b. Harmful impact exists in minds of those who experience them
    c. Factors determine how a person reacts to and copes with stress
        (1) When they have to cope alone; no social support
        (2) When they feel helpless or unable to control
        (3) Caused by intentional or careless behavior of another
    d. Confident person may view stressors as challenges
    e. Introverted or shy person may be traumatized

D. Measuring Stress
  1. Schedule of Recent Experience (SRE) examples
    a. Major changes in eating or sleeping habits
    b. Being fired from work
    c. Death of a relative or close friend
    d. Major business readjustment
    e. Each event given weight of amount of adjustment to cope
  2. Life Experience Survey (LES)
    a. Respondents rate positive or negative impact of event
    b. More sensitive to cultural influences
  3. Hassles Scale
    a. How much hassle in prior month
    b. Minor problems—losing things, meetings, forms, sudden guests

E. Effects of Stressors
  1. Three stages of *general adaption syndrome*
    a. Alarm reaction—*flight-or-fight response*
    b. Stressor persists—*stage of resistance*
    c. Stressor continues long enough—*stage of exhaustion*

II. Reactions to Stress (pp. 160-167)
  A. Physiological Reactions
    1. Alarm Reaction—*hypothalamic-pituitary-adrenalcortical axis* acts
      a. Hypothalamus secretes corticotropin—releasing hormone (CRH)
      b. CRH starts chain of physiological and biochemical defenses
        (1) Pituitary secretes *adrenocorticotrophic hormone* (ACTH)
        (2) Adrenal glands release *adrenal corticosteroids*-hormones
        (3) Autonomic nervous system shuts down
        (4) Heart rate, blood pressure, respiration, glucose increase
        (5) Pupils dilate, muscles tense, immune responses slow
        (6) CRH stops, completing *negative feedback loop*
      c. Hypothalamus releases epinephrine and norepinephrine
        (1) Catecholamines stimulate heart rate, raise blood pressure
        (2) Stimulate central nervous system—attention, concentration
        (3) Heightened anxiety or even panic accompany changes
      d. Two stress alarms interact, produce adaptive changes
        (1) Activate production of *endogenous opioids*

      (2) *Endorphins* regulate cardiovascular activity, relieve pain, facilitate psychological coping with stress
      (3) Physical exercise releases endorphins (stress coping)
    2. Experiencing the Alarm Reaction
     a. During stressor
      (1) Perceptual, cognitive, behavioral adjustments made
      (2) Attention riveted on the stressor
     b. After stressor
      (1) Arms and legs shake; heart thumps; breath in gasps
      (2) Dizziness common; knotted up stomach
    3. Reactions to Prolonged Stress
     a. Stressor persists; person enters resistance phase
     b. Prolonged stress hormones—chronically high blood pressure, damages muscle tissue, inhibits body's ability to heal
     c. Sustained corticosteroids—wear and tear on part of nervous system
     d. *Immunosuppression*—physical illnesses such as cancer
 B. Stress and the Immune System
    1. Compromised immunity result of
     a. Sleep deprivation, final examinations, divorce, loss of loved one, caring for chronically ill relatives
     b. Depressed or angry mood, negative thinking, conditioned stimuli
    2. Components of the Immune System
     a. *Innate immunity*—present from birth—first defense against pathogens
      (1) Skin wards off germs
      (2) Mucus contains chemical to fight virus
     b. *Specific immunity*—acquired, not innate
      (1) Detection of the invading pathogen
      (2) Destruction of pathogens using T and B *lymphocytes*
      (3) Detection done by *macrophages*—find pathogens by *antigens*
      (4) Macrophages use chemical messenger—*interleukin-1*
      (5) Interleukin-1 calls in T-cells and activates them for battle
      (6) *T-helpers* secrete interleukin-2 to call more t-cells, b-cells
      (7) T-cells produced in thymus; b-cells in bone marrow
      (8) Killer t-cells use chemical warfare, destroy pathogens
      (9) B-cells divide into plasma cells; release *antibodies*
      (10) Memory t-cells, b-cells react if pathogen comes back
      (11) *Suppressor t-cells* call off the troops when war is won
      (12) Stop killer cells from creating *autoimmune disease*
    3. Stress and Psychological Disorders
     a. Psychological reactions become maladaptive if last too long
     b. Effects—anxiety, helplessness, frustration, hostility, sleeplessness
     c. Severe stress contributes to several specific mental disorders
     d. Examples—sleep, adjustment, PTSD, dissociative, and somatoform

III. Sleep Disorders (pp. 167-173)
   A. The Process of Sleep
      1. EEG measure used in *polysomnographic (PSG) assessment*
         a. PSG done while person observed in sleep laboratory
         b. Biological measures of muscle and eye movements, heart activity
      2. Stages of Sleep
         a. Stage 1—light sleep, can be easily awakened
         b. Stage 2—sleep deepens; changes in brain activity
         c. Stage 3-4— deep or *delta* sleep-slower delta brain waves
         d. Immune system thought to replenish in deep sleep
         e. Stage 5— light sleep in which REM occurs (1-4 are non-REM)
         f. During REM sleep muscles so relaxed, person is almost paralyzed
         g. Locus coeruleus does not release norepinephrine during REM sleep
         h. Deprived of REM sleep; retention of material poor for previous day
         i. Person passes through full sleep cycle 4 to 6 times each night
      3. Biological Regulation of Sleep
         a. *Circadian rhythms*—sleep happens about every 24 hours
         b. Body is equipped with biological clock maintaining rhythms
         c. Clock in *supra chiasmatic nucleus* of hypothalamus
         d. Eyes sense darkness; pineal gland begins to produce *melatonin*
   B. Types of Sleep Disorders
      1. DSM-IV classifies sleep disorders in four major categories
         a. Sleep disorders related to another mental disorder
         b. Sleep disorders due to a general medical condition
         c. Substance induced sleep disorders
         d. Infant sleep disorder
      2. Arise from interaction of biological, psychological, behavioral, cultural
      3. Dyssomnias
         a. Primary dissomnia—so much trouble falling asleep or staying asleep that one suffers significant distress or impairment
         b. Many insomniacs engage in more active thinking at night
         c. Dyssomnias
            (1) Infant sleep disturbance affects 15-25% of infants
            (2) primary hypersomnia—excessive sleepiness
            (3) narcolepsy—suffers sudden attacks REM sleep, *cataplexy*
      4. Parasomnias
         a. *Nightmare disorder*—repeated frightening dreams
         b. *Sleep terror disorder*—wakes with scream or panicky cry
         c. *Sleepwalking disorder*—person leaves bed and roams about
   C. Treatment of Sleep Disorders
      1. Most common treatment for insomnia is medication
         a. Prescription drugs: Halcion, Dalmane, Valium
         b. Hypersomnia treated with Ritalin (stimulants)
         c. Narcolepsy treated with antidepressants
      2. Drugs have disadvantages
         a. Sleepiness during the daytime

                b.   Often induce dependence
                c.   When discontinued, problem worse than when started
          3.   Psychological treatments for insomnia
                a.   Relaxation techniques counter tension
                b.   Cognitive therapy reduce tendency to ruminate and worry
                c.   Sleep hygiene counseling most effective
                      (1)   Not using caffeine or alcohol before bedtime
                      (2)   Going to bed same time every night; rise same time
                      (3)   Only sleep and sex in bedroom; no work or TV
IV.   Adjustment Disorders (pp. 173-179)
        A.   DSM-IV Classification
            1.   Significant behavioral, psychological symptoms in response to stressor
            2.   Symptoms occur within 3 months after; last no longer than 6 months
            3.   Chronic last longer (e.g. financial setbacks associated with divorce)
            4.   Symptoms exceed what would be normally expected from exposure
            5.   Five subtypes of adjustment disorders
                a.   Adjustment disorder with anxiety
                b.   Adjustment disorder with depressed mood
                c.   Adjustment disorder with disturbance of conduct
                d.   Adjustment disorder with mixed disturbance emotions and conduct
                e.   Adjustment disorder with mixed anxiety and depressed mood
            6.   Mixed common among adolescents; depressed subtype among adults
            7.   Typical mild and of limited duration; sort of "wastebasket" category
        B.   Triggers for Adjustment Disorders
            1.   Stressors That Give Rise to Adjustment Disorders
                a.   Can be one-time events (divorce or repeated occupational failure)
                b.   May last a short time (earthquake)
                c.   Stretch on lengthy period (chronic illness of a loved one)
            2.   Adjustment Disorders and Natural Disasters
                a.   Adjustment disorder with mixed disturbance of emotion
                b.   Fear of leaving home, fear someone at home is hurt
                c.   Forgetful of little things, frequent nightmares
            3.   Adjustment Disorders and Technological Disasters
                a.   Severity of psychological problems related to extent or length of exposure to the danger
                b.   Floods—higher the water; longer person in them; more serious it is
                c.   Israeli children (Persian Gulf War) missiles near homes, families
            4.   Adjustment Disorders and Interpersonal Stressors
                a.   Development of Social Readjustment Rating Questionnaire
                b.   People rated divorce and marital separation as 2nd and 3rd most upsetting life events possible (1st is death of spouse)
                c.   Interpersonal problems often chronic; impact all family members
                d.   Involve loss of social support; usually involve shame
        C.   Treatment of Adjustment Disorders
            1.   Enhancing Problem-Focused Coping
                a.   Strengthening person's ability to solve problems is effective

    b. Successful in divorce, occupational stressors, financial setbacks
    c. Particular success in coping skills of children and adolescents
    d. Goal attained through friends or family or formal counseling
    e. Effective problem solving therapy follows seven steps
      (1) Define the problem clearly
      (2) Identify alternative strategies
      (3) Evaluate short-term and long-term consequences
      (4) List several alternative tactics for general strategy
      (5) Choose tactic that appears to have best chance of resolving
      (6) Act on decisions reached in previous steps
      (7) Assess; if problem not resolved, return to earlier stages
  2. Enhancing Emotion-Focused Coping
    a. Expressing feelings about stressor unburdens; allows new thoughts
    b. Writing ventilates negative feelings, clarifies, considers new ways
    c. Study (Pennebaker et al., 1988)
      (1) 25 students wrote about traumatic events in their lives
        (a) Showed better immune system functioning
        (b) Made fewer visits to the health center
        (c) Reported less emotional distress
      (2) 25 students wrote about trivial events in their lives
        (a) Showed less immune system functioning
        (b) Made more visits to the health center
        (c) Reported more emotional distress
    d. Another study—students wrote or spoke about traumatic events
      (1) Wrote or spoke only 20 minutes per week
      (2) Better immune control over Epstein-Barr antibodies
    e. Writing or talking improves functioning even years after event
    f. Survivors of Nazi Holocaust during World War II
      (1) Disclosed strong negative feelings in interview 40 years later
      (2) Demonstrated greater improvements in health
    g. Disclosure may cause short-term surge in negative emotions
    h. Long-term effects of emotion-focused coping largely positive
    i. Emotional disclosures relieves negativity, increases confidence
    j. As confidence grows, individual releases pessimism
    k. *Dispositional optimism*—good things will eventually happen
  3. Enhancing Social Support
    a. Therapists help clients become more receptive to social support
    b. Client may want an image of sturdy independence
    c. Client thinks turning to others "sign of weakness"
    d. They will lose respect of others
    e. Therapists counter—how does client feel when asked to help
    f. Client admits closeness to those who need help

5 Stress, Sleep, and Adjustment Disorders

LECTURE MAKER 5.1

Purpose To provide a self-awareness instrument that quantitatively defines stress and predicts effects. (pp 159-163)

Lecture Introduction Present stress definition, summarize stress effects and reactions, and describe the general adaptation syndrome. Introduce the Holmes and Rahe Stress Test. Duplicate copies for students to individually and anonymously complete.

Demonstration With students' reflection on their own scores, discuss the implication of high scoring and illness.

Lecture Capsule Review the autoimmune system suppression effects as a result of cumulative and massive stress. Discuss the "mind/body" connection and health preserving behaviors.

LECTURE MAKER 5.2

Purpose To demonstrate strategies for cognitive change, enhance self esteem, and facilitate positive coping techniques. (pp. 164-167)

Lecture Introduction Brief the students on cognitive attitude change, affirmations, and self esteem enhancement. Relate coping styles to stress reactions and effects.

Demonstration These activities may be assigned or extra credit but they can be demonstrated in class and followed up in a later discussion.
1. Stop-Think—Get a box of medium to large rubber bands and pass one out to each student. Put one rubber band on your wrist and discuss the snap-the-rubber-band-when-you-have-a-negative-thought technique. This technique can be applied to smoking, nail-biting and other habits. Explain the aversive and immediate conditioning as it relates to thought processes.
2. Self Affirmations—Be prepared for giggles with this demonstration but assure the students that it is an effective self esteem building tool. Assignment: write 5 self affirmations a day, read them aloud and practice smiling at themselves in the mirror. Demonstrate (even as they laugh). Collect summaries of their affirmation experiences and read excerpts later.
3. Fun Things to Do—Ask students what they enjoy spending time doing. You can take suggestions and write them on the board or collect their personal lists to share in class. *Note that many pleasurable experiences cost no money and are easily accessible. Relate this list to positive coping techniques for stress relief and release.

Lecture Capsule Relating stress to the individual student's life internalizes this material nicely. Concepts come alive and make sense. You can weave much of the chapter around these demonstrations.

☺**Things to do to treat yourself**☺

      A   OP $ W

1. Walking

2. Jogging

3. Playing a game

4. Listening to music

5. Going to the beach

6. Singing

7. Fishing

8. Meditating

9. Your idea

A=can be done alone

OP=need other people

$=needs money

W=done in past week

Social Readjustment Rating Scale 5.1

The amount of life stress a person has experienced in a given period of time, say one year, is measured by the total number of life change units (LCUs). These units result from the addition of the values (shown in the right column) associated with events that the person has experienced during the target time period.

Rank	Life Event	Mean Value
1	Death of spouse	100
2	Divorce	73
3	Marital separation	65
4	Jail term	63
5	Death of close family member	63
6	Personal injury or illness	53
7	Marriage	50
8	Fired at work	47
9	Marital reconciliation	45
10	Retirement	45
11	Change in health of family member	44
12	Pregnancy	40
13	Sex difficulties	39
14	Gain of new family member	39
15	Business readjustment	39
16	Change in financial state	38
17	Death of close friend	37
18	Change to different line of work	36
19	Change in number of arguments with spouse	35
20	Mortgage over $10,000	31
21	Foreclosure of mortgage or loan	30
22	Change in responsibilities at work	29
23	Son or daughter leaving home	29
24	Trouble with in-laws	29
25	Outstanding personal achievement	28
26	Wife begin or stop work	26
27	Begin or end school	26
28	Change in living conditions	25
29	Revision of personal habits	24
30	Trouble with boss	23
31	Change in work hours or conditions	20
32	Change in residence	20
33	Change in schools	20
34	Change in recreation	19
35	Change in church activities	19
36	Change in social activities	18
37	Mortgage or loan less than $10,000	17
38	Change in sleeping habits	16
39	Change in number of family get-togethers	15
40	Change in eating habits	15
41	Vacation	13
42	Christmas	12
43	Minor violations of the law	11

Source: Thomas H. Holmes and Richard H. Rahe "The Social Readjustment Rating Scale," *Journal of Psychosomatic Research, II* (1967), 213-218

RESOURCES

Associations   The Association for Applied Psychophysiology and Biofeedback
Organizations   10200 W. 44th Avenue
Suite 304
Wheat Ridge, CO 80033-2840
USA
1-800-477-8892 / 303-422-8436
AAPB @ resourcenter.com

Media

Facing Reality (McG, 12 min)
Defense Mechanisms renewed

A Perfectly Normal Day (CCF, 28 min)
How to cope with everyday stress

Stress (PCR, 11 min)
A demonstration of Selye's general adaptation syndrome

Nietzel et al., *Abnormal Psychology*, Transparencies

Chapter Five

	Text Figure Number	Text Page Number

31. The Process of Stress...5.1.............155

32. Schematic Diagram of the Biological Basis of Stress Response...............160

33. Activation of the Autonomic Nervous System...........................5.2.............161

34. Physiological Stress Responses..5.3.............162

6 Psychological Factors and Health

CHAPTER OUTLINE

I. Mind, Body, and Health Psychology (pp.0 184-188)
   A. *Health psychology*—specialty devoted to studying "psychological influences on how people stay healthy, why they become ill, and how they respond when they do get ill"
      1. Health psychologists concentrate on
         a. Understanding how psychological and physiological factors interact to influence illness and health
         b. Identifying *risk factors* for sickness; *protective factors* for health
         c. Developing and evaluating techniques for promoting healthy behaviors and preventing unhealthy ones
         d. Developing and evaluating psychological interventions that contribute to the effective treatment of illness
      2. Behavioral medicine—integrates behavioral science and biomedical knowledge into interdisciplinary effort to understand, treat, prevent illness
      3. Health psychology and behavioral medicine follow *biopsychosocial model*; physical illnesses outgrowth of biological vulnerability, psychological processes, and social conditions
      4. Sir William Osler (1849-1919) father of behavioral medicine; believed many symptoms heart disease brought on by anger, worry, or sudden shock
      5. Major risk factors for developing chronic illnesses are *behaviors* (smoking, unhealthy eating habits, alcohol abuse)
      6. Psychological factors in physical illness (onset or severity)
         a. Heart disease
         b. Ulcers
         c. Asthma
         d. Stomach disorders
         e. Cancer
         f. Arthritis
         g. Headaches
         h. Hypertension
      7. Modern behavioral science psychological factors influence on all diseases
   B. Classifying Psychological Factors Affecting Health
      1. More difficult to sharply divide "physical" from "mental"
         a. Schizophrenia and major depression entail mixture
         b. Depression adversely affects course of diabetes
         c. Diabetes ultimately leads to clinical depression
      2. DSM-IV deals with dilemma three ways
         a. Axis III—general medical conditions related to mental disorder
         b. Special rules for classifying mental disorders caused by drugs, medical conditions
         c. Directs clinicians to use multiple diagnoses to classify *all* conditions of given patient

    3. No diagnosable medical condition explains symptoms in somatoform disorder
    4. Factitious disorders—person fakes or exaggerates physical or psychological symptoms to play role of one who is sick (mental disorder)
    5. *Malingering*—not a mental disorder, deliberately faking symptoms for tangible gain or avoidance of unwanted obligations
  C. Linking Psychosocial Factors and Illness
    1. Various illnesses result from specific unconscious emotional problems
     a. Ulcers linked to oral conflicts
     b. Migraine headaches to repressed hostility
    2. Question not *whether* psychological factors are linked, but *how*
     a. Disease can cause psychological changes
     b. Disease and psychological conditions both influenced by common underlying biological process
     c. Psychological and social influences exert influence on biological
     d. Psychological and social influence encourage unhealthy behavior
II. The Psychology of Getting Sick (pp. 188-201)
  A. Psychological Factors in Cardiovascular Diseases
    1. Coronary Heart Disease
     a. Over half a million Americans die from CHD every year
     b. Main cause is *atherosclerosis*
      (1) Flow of blood to heart is reduced by *plaque*
      (2) Plaque damages arterial walls leads to *aneurysms*
     c. Two most serious clinical consequences of CHD
      (1) *Angina pectoris*—chest pains due to lack of oxygen
      (2) *Myocardial infarctions*—heart attacks—blood to heart cut off
    2. Hypertension
     a. High blood pressure puts strain on heart
     b. Left untreated, kidney problems, heart failure, strokes
     c. *Essential hypertension*—not caused by organic factors
    3. Stress and Cardiovascular Diseases
     a. Genetics and sociocultural factors cannot explain CHD, hypertension
     b. Scientists study role of stress and personality characteristics
     c. Manuck studied monkeys' responses to different stressors
    4. People react to threatening stimuli and other stressors with
     a. Increases in heart rates, pronounced changes in blood pressure
     b. Changes in levels of epinephrine, norepinephrine, sodium secretion
    5. Psychological factors affect meaning and therefore impact of stressors
     a. When people think they have no control over stressful event; experience anxiety or fear
     b. Surge in heart rate or "butterflies in the stomach"
     c. Greatest reactivity to stressors—hostility or competitiveness
    6. Ethnicity, gender, and age related to tendency or overreact
     a. Black Americans, men, older people higher rates heart disease
     b. Greater-than-average blood pressure responses to stressors

7. Identifying the Type A Behavior Pattern
   a. The *"hurry sickness"* characteristics
      (1) Highly competitive, driving hard to achieve maximums
      (2) Success in terms of quantity of work finished
      (3) Amount of recognition received too important
      (4) Pursuit of visible success is relentless
      (5) Heightened sense of *time urgency*
      (6) Restless, edgy, and nervous
      (7) Always dissatisfied with what they accomplish
      (8) Strive to maintain control as much as possible
   b. Type B behavior patterns
      (1) More relaxed; feel less time pressure in their lives
      (2) Less controlling, hostile, and competitive
      (3) Thrive on tasks that require careful analysis; concentration
8. Does Type A Behavior Cause CHD?
   a. Western Collaborative Group Study
      (1) 3,500 men ages 39-59 for 8.5 years
      (2) Type A men twice as likely to have heart attacks
   b. Framingham Heart Study
      (1) 1600 men and women followed for 8 years
      (2) Twice as many participants (A) developed CHD
   c. National Heart, Lung, and Blood Institute
      (1) Type A risk factor equal in magnitude to smoking
      (2) Type A same risk as high levels LDL cholesterol
   d. Negative Affect and CHD
      (1) Most risky component Type A—hostility, anger, cynicism
      (2) Cynicism and distrust greater risk for CHD
      (3) Chronic negative emotions create risk for CHD
      (4) Anxiety significantly predicted hypertension
      (5) *Vital exhaustion* (burnout) fatigue, dejection, defeat, irritability leads to risk for angina and heart attacks
      (6) Depression, aggressive competitiveness, anger leads to CHD
   e. Some Tentative Conclusions About Type A and CHD
      (1) Type A overreact physiologically to threat or anger
      (2) Competitiveness and hostility create conflict
      (3) Frequent angry outbursts lead to rapid swings in hormones
      (4) Chemical changes weaken arteries
      (5) Type A too busy to go to doctor, eat balanced diet, get enough sleep, engage in regular exercise
      (6) They eat on the run, consume excessive caffeine, and smoke tobacco
      (7) These unhealthy *behaviors* more critical to development of CHD than biological effects
      (8) Unhealthy behaviors and emotional driven wear and tear on cardiovascular system may be complete explanation CHD

B. Psychological Factors and the Immune System
1. Psychological characteristics increase disease risks via biological mechanism
   a. Influence on immune system-body's defense system
   b. *Psychoneuroimmunology*—study of how brain, immune system, and psychological processes affect each other
   c. Study done—rats inhibit immune system by Pavlovian conditioning
   d. Psychological process (learning) influence immunity
2. *Anticipatory nausea*—adult cancer patients vomit 24 hours before drugs
3. Patients associate chemotherapy (unconditioned responses) with sights, sounds, and smells of hospital (conditioned stimuli)
4. Stress, the Immune System, and Illness
   a. Rates of children's infections increase when family under stress
   b. Interpersonal stressors can impair immunological functioning
   c. Healthy students suffer decline in immune systems at finals
5. AIDS
   a. Caused by *human immunodeficiency virus type 1*
   b. Destroys immune system's T cells
   c. 650,000 to 1 million Americans are HIV positive
   d. 20 million people worldwide
   e. Fourth leading killer of American women 18-44—linked to
      (1) Increases in women's poverty
      (2) Use of intravenous drugs
      (3) Sexual abuse victimization
   f. Psychological factors implicated in AIDS
      (1) Most cases of AIDS can be prevented by avoiding
         (a) Heavy use of alcohol or drugs before sex
         (b) Sexual activity with multiple partners
         (c) Partners with an unknown sexual history
         (d) Sexual activity without condoms
         (e) Sharing of needles used to inject drugs
      (2) Improvements in psychological functioning will be accompanied by a fortification of immune system
6. Cancer
   a. Normally cells in body divide in orderly fashion
   b. Out-of-control division leads to tumors (*metastasized)* growth
   c. Triggers—age, radiation, chemicals, environmental hazards
   d. Psychosocial factors
      (1) Mildly related to ethnicity and gender
      (2) Unhealthy habits—smoking; high level of fatty foods
   e. Certain personality types
      (1) Type C—overly conforming, emotionally blunted; appears calm on outside; denies, represses emotional turmoil
      (2) Type C feel hopeless and powerless to control own lives

C. Social Factors and Illness
  1. Stressors less likely to adversely affect people in high levels social support
     a. May buffer negative effects of stressor
     b. May increase individual's sense of well-being
     c. Socially competent have many friends; maintain better health
  2. *Socioeconomic status* measured by one's income, education, occupation
     a. Reflects person's standing relative to others in a society
     b. Strong relationship between SES and health
  3. Two studies measured *standardized mortality ratios* (ratio of deaths that actually occur to deaths that are naturally expected
     a. Lower peoples SES , greater the chance of unexpected death
     b. Lower SES, greater the rate of illness
     c. SES affects biochemical processes which in turn lead to poor health
     d. Poor basic nutrition, less medical care, exposure to hazards
  4. Psychological Functioning
     a. Social class inversely related to strong negative emotions
     b. Depressive symptoms, depression more likely among SES
     c. Hostility and chronic antagonism higher among SES
  5. Stressors
     a. People of SES face more negative life events
     b. Have fewer resources at hand to cope with stressors
  6. Unhealthy Behaviors
     a. Smoking consistently more common among less-educated
     b. People less likely to engage in physical exercise
     c. Obesity associated with lack of exercise
     d. No time to attend smoking prevention or cessation classes
     e. No motivation to stop smoking or to lose weight
     f. Unhealthy behaviors and poor nutrition lead to greater depression, increased levels of fewer adequate coping skills

III. The Psychology of Getting Well and Staying Well (pp. 201-211)
  A. Most effective interventions involve a combination of treatment techniques
     1. Training in a stress-reduction technique
        a. Relaxation training
        b. Biofeedback
        c. Hypnosis
        d. Meditation
     2. Cognitive restructuring—more adaptive ways to think about problem
     3. Offer behavioral medicine interventions in a group context
        a. Ongoing social support for members
        b. Social support provides modeling; social reinforcements
        c. Tangible aid—food, transportation, child care, financial assistance

B. Interventions for Cardiovascular Diseases
   1. Behaviors related to obesity, high LDL levels, major stressors, lack of aerobic fitness, high sodium levels, risk factors for hypertension and CHD, targeted for psychological intervention
      a. Weight reduction achieve 1 pound per week for 1 or 2 years
      b. Relapse rates in smoking cessation discouragingly high
      c. Type A behavior can be changed yielding health benefits
C. Preventing and Coping With AIDS
   1. Cognitive-behavioral techniques modify high-risk behavior
   2. Participants increased use of condoms, resistance to sexual coercion, knowledge of AIDS risks
D. Psychological Interventions and Cancer
   1. Educational programs, group and individual therapy, behavioral therapy improves psychological and physical well-being of cancer patients
      a. A year of weekly group meetings improved survival of women
      b. Patients reported less distress and fatigue, higher energy level
      c. Those receiving hypnosis reported no increase in pain
      d. Group therapy patients lived twice as long
E. Increasing Compliance with Treatment Regimens
   1. Prescribed treatment for medical illness being effective depends on
      a. Treatment needs to be correct
      b. Patient need to follow through with the treatment
   2. Systematic attempts to increase medical compliance in categories
      a. Educating patients about importance of compliance
      b. Modifying the treatment plan to make compliance easier
      c. Using behavioral and cognitive-behavioral techniques in increase patient' ability to maintain compliance
F. Interventions for Promoting Health
   1. Half of 2 million deaths could be prevented by changes in six behavioral risk factors— use of tobacco; abuse of alcohol and illegal drugs; unhealthy eating habits; infrequent use of seat belts; failure to obtain and comply with medical treatments (immunizations); risky sexual practices
G. The *Health Belief Model* (HBM)
   1. Key factors
      a. How susceptible to a given illness they believe themselves to be and how severe they think the illness would be
      b. How effective and feasible versus how costly and difficult they perceive a prescribed treatment to be
      c. How much they are bothered by internal cues and motivated by external cues that promote lifestyle changes
   2. Community-based prevention programs can be successful, combine mass media campaign with individual counseling on how to change health habits

6   Psychological Factors and Health

LECTURE MAKER 6.1

Purpose To define and illustrate defense mechanisms. (pp. 201-210)

Lecture Introduction Review the purpose of defense mechanisms and definitions.

Demonstration Write a series of scripts (like the following) to be given to two students to "act out" in front of class:

Student 1: You are the mother of a 15-year-old boy and found drug paraphernalia in his sock drawer. Confront him.

Student 2: You are a 15-year-old boy. Use denial in your reply to your "mother".

Student 1: You and a friend are considering seeing an R-rated movie. You would like to go. Ask your friend.

Student 2: You would really like to see the R-rated movie with your friend. When she asks you use reaction formation.

Student 1: You are discussing the grade you got on the test in Psychology. You got a "C" and you are fairly satisfied. Ask your friend what they got on the test.

Student 2: You got a "C" on your test in Psychology and you are furious over this injustice. Use rationalization.

Lecture Capsule You will find that the more students you can get involved with this the more fun you will have. There is usually a couple students who think they can do a better job than the last one. It is really interesting to find out just how dramatically insightful some of them can be.

LECTURE MAKER 6.2

Purpose To personalize for the students the concepts of concern to health psychologists. (pp. 184-188)

Lecture Introduction Introduce health psychology and the focus on the interaction of psychological and physiological factors in illness and health. Identify risk factors for sickness and protective factors for health. Also introduce behavioral medicine which integrates behavioral science and biomedical knowledge.

Demonstration Have the students complete the family health check list. Encourage them to add other dimensions that they can think of that influence their health (for the bottom half of the checklist). The fewer checks, the healthier the family member. Next have students compose a positive list of health-oriented behaviors for themselves.

Lecture Capsule This simple review and checklist often prods students into internalizing the information form this section of the chapter. Although they may still believe in their relative "vulnerability", the family "behaviors" and illnesses are eye-opening.

FAMILY HEALTH CHECKLIST 6.2

	Mother	Father	Siblings	Self
Heart Disease				
Ulcers				
Asthma				
Stomach Disorders				
Cancer				
Arthritis				
Headaches				
Hypertension				
UnhealthyEating Habits				
Drug/Alcohol Abuse				
Smoking				
Always Feeling Pressured/Stressed				
Anxious A Lot				
Minimal Exercise				
Frequent Negative Thoughts/Comments				

RESOURCES

General

AIDS Action Committee
661 Boylston
Boston, MA 02116
617-437-6200, ext. 216
(Women's Education)
617-536-7733 (AIDS Action Line)

AWARE
San Francisco General Hospital
995 Potrero Avenue
San Francisco, CA 94110
415-476-4091

Gay and Lesbian Counseling Services
6 Hamilton Place
Boston, MA 02108
617-542-5188

AIDS
1555 Wilson Boulevard, Suite 700
Rosslyn, VA 22209

Surgeon General's Report on AIDS
National AIDS Information Clearing
House of Centers for Disease Conrol
P.O. Box 6003
Rockville, MD 20850
800-342-7514

Women's AIDS Network
333 Valencia Street
San Francisco, CA 94103
415-864-4376

Women's AIDS Project
8235 Santa Monica Boulevard
West Hollywood, CA 90045
213-650-1508

Gay Men's Health Crisis, Inc
Publications Orders
Box 274, 132 West 24th Street
New York, NY 10011
212-807-7517

San Francisco AIDS Foundation
333 Valencia Street
San Francisco, CA 94103
415-864-4396 (business line)
415-863-AIDS (hotline)

Women and AIDS Counseling Group
Stuyvesant Polyclinic
137 Second Avenue
New York, NY 10003
212-674-0220

Women and AIDS Project
1209 Decater Street, N.W.
Washington D.C. 20011

AIDS Project of Los Angeles
3570 Wilshire Boulevard, Suite 300
Los Angeles, CA 90010
213-738-8200 Office
213-876-AIDS Hotline

AIDS and Safer Sex for Women
Fenway Community Health Center
16 Haviland Street
Boston, MA 02115

What Women Should Know About AIDS
Network Publications
P. O Box 1830
Santa Cruz, CA 95061-1830

National Initiative for AIDS and HIV
Prevention Among Adolescents
1025 Vermont Avenue, N.W.
Suite 210
Washinton, DC 20005

Teens Teaching AIDS Prevention
3030 Walnut Street
Kansas City, Missouri 64108

National Association of People with AIDS
P.O. Box 34056
Washington, DC 20043

Mothers of AIDS Patients
C/O Barbara Peabody
3404 E Street
San Deigo, California 92102

The Henry Nichols Foundation
P.O. Box 621
Cooperstown, New York 13326

National Council of Churches
AIDS Task Force
475 Riverside Drive, Room 572
New York, New York
212-870-2491

Sex Information and Education Council
of the United States (SIECUS)
130 West 42nd St., Suite 2500
New York, NY 10036
212-819-9770
A national clearing house for information about sexuality, SIECUS provides bibliographies on topics involving human sexuality, and can direct callers to agencies, hotlines and other resources to help them with their personal questions regarding AIDS or other sexual topics.

American Association of Physicians for
Human Rights
P.O. Box 14366
San Francisco, California 94114
415-558-9353

Center for Prevention Services
Centers for Disease Control
1600 Clifton Road, NE
Atlanta, GA 30333

National AIDS Information Clearinghouse
Education Database Distribution
P.O. Box 6003
Rockville, Maryland 20850

UsS. Public Health Service
Public Affairs Office
Hubert Humphrey Building, Re 725-H
200 Independence Avenue, SW
Washington, DC 20201

American Red Cross
AIDS Education Office
1730 D Street NW
Washington, DC 20006
202-737-8300

National AIDS Network
729 8th Street, SE
Washington, DC 20003

National STD Hotline
800-227-8922

National Herpes Hotline
Herpes Resource Center
Box 100
Palo Alto, CA 94302
919-361-8488

Nietzel et al., *Abnormal Psychology*, Transparencies

Chapter Six

	Text Figure Number	Text Page Number

35. Personality and Environmental Influences on Disease.........................6.1.............189

7 Anxiety Disorders

CHAPTER OUTLINE

I. Fear and Anxiety Gone Awry (pp. 216-218)
    A. Anxiety Disorders
        1. Fear and anxiety lie at core
            a. Fear—set of responses to specific perceived danger
            b. Anxiety—diffuse sense of apprehension aversive event will occur
        2. Both emotions expressed through three channels
            a. Cognitive distress, distortions, and ruminations
            b. Physiological arousal
            c. Behavioral disruptions and avoidance
        3. Freud
            a. *Neuroses*—chronic anxiety, unhappiness, and guilt
            b. Resulted from conflicts among the id, ego, and superego

II. The Phobias (pp. 218-225)
    A. Term from Greek deity, Phobos, son of Ares, god of war
        1. Irrational, excessive fear
        2. Causes intense emotional distress and interferes significantly with life
    B. Specific Phobias
        1. Intense, persistent fear of specific objects or situations
        2. Objectively poses little or no actual threat
        3. DSM-IV
            a. It must cause intense distress each time person is exposed
            b. Must interfere with one's educational, occupational, or social life
        4. *Animal phobias*—snakes, mice, spiders, cats, and dogs most common
        5. *Blood, injections, and injury* very common cluster of phobias
            a. Fainting occurs readily
            b. Fear results in reluctance to seek medical help, impairs health
        6. *Situational*—fear of closed places: elevators, tunnels, airplanes, small rooms
        7. *Natural environment*—storms, deep water, heights
    C. Social Phobia
        1. Excessive fear of being evaluated and possibly embarrassed
        2. Most common—speaking or performing in public, meeting strangers
            a. Many people function by avoiding situation
            b. Underachieve at school or work, less likely to marry
        3. Social phobias develop later in life; are *cultural general*
            a. Japan, Asia—*interdependent* or *collective*, how they offend others
            b. Westerners more *independent*, concerned how others think of them
            c. *Culture-specific*—TKS in Japan
    D. Causes of Phobias
        1. Psychoanalytic Formulations—Sigmund Freud
            a. Unconscious fear of castration (animal phobias in young males)

    b. Hans (Oedipal) incestuous desire for mother, feared castration
    c. Fear is transferred to horse, thus rational fear
    d. Social phobias from unconscious impulses from sexual urges
  2. Behavioral and Cognitive Factors
    a. John B. Watson, American behaviorist
    b. All emotional learning developed from conditioning responses
    c. Due to direct traumatic experience with formerly neutral object
    d. Could be extinguished by deconditioning
    e. Bandura—conditioning responses incomplete explanation
    f. Direct conditioning and through observation
    g. Modeling and vicarious conditioning
    h. Can develop by hearing or reading vivid accounts of danger
  3. Biological Theories
    a. Genetic component
      (1) Appear more often in monozygotic twins
      (2) Concordance rate higher for specific, social, agoraphobia
    b. Neurological difference
      (1) Particularly prone to excessive physiological activity
      (2) Levels of brain's neurotransmitters are disturbed
        (a) GABA inhibits post synaptic activity
        (b) If low, neurons fire more rapidly increasing anxiety
        (c) Benzodiazepines increases activity of GABA
      (3) Intense fear originates in *amygdala* in limbic system
        (a) Limbic system regulates emotions
        (b) Triggers adrenal gland, produces epinephrine
      (4) Deficiencies in neurotransmitter to inhibit neuron activity
    c. Environmental experiences, informational processes, family history
  4. Diathesis-Stress Model
    a. Combination of genetic predisposition, environmental experiences
    b. Preparedness theory—biologically prepared to develop fears
      (1) Snakes and spiders dangerous to our ancestors
      (2) Inherit the capacity to acquire fears, not fears themselves
      (3) Single traumatic exposure sufficient to acquire phobia
      (4) Certain people have *inborn* neurological capacity
      (5) Susan Mineka and Michael Cook—rhesus monkey studies
E. Treatment of Phobias
  1. Systematic Desensitization
    a. Teach client muscle relaxation (leads to calmness)
    b. Construct an anxiety hierarchy
      (1) Imagine least frightening moving up list to most frightening
      (2) Success when client remains calm imaging most frightening
  2. Exposure procedures
      (1) Principle of extinction basis
      (2) Fear response acquired by US with CS
      (3) Extinguish fear response—exposures CS in absence of US

                (4)   Graduate hierarchy to *live, not imaginary* exposures
                (5)   Virtual reality now being used
      3.   Flooding
          a.   Exposes client to most intense stimuli
          b.   Initial increase in anxiety followed by rapid fear reduction
          c.   20-session flooding superior to medication for social phobia
      4.   Modeling Procedures
          a.   Albert Bandura—fearful client observes model
          b.   Model interacts with feared stimuli without fear
          c.   Participant Modeling
                (1)   Combination of *in vivo* exposure and modeling
                (2)   Therapist demonstrates feared behavior; then assists client
                (3)   Behavioral progress engenders confidence
                (4)   Confidence reduces fear behavior
III.   Panic Disorder and Agoraphobia (pp. 225-232)
      A.   Characteristics and Prevalence
          1.   *Panic attacks*—periodic and unexpected attacks of intense anxiety
              a.   Person develops persistent anxiety of another attack
              b.   Fears next attack will be uncontrollable
              c.   Symptoms: attacks come "out of the blue"
                    (1)   Racing heart (tachycardia)
                    (2)   Sweating
                    (3)   Trembling
                    (4)   Choking or smothering
                    (5)   Chilling
                    (6)   Dizziness
                    (7)   Nausea
                    (8)   Shortness of breath
              d.   So strong can cause derealization or depersonalization
          2.   *Agoraphobia:* Fear of open places—Greek, agora means marketplace
              a.   Panic attacks may cause
              b.   Basic fear—having panic attack away from "safe" place
              c.   Follows series of unpredictable, uncontrollable panic attacks
              d.   Attack in certain place leads to avoidance of that place
              e.   Too many places; agoraphobic becomes housebound
              f.   Agoraphobics suffer "fear of fear"
              g.   Panic disorder with agoraphobia renders clients vulnerable
                    (1)   Frequent use of alcohol
                    (2)   Self and prescribed medications potentially addictive
                    (3)   Frequently suffer depression; risk of possible suicide
          3.   Prevalence
              a.   1.5 to 3.5% in world, high as 9% of adults in U.S.
              b.   Females more frequent; no difference in ethnic groups (U.S.)

    c. Higher in African-Americans
      (1) High prevalence of *sleep paralysis*
      (2) Inability to move body, visual hallucinations, acute fear
 B. Causes of Panic Disorder and Agoraphobia
   1. Psychodynamic Formulations
    a. Freud
      (1) Unresolved Oedipal complex
      (2) Unconscious temptation to act out sexual impulses
    b. Object Relations Theory more recent
      (1) Agoraphobia is unresolved separation anxiety
      (2) Parents did not answer infant's need for security
      (3) Fears are reactivated later in life
   2. Biological Factors
    a. Panic disorder and agoraphobia run in families
    b. 17% of family some disorder, female relatives 46%
    c. Greater concordance with monozygotic twins
    d. Inherited neurophysiological and biochemical mechanisms
    e. Intense terror is primitive alarm system
    f. Neurological center, locus coerulus (removal ends panic)
    g. Amygdala and frontal and temporal lobes involved
   3. Diathesis-Stress
    a. Panic attacks begin as false alarms
    b. Misperceptions escalate into repetitive thoughts
    c. Anxiety drives activation of sympathetic nervous system higher
    d. *Learned alarms* cause anxious apprehension
    e. Triggering substance mimics internal cues—real attack follows
 C. Treatment of Panic Disorder and Agoraphobia
   1. Cognitive Behavioral Treatment
    a. Misinterpretation of physical sensations as sign of danger
    b. Treatment package
      (1) Breathing retraining
      (2) Interceptive exposure to somatic cues
      (3) Cognitive restructuring
      (4) Group settings as effective as individual
    c. Panic control above 3 treatments and educate to not catastrophize
    d. Agoraphobia, same as above and exposure or flooding
   2. Drug Treatments
    a. Antidepressants (imipramine or phenelzine)
      (1) Reduce panic symptoms
      (2) Side effects cause client to stop medication
    b. Anxiolytics (benzodiazepines)
      (1) Facilitate actions of inhibitory neurotransmitter
      (2) Clients can become dependent or addicted

     c. Combination of psychological and pharmacological more effective than either alone
       (1) Drugs for panic
       (2) Cognitive-behavior therapy for agoraphobic avoidance

IV. Obsessive-Compulsive Disorder (pp. 232-237)
  A. *Obsessions*—unwanted, disturbing, often irrational thoughts, feelings, or images that people cannot get out of their head
    1. Not preoccupation or daydream
    2. Involve frightening images or aggressive urges
    3. Most common
     a. Fear of contacting dirt, germs, touching infected people or objects
     b. Disgust over body waste or secretions
     c. Undue concern job has not been done adequately
     d. Fear of committing a crime or hurting someone
     e. Fear of shouting obscenities or insults
     f. Fear of thinking anti-religious or sexual thoughts
     g. 80% compelled to take action to suppress or ease anxiety, guilt
  B. *Compulsions*—repetitive, nearly irresistible acts that temporarily neutralize obsessions or relieve their anxiety
    1. Common compulsive rituals
     a. Repetitively washing one's hands or other contaminated objects
     b. Checking doors, windows, water or gas taps
     c. Counting objects a precise number of times, repeating actions
     d. Hording items—old newspapers, mail, used and useless items
     e. Putting dishes and silver in precisely aligned pattern
    2. Client tries to resist performing rituals (understands excessive)
    3. Impulse to act in that way to reduce tension wins out
  C. Characteristics and Prevalence
    1. Characteristics
     a. No pleasure in compulsive behavior
     b. Performed in response to obsessional thought
     c. Not like over-eating, gambling, drinking, drug abuse
     d. OCD rituals highly debilitating (Howard Hughes' isolation)
    2. Related disorder
     a. *Tourette's Disorder*
     b. Tourette's and OCD share genetic vulnerability
    3. Prevalence of Obsessive-Compulsive Disorder
     a. Between 2-3% of U.S. adults and 1% of children
     b. Onset in early childhood predominately male
     c. Adult-onset cases predominately female
     d. Gender role differences (women are cleaners)
  D. Causes of Obsessive-Compulsive Disorder
    1. The Role of Genetics
     a. OCD's association with Tourette's syndrome
     b. Contributions in family and twin studies

    c. 30% family members vs. 17.1% in controls
    d. Inherited general diathesis rather than genetic
   2. Neurobiological Factors
    a. Neurotransmitter *serotonin* influences emotions, regulates sleep
    b. OCD may be triggered by low levels of serotonin
    c. Antidepressants effectively block re-uptake of serotonin
    d. Blockage may allow neuron receptors to adapt therapeutically
    e. When brain areas over-activated results in repetition seen in OCD
    f. Large proportion patients with head injuries, neural disease OCD
   3. Cognitive-Behavioral Factors
    a. Reactivity and obsessive thinking increase during heightened stress
    b. Obsessive thoughts very anxiety-provoking
    c. Ritualistic behaviors/thoughts used to neutralize anxiety
    d. Panic clients distressed by physical ;compulsive by thoughts
    e. Strive to undo thoughts through compulsive behavior
  E. Treatment of Obsessive-Compulsive Disorder
   1. One of most difficult to treat
   2. Desperate clients submitted to psychosurgery *cingulotomy*
    a. Small amount of tissue in cingulum is destroyed
    b. Improvement in minority; questionable treatment
   3. Two approaches shown consistent success
    a. Drug therapy
     (1) Clominpramine (blocks serotonin-uptake)
     (2) 50-75% improvement, symptoms return quickly
    b. Cognitive Behavior therapy
     (1) Sometimes combined with drug treatment
     (2) Based on extinction model
     (3) Combined exposure and response prevention
V. Generalized Anxiety Disorder (pp. 237-240)
  A. Anxiety not focused on any particular time, situation, or person
   1. Clients experience "free-floating anxiety, overwhelmed by expectations
   2. Dominates their lives, interferes with daily activities
   3. Symptoms
    a. "Keyed-up, irritable, tense, easily fatigued
    b. Trouble concentrating, difficulty getting to sleep
    c. Constant intense worry and negative thoughts
    d. Half of time anxious worry that is not productive
   4. Prevalence
    a. Under 30 years; more females
    b. 6.6% females and 3.6% males (adults) some time in life
    c. Highest overall African-American males
    d. Lower socioeconomic levels particularly vulnerable
  B. Causes of GAD
   1. Basic anxiety state from which other disorders develop
   2. Response to chronic economic stressors (not disorder)

3. Might be attempt to maintain tight control
4. Worry to avoid anxiety
C. Treatment of GAD
 1. Cognitive-behavioral treatment
    a. *Cognitive restructuring*
       (1) Replace irrational thought with rational
       (2) Relaxation training
       (3) Combination of both
    b. *Non-directive therapy*
       (1) Self-reflection in calm, relaxed atmosphere
       (2) Relaxation training
       (3) Combination of both
 2. Drug Treatments
    a. Antidepressant medications (not clear how they work)
    b. Benzodiazepines (Valium, Xanax, and Serax)
    c. Long-term effects a problem
       (1) Physical dependence
       (2) Do not seem to produce lasting reduction in anxiety

VI. Posttraumatic Stress Disorder (pp. 240-247)
 A. Severe trauma experienced—weeks later still intense fear-related reactions
    1. Trauma threatened the victim or someone close with mortal danger
    2. Symptoms
       a. Frequent reexperiencing of events (flashbacks)
       b. Repeated nightmares or dreams
       c. Persistent avoidance of stimuli associated with trauma
       d. General numbing or deadening of emotions
       e. Increased startle responses or difficulty sleeping
       f. May not emerge for months or years after event
       g. Must last longer than a month to qualify as PTSD
    3. Prevalence of PTSD not clear
 B. Causes of PTSD
    1. Traumatic Experiences
       a. War
       b. Natural disasters (tornados, earthquakes, floods)
       c. Serious accidents
       d. Torture
       e. Abuse (physical and sexual assault)
    2. Situation directly threatening one's bodily integrity or life
    3. Belief that one's life is in danger and one has no control
    4. Posttrauma Events
       a. Amount of social support crucial
       b. Larger the network of friends or relatives, better person copes
       c. Victim feels no one to turn to for help or discussion of fears

             d.   Vietnam Vets had reduction in friends and social supports
             e.   Victim believes world dangerous place (generalizes)
        5.   Individual Differences
             a.   Before war profiles of soldiers who developed PTSD
                  (1) Overly concerned with functions (stomach or head pains)
                  (2) Social maladjustments, including legal difficulties
                  (3) More passive, inner directed, more aesthetic interests
                  (4) Highly sensitive to criticism, suspicious of others
                  (5) Socially introverted; more severe symptoms
             b.   Risk of PTSD greater among people having
                  (1) Depression
                  (2) Social withdrawal
                  (3) Sense of being unable to control stressors
                  (4) Genetic predisposition contributes to nearly all symptoms
                  (5) Excessive surges neurotransmitters; hypersensitivity in brain
        6.   Behavioral and Cognitive Factors in PTSD
             a.   Behavioral theories focus on *two-factor conditioning*
                  (1) Classical conditioning and operant conditioning
                  (2) During trauma, neutral stimuli become conditioned emotions
             b.   CSS later elicit terror, anxiety as memories flood back
                  (1) Victim tries to avoid stimuli to reduce anxiety
   C.   Treatments for PTSD
        1.   Best results from behavioral and cognitive approaches
             a.   Direct exposure
                  (1) Can be either imaginal or *in vivo*
                  (2) Includes relaxation training, etc.
                  (3) Develop new coping skills
                  (4) Extinguish emotional reactions to stimuli
             b.   Cognitive therapy
                  (1) Activate the fear network
                  (2) Provide experiences incompatible with information there
                  (3) Allows rational information to enter network
             c.   Cognitive Processing Therapy
                  (1) Writing about the meaning of the event
                  (2) Identifying and challenging erroneous beliefs
             d.   Drug Treatments
                  (1) No single drug able to reduces all symptoms in PTSD
                  (2) Drugs useful in alleviating specific clusters of symptoms
                       (a) Reexperiencing symptoms respond to antidepressants
                       (b) Avoidant/numbing symptoms respond to selective serotonin reuptake inhibitors
                       (c) Arousal symptoms improve most with antiadrenergics

7 Anxiety Disorders

LECTURE MAKER 7.1

Student Assignment Read pages 29-33 in Case Studies in Abnormal Behavior to supplement text.

Purpose To introduce the concept of conditioned emotional responses, the case of conditioning and generalizable nature. (pp. 220-223)

Note**** This demonstration requires a few practice runs and is not for the faint of heart. You can inform your students in advance that you will be conditioning them emotionally in the first five minutes of class and give them the option of participation.

Lecture Introduction Review the essential of John Watson's 1920 experiment with Little Albert. Include necessary information on conditioning, generalization, extinction and the possible function of these concepts in phobia development or anxiety induction.

Demonstration Take your text book to class. Without any reference to what you doing, at your ready point in the introduction; hold up your free hand and say, "Ready?" and then slam the book on a table. Students should startle in response to the loud and unexpected noise. Ask the students if they felt an increase in their heart rate and how they felt, in general, with the startle response. Also ask the students what their immediate thoughts were. Welcome them to the world of Little Albert. Speak for a minute or so about the effects of this demonstration and then without warning or reference, hold up your free hand and say, "Ready?" and begin the same slam-the-book motion but do not slam the book down. Watch closely for student responses. A few students (at the very least) should visibly cringe. Ask the students again how they feel physically in general, and what their thought processes included. What cues had they generalized their emotional response to and why?

Lecture Capsule Following this demonstration ask the students how they would proceed to remove this unwanted anxiety/fear response to the learned cues. Introduce Mary Cover Jones and Little Peter, review extinction concepts, and present systematic desensitization information. Students can now use their own, non-threatening experience to identify with the historical subjects of Albert and Peter and work the concept through a personal experiential framework.

LECTURE MAKER 7.2

Student Assignment	Read pages 40-46 in Case Studies in Abnormal Behavior to supplement text.
Purpose	To introduce the concept of anxiety, measurement of anxiety, and demonstrate cognitive impact on arousal.(pp. 231-233)
Equipment	Biofeedback Monitor (Can be purchased at Radio Shack for $15, needs 9v battery). Has two Velcro finger cuff leads, select any two fingers but I prefer to have a non-cuff finger between the 2 cuffs.
Lecture Introduction	Ask for a volunteer from class to be attached to the monitor. As you attach the finger cuffs, explain that there is no shock or pain. This monitor will increase the noise level as the individual's anxiety level increases, and vice versa. Tell the student to relax, think pleasant thoughts and listen. You will return to them in a few minutes. Begin a discussion of topical material to give the subject time to calm down the noise from the monitor. Introduce and relate the channels of emotional expression: cognition, behavior, and physiological arousal. Discuss the salient features of Bess's obsessive-compulsive disorder. Identify her initial obsessive thoughts and how they caused her anxiety and helped to shape her subsequent behavior patterns. Follow with the latter obsessive thoughts and compulsive rituals. What do the rituals do to and for Bess?
Demonstration	When the noise has lowered noticeably, turn around to the subject and announce firmly, "I'd like everyone to look closely at the subject right now." Within three to four seconds, the monitor noise should be increasing dramatically, much to the chagrin of the subject and giggles of the class. All it takes is eyeballs-focused-on-the-subject to cause enough cognitive stress to be indicated by the biofeedback monitor. From here, the twists are up to the instructor. Questioning is fun and so is leaving the subject attached to the monitor as you lecture, which generally results in the noise almost disappearing.
Lecture Capsule	Discuss the demonstration, what happened and what it means. You might want to add a segment on "lie detectors." Using everyday anxiety as an example, ask the students how the Biofeedback Monitor might be used effectively. Could this type of technique be used therapeutically? Could Bess have benefitted from biofeedback training? What role might biofeedback play in systematic desensitization therapy? This demonstration impresses the class and is quite a success. It can be used for many introductions, especially anxiety and stress.

LECTURE MAKER 7.3

Purpose To inform students about anxiety disorders and involve them in National College Anxiety Disorders Screening Day

Lecture Introduction In 1996 Freedom From Fear, a non profit mental health advocacy organization, established *National Anxiety Disorders Screening Day*. The event which takes place in May has had an attendance of more than 65,000 individuals. The purpose of NADSD is to educate consumers about anxiety disorders, *America's most common mental illnesses* and to help sufferers find treatment.

Each year more than 28 million people will suffer from an anxiety disorder which will greatly impair their lives. Quite often these illnesses start in late adolescence or early adulthood, the college age student. National College Anxiety Disorders Screening Day has been established and will take place on the first Wednesday in May every year. NCADSD is an educational/screening program during which the college students learn about anxiety disorders and other mental illnesses.

This program utilizes a video with accompanying screening questionnaire and literature designed for college students. NCADSD can help educate the student body and guide appropriate students to treatment. The main anxiety disorders focused in the program are: Panic Disorder; Generalized Anxiety Disorders; Obsessive-Compulsive Disorder; Social Phobia; and Post Traumatic Stress Disorder

Lecture Capsule The screening day is an education event that can benefit all students, not only those who think they may have symptoms of an anxiety disorder. Students will learn to recognize the symptoms of anxiety disorders and will receive free literature about anxiety disorders and other mental illnesses. They will learn what services are available on campus and in the area.

Miscellaneous Demonstrations 1. Select a relatively popular television program. Identify two or three majorplayers and dominant dramatic personality features. Play a five minute or so pre-recorded clip (made at home and used for educational purposes only) in class. Ask students to identify any potential abnormal behavior and possible DSM-IV classification (s). This is usually great warm up material and enjoyable for all.
2. Select a major disaster that the students are fairly certain to recognize. Briefly describe the catastrophe and ask students to conjecture what survivors of the crisis might experience as PTSD symptoms and under what circumstances.

3. There are a wealth of excellent Vietnam war movies available for rent:
   Deer Hunter
   Full Metal Jacket
   Platoon
   Apocalypse Now
   Born on the Fourth of July
   Coming Home

Any of these videos can be stopped at an appropriate vignette selected by the instructor and played in class for educational purposes. Selected characters powerfully enact DSM-IV criteria for PTSD and students respond well to these examples. Relate the movie to Case Study of the Postman.

NATIONAL COLLEGE ANXIETY DISORDERS SCREENING DAY
MAY 1998

WHAT IS NATIONAL COLLEGE ANXIETY DISORDERS SCREENING DAY?

The National College Anxiety Disorders Screening Day (NCADSD) is an education/screening program during which college students learn about anxiety disorders, view a video, obtain free literature about anxiety disorders and other mental illnesses, have the opportunity to complete an anxiety disorders questionnaire and have the results reviewed by a clinician. The program is implemented by the staff of the sponsoring facility. The materials for the program will be supplied by the NCADSD office. The program is not a substitute for psychiatric evaluation and no formal diagnosis is given. A referral for a complete evaluation is provided if indicated.

The NCADSD program will be held during the month of May, 1998. Each college determines the specific date and time.

WHO SPONSORS A SCREENING?

Sponsors must be college health or counseling centers. Hospitals, health centers, or private physicians who specialize in anxiety disorders may sponsor a screening provided they collaborate with a college. It is the responsibility of the sponsor/site to have an adequate staff of doctors or mental health professionals available to review the screenings forms.

WHO SHOULD ATTEND?

The screening day is an educational event that can benefit all students, not only those who think they may have symptoms of an anxiety disorder. Students will learn how to recognize the symptoms of anxiety disorders and will receive free literature about anxiety disorders and other mental illnesses. They will learn what services are available on campus and in the area.

WHY SHOULD YOU ORGANIZE A NCADSD?

NCADSD is an excellent opportunity for colleges/universities to promote the services that are available on campus. The event is to improve students' awareness of on campus services and how to utilize them.

WHAT DOES THE NCADSD OFFICE PROVIDE?

Planning and Promotion Guide
A step by step "How To" guide to organize the event including promotion and advertising ideas, information on the various anxiety disorders and available treatments, and guidelines for organizing the screening day.

Video (The video is used in conjunction with a specifically designed questionnaire to identify the symptoms of anxiety disorders) The video features college students discussing their anxiety disorders and the impairment the illness brought to their lives. It emphasizes how the illness developed, how it affected their lives and how they got treatment.

Screening and Educational Materials
Screening questionnaires and criteria for evaluating anxiety disorder symptoms
Consumer education materials including brochures and handouts. Promotional materials such as posters and fliers

SCREENING SITE REQUIREMENTS

The screening site must provide the following:
- Site Director
- Mental health professionals to conduct review of screening forms with participants-10-15 minutes per participant
- A meeting room for the screening with appropriate equipment
- Publicity on college campus
- Referrals for individuals who have symptoms of a psychiatric illness if further evaluation is indicated.

SPONSORS

American Academy of Child and Adolescent Psychiatry • American College Counseling Association
American College Health Association • American Psychiatric Association • American Psychological Association
Association for University and College Counseling Center Directors • Freedom From Fear
National Council of Schools and Programs in Professional Psychology
The National Institute of Mental Health • Zeta Phi Beta

NATIONAL COLLEGE ANXIETY DISORDERS SCREENING DAY
Registration Form

The National College Disorders Screening Day is a program of the National Mental Illness Screening Project

Before completing this form, please note:
- This program is designed for a college population only and must occur either on campus or in conjunction with a college or university health or counseling center.
- Please complete all questions. Each site must have a separate registration form, copies are acceptable.
- Please retain copies for your records.

The NCADSD office need both your completed registration form and fee in order to process your registration. Please enclose payment with this form.

1. Sponsor Name:_____
   (Please enter the name of the department sponsoring the event as well as the name of the college or university.)

Participated in National Anxiety Disorders Screening Day 1997?   Yes_____ No_____

Sponsor Address (No P.O. Boxes)_____

_____
City   State   Zip

Contact Person:_____

Contact Person Phone: ( )_____   Fax: ( )_____

If the Sponsor is not a college, please tell us which college you are working with:
For example, the sponsor may be a hospital or a private practitioner sponsoring the screening day on a college/university campus. Please enter the information below:

Name of College/University:_____

College/University Address:_____

_____
City   State   Zip

College Contact:_____

College Contact Phone:( )_____   Fax: ( )_____

Registration Deadline: December 15, 1997   Registration Fee: $100
Mail Form(s) with registration fee(s), payable to Freedom From Fear (FedTax # 13-3363064) to:
**National College Anxiety Disorders Screening Day
C/O Freedom From Fear
308 Seaview Avenue, Staten Island, N.Y. 10305
Phone: (718) 351-1717   Fax: (718) 667-8893**

RESOURCES

General
Dean Foundation
Obsessive Compulsive Information Center
8000 Excelsior Drive, Suite 302
Madison, WI 53717-1914
Telephone 608-836-8070

Computer data base of over 4,000 references updated daily. Computer searches done for nominal fee. No charge for quick reference questions. Maintains physician referral and support group lists

Obsessive Compulsive Foundation
P.O. Box 70
Milford, CT 06460
Telephone 203-878-5669

Offers free or at minimal cost brochures for individuals with the disorder and their families. In addition videotapes and books are available. A bimonthly newsletter goes to members who pay an annual fee of $30.00. Has over 250 support groups nationwide.

Tourette Syndrome Association, Inc.
42-40 Bell Boulevard
New York, NY 11361-2874
Telephone 718-224-2999

Publications, videotapes, and films available at minimal cost. Newsletter goes to members who pay an annual fee of $35.00

American Psychiatric Association
1400 K Street, N.W.
Washington, DC 20005

American Psychological Association
750 First Street N.E.
Washington, DC 20002

Anxiety Disorders Association of America
6000 Executive Boulevard, Suite 513
Rockville, MD 20352
(Include $3 for postage and handling)

Association for the Advancement of Behavior Therapy
305 Seventh Avenue
New York, NY 10001

National Alliance for the Mentally Ill
200 North Glebe Road, Suite 1015
Arlington, VA 22203-3754

National Anxiety Foundation
3135 Custer Drive
Lexington, KY 40517-4001

National Depressive and Manic Depressive Association
740 North Franklin Street, Suite 301
Chicago, IL 60601

National Institute of Mental Health
Publications List
5600 Fishers Lane, Room 7C-02
Rockville, MD 20857

National Mental Health Association
1201 Prince Street
Alexandria, VA 22314-2971

Media

Anxiety: Decision at the Synapse (Abbot Laboratories, 27 min.) An oldie but goodie, this reviews the causes, physiological response, symptoms and therapy for anxiety.

Anxiety: The Endless Crisis (IU, 59 min.) This is long and old but it is recommended as an overview.

Biofeedback: Listening to Your Head (IDEAL, 22 min) This demonstrates the basic process of gaining cognitive control over autonomic process, specifically brain wave conditioning, and its use in disease and emotional disorders.

Fighting Fear With Fear (McG, 26 min.) One video of a CBS series on implosive therapy for phobia treatment.

Obsessive-Compulsive Neurosis (McG, 30 min.) This contains examples and interpretations of OCD

Pathological Anxiety (PCR-2122, 30 min.) As a very old case study with panic attacks, this illustrates the same basic disorder years ago. Good for history and continuity.

The Obsessive-Compulsive Neurosis (McG, 28 min.) Presented is a case study, symptoms and therapy for OCD.

Anxiety Disorders, Professional New Diagnostic Issues Series
American Psychiatric Press Inc. and Allyn & Bacon
This series of three clinical programs reveal additions and changes from DSM-III-R to DSM-IV for mood, psychotic, and anxiety disorders. Each videotape focuses on one particular area of psychiatric diagnosis and contains enaactments of three outstanding clinicians' actual patient . Each videotape begins with an introductory discussion between the clinician and the moderator. The clinician then conducts three 10-minute psychiatric diagnostic interviews. Following each interview, the clinician and the moderator discuss the taped segments and comment on issues illustrated during the interviews. These issues include:

> How the new DSM-IV diagnostic criteria were utilized in the interview.
> How diagnostic markers were elicited.
> How interpersonal issues, as well as diagnostic markers, were identified.

The interviews utilize reference data to examine conclusions reached during the interview. Each tape also demonstrates good interviewing techniques and highlights the development of good doctor-patient relationship. A printed list of relevant issues highlighted in interviews and elaborated in the clinical discussions is enclosed.

Andrew E. Skodol II, M.D., is Associate Professor of Clinical Psychiatry at the College of Physicians and Surgeons of Columbia University. He is co-author of the *DSM-IV Casebook*, as well as a member of the DSM-IV Multiaxial Work Group. He is especially noted for his extensive teaching in areas of differential diagnosis and clinical psychiatry.

Ian Alger, M.D., is Moderator and Executive Producer of the DSM-IV New Diagnostic Issues Videos; faculty member in the residency training program, New York Hospital-Cornell Medical Center; Multimedia Consultant to the American Psychiatric Association's Psychiatric Services; and Editor of the american Psychiatric Press Video Series.

Obsessive-Compulsive Disorder Pharmacotherapy and Psychotherapy
American Psychiatric Press Inc. and Allyn & Bacon
These new and richly comprehensive videotapes are based on material recently presented by the distinguished facult at West and East Coast conferences on treatments of psychiatric disorders, sponsored by the American Psychiatric Association. For those who did not attend these conferences, these videotapes present the unusual opportunity to listen and watch these clinicians discuss four of the most critically important psychiatric disorders.

John H. Griest, M.D., is Distinguished Senior Scientist at the Dean Foundation for Health, Research, and Education and is currently Clinical Professor of Psychiatry at the Universtiy of Wisconsin Medical Scholl, Madison, Wisconsin. Dr. Griest is also Director of the Lithium and Obsessive-Compulsive Information Centers at the Dean Foundation.

Ian Alger, M.D. is Executive Producer of the Treatments of Psychiatric Disorders Videotape Series; Clinical Professor of Psychiatry, The New York Hospital-Cornell Medical Center; Multimedia consultant to the American Multimedia Consultant to the American Psychiatric Association's Psychiatric Services; and Editor of the american Psychiatric Press Video Series.

For additional video resource materials, please contact your Allyn & Bacon representative.

Nietzel et al., *Abnormal Psychology*, Transparencies

Chapter Seven

	Text Figure Number	Text Page Number
36. Prevalence of Anxiety Disorders	7.1	217
37. Some Common Forms of Object Phobias		218
38. A Diathesis-Stress Model of Phobias	7.2	223
39. Criteria for Panic Attack		226
40. Criteria for Obsessive-Compulsive Disorder		233
41. Criteria for Posttraumatic Stress Disorder		242

8 Dissociative and Somatoform Disorders

CHAPTER OUTLINE

I. Dissociative Disorders (pp. 253-263)
   A. Definition—process by which the normally integrated processes of consciousness, memory and personal identity become splintered.
       1. Dissociation
          a. Not being able to remember important personal experiences
          b. Becoming confused about identity and acting as if new identity
          c. Feel as if objects around person are not real
          d. Emotionally detached, as if client is outsider watching a movie
       2. Somataform
          a. Physical symptoms appear that suggest medical disorder with no adequate medical explanation
          b. Symptoms expression of underlying emotional conflicts
   B. Cultural Perspectives on Dissociation
       1. Described throughout history
          a. Greek and Roman mythology
          b. Christianity—belief person's soul could be possessed by spirits
          c. Witch hunts—women's personalities taken over by demons
       2. Described across cultures
          a. India—another self temporarily "takes over" leaving no memory
          b. *Ataque di Nervios*—response to stress in Latin American countries
          c. American Indian—*shaman* induce trances, communicate spirits
       3. If it does not lead to impairments, personal distress, not called a disorder
   C. Symptoms and Types of Dissociative Disorders
       1. Symptoms
          a. *Amnesia*—loss of person's memory not by organic injury or illness
          b. *Depersonalization*—observing self from outside body
          c. *Derealization*—objects in the external world are strange or unreal
          d. *Identity confusion*—uncertainty about person's own identity
          e. *Identity alteration*—person has assumed a new identity
       2. DSM-IV Classifications
          a. Dissociative amnesia
          b. Dissociative fugue
          c. Depersonalization disorder
          d. Dissociative identity disorder
          e. Dissociative disorder not otherwise specified
              (1) Significant psychopathology, no criteria for other disorders
              (2) *Dissociative trance disorder*
                  (a) Involuntary trance state not cultural or religious
                  (b) Associated with trauma or long confinement

3. Dissociative Identity Disorder
   a. *Multiple personality disorder* (dual personality)
   b. *Three faces of Eve; Sybil; The Minds of Billy Milligan*
   c. Childhood trauma, often abuse, plays central role in explanation
4. Symptoms and Prevalence of Dissociation Identity
   a. Personality appears as separate identities or parts
   b. Two or more separate, coexisting personalities (*alters*) with different memories, behavior patterns, emotions
   c. Alters assume control of functioning in different situations
   d. *Host personality*, primary identity in charge most of the time
      (1) One alter prim and proper, another flamboyant
      (2) Male and female alters appear in one individual
      (3) Host typically seeks psychological treatment
      (4) Host troubled by low self-esteem, depression, and recurrent nightmares; suicidal thoughts or self-mutilation thoughts, headaches, other physical concerns
      (5) One alter typically powerful, dominant, protector for host
   e. Personality fragments
      (1) Not as well developed as alters
      (2) Represent one emotion (rage, etc)
5. Switching
   a. Process of changing from one personality to another
   b. Stimulated by anxiety, flashbacks of prior traumas
   c. Sometimes when clients begin to recall childhood
   d. Generally no voluntary control
   e. Aware of lost time, but not of alter's appearance or actions
6. Prevalence
7. Small-scale study—just over 1%
8. 9 times more frequently in women
9. First diagnosis in late 20's or early 30's

D. Is Dissociative Identity Disorder a Real Clinical Disorder?
   1. Those who doubt the condition
      a. Culture-bound syndrome, does not meet necessary criteria
      b. Somatic, psychological, cognitive factors overlap other disorders
      c. Some clinicians believe it a severe subtype of PTSD
   2. Proponents
      a. Some alters right handed, host left handed
      b. Some alters need glasses, host does not
      c. Allergic reactions different for host and alter
      d. EEGs of alters different from host
      e. Host is color-blind, alter sees colors

E. Other Dissociative Disorders
   1. *Dissociative Amnesia*
      a. Sudden loss of memory for personally important information not caused by medical condition or other mental disorder

                (1) Follows stressful event (suicide attempt, violent assault)
                (2) Takes several forms
                    (a) *Localized amnesia* loss of memory for period of time
                    (b) *Selective amnesia* remember only some of events
                    (c) *Generalized amnesia* total loss for entire life
                    (d) *Continuous amnesia* from trauma to present time
                    (e) *Systematized amnesia* certain classes of information
                (3) Only localized and selective lift rapidly and completely
                (4) *Malinger*—fake amnesia to avoid punishment
                (5) *Sodium amytal* (truth serum) helps determine validity
        2. Dissociative Fugue
            a. Person leaves home or work, travels to new location
            b. Do not remember prefugue life; after may not remember episode
            c. Happens twice as often in men as women
            d. Recover spontaneously and quickly; recurrence rare
        3. Depersonalization Disorder
            a. Depersonalization and derealization occur together
            b. Person feels like robot or actor in dream or movie
            c. Some feel they have left their bodies, hovering above them
            d. Movement and speech outside personal control
            e. Affects women more than men
II. Causes and Treatment of Dissociative Disorders (pp. 263-273)
    A. Vulnerability to Dissociative Disorders
        1. Imaginative Involvement
            a. Ability to become absorbed in imaginings contributes
            b. Two thirds fantasy proneness persons meet criteria for disorder
            c. 50% high fantacizers had episode of major depression
            d. Leads to demoralization and greater vulnerability to stressors
        2. Hypnotizability
            a. Hypnosis—person displays suggestions given while "under"
            b. People differ in how *suggestible* they are
            c. Dissociative persons higher on measures of hypnotic sensitivity
        3. Childhood Trauma
            a. Increased risk for those with early childhood trauma
            b. Pattern of coping through dissociation established early childhood
        4. Conclusions
            a. Diathesis-stress model has not been supported
            b. Disorders diagnosed in U.S. and among women
            c. Hypnotizability, trauma, and child abuse rates do not differ enough
    B. Causes of Dissociative Identity Disorder
        1. Trauma-Dissociation Model
            a. In 70s therapists link severe childhood abuse
            b. Sexual abuse, particularly incest, most common reported
            c. Combination of sexual and physical abuse next common

    d. Ritualistic abuse, repetitive, lurid or sadistic
     (1) Inserting objects into the child's vagina or anus
     (2) Binding and torturing the child
     (3) Locking child up in small spaces (closets)
    e. Some not endured but witnessed such as murder of family member
    f. If repeatedly traumatized, became adroit at *mental* escape
     (1) In that state a separate memories, feelings, and behaviors
     (2) Episodes form beginnings personality fragments
     (3) In adulthood, stressful situations bring back alter identities
  2. Evaluating Trauma Dissociation Models
    a. Value is uncertain, not established
    b. Difficult to prove; documented by adults' retrospective recall
    c. Evidence that false memories can be implanted
    d. Therapists find it difficult to distinguish authentic recollections
    e. Well documented abuse, remembered, but no dissociation
  3. Sociocultural Model
    a. *Enactment* of multiple identities serves personal goals
    b. Enacted by individuals culturally or socially disadvantaged
    c. Acting possessed by spirits acceptable way of expressing distress
    d. In U.S. dissociative identity disorder acceptable
    e. Therapists can encourage alter personalities to emerge
  4. Evaluating the Sociocultural Model
    a. Role enacted by persons with psychological problems
    b. Not *all* cases are fabrications
C. Treatment of Dissociative Disorder
  1. Long-term prognosis not favorable
  2. Most patients chronic impairments
  3. "Real" personality will emerge after alters *fused* or integrated
  4. One approach involves 2 to 3 years of psychotherapy
    a. Initial phase—trusting relationship with the client
    b. Second—establish communication and cooperation among alters
    c. Hypnosis used to facilitate access to memories, communicate with alters, patient confronts and releases painful emotions. Cognitive-behavior techniques—client asked to give up dissociative defenses; allow painful memories, gain sense of control over them
    d. Third—client strengthens new coping mechanisms; works through grief of acknowledging past trauma and relegates it to past; begins to build integrated personality that subsumes former alters
    e. Final—client learns to cope with new way of living; trauma no longer lurks in memory as a threat
    f. Continues focus on facing problems without dissociative strategies
    g. Other difficulties (depression, anxiety, substance abuse) attention
  5. Some clinicians treat the depression and anxiety only
  6. Some clinicians respond to only one personality; refuse to reinforce alters
  7. No medication has been found to address *core* symptoms

III. Somatoform Disorders (pp. 273-283)
    A. Somatization Disorder
        1. Emotional distress is converted into physical symptoms
        2. Widespread but not necessarily pathological condition
        3. Bodily symptoms serve as barometer of emotional well-being
            a. Stomach cramps or diarrhea when pressures increase
            b. Headaches or migraines when emotionally upset
        4. Clinical conditions
            a. Expression of psychological distress via physical symptoms
            b. Heightened sensitivity to bodily cues
            c. Misinterpretation of emotions as signs of physical illness
        5. Physical symptoms *feel real* to patients (not malingering)
        6. Differs from *factitious disorder* (person pretends in order to seen as sick)
        7. Medical illness more acceptable than mental illness; reluctance to consider psychological explanations for physical symptoms
            a. Leads to unnecessary testing
            b. Excessive use of medications
            c. Invasive medical procedures that can produce serious side effects
            d. Patients 9 times more expensive to treat than typical patient
    B. Hypochondriasis
        1. Hypochondriasis patients focus on few select symptoms
            a. Preoccupied with fear of having serious medical illness
            b. Originates from misinterpretation of a bodily sensation
            c. Persists after medical evaluations confirm nothing is wrong
        2. So consuming person cannot work or manage relationships
            a. Never reaches delusion proportions
            b. Some realize fears exaggerated, still cannot control them
            c. Relationships with family, friends, health care strained
        3. Symptoms appear during episodes of depression, abate as depression lifts
            a. Associated with anxiety disorders
            b. Routine sensations misinterpreted leading to alarm or arousal
            c. More frequent and severe somatic symptoms than panic groups
            d. Less positive social and occupational functioning
    C. Conversion Disorder
        1. *Pseudoneurological* symptoms
            a. *Motor* deficits such as difficulties swallowing, poor balance or coordination, paralysis or weakness of the arms or legs, loss of the voice, and urinary retention
            b. *Sensory* deficits such as the loss of sensation to touch or pain, double vision, blindness, and deafness
            c. *Seizure-like* symptoms
        2. Symptoms may come and go
            a. Person inadvertently uses "paralyzed" limb

    b. Complaint does not correspond to body's sensory systems
    c. *Glove anesthesia*—loss of sensation in hand when damage would run entire length of arm and hand
  3. One-third strangely indifferent (*la belle indifference*)
  4. Observed more often among women, rural populations, lower socioeconomic groups, most likely to affect children

D. Pain Disorder
  1. Pain number one reason people seek medical attention
  2. Pain disorder diagnosed
    a. Person's predominant clinical complaint is pain
    b. Psychological factors play role in causing or maintaining
    c. Pain is not intentionally produced
    d. *Acute pain disorder*— less than 6 months
    e. *Chronic pain disorder*— 6 months or longer
  3. Common and expensive
    a. 10-12% of population of U.S.
    b. Costs of pain total— $90 billion per year
    c. 20 million tons of aspirin annually
  4. Pain intensified when people feel anxious or depressed, feel no control

E. Body Dysmorphic Disorder
  1. Dysfunctional preoccupation with one particular physical aspect
    a. So all-consuming person avoids social contact
    b. Repeatedly check looks in mirror
    c. Spend hours each day in self-devised remedies
  2. Preoccupation leads to paranoid ideas others are scrutinizing
  3. Concern is totally out of proportion to reality

F. Causes of Somatoform Disorders
  1. Diathesis-Stress model most useful
    a. Predisposition to somatoform disorders combination of biological and psychological vulnerabilities—higher levels of negative emotions, deficiencies in ability to inhibit behavior, neurological abnormalities, hypersensitivity to physical sensations, traits such as private self-consciousness and neuroticism, a history of physical illnesses, family members who display illness
    b. One or more of these factors interacts with long-term stressors, intense emotional conflicts, or a severe trauma to increase probability that person will experience physical symptoms associated with emotional arousal
    c. Symptoms likely to be interpreted and experienced as signs of illness rather than mental disorder if sociocultural conditions support, if individual lacks sufficient medical knowledge, or if environment provides reinforcement for interpretation
  2. Biological and Psychological Vulnerabilities
    a. Conflicting evidence in role of genetics
      (1) Conversion disorders cluster within families

     (2) Neurological abnormalities constitute vulnerability
    b. Conversion symptoms located on left side of body
     (1) Right hemisphere of brain controls
     (2) Abnormality in right hemisphere (negative emotions)
    c. Organic brain disease or neuropsychological abnormality
    d. Organic factors increase vulnerability
    e. May be *somatosensory amplifier*—-perceive normal bodily sensations as more intense and disturbing
    f. *Private self-consciousness*—person prone to concentrate on internal sensations and private thoughts
    g. *Negative affectivity*—people worry, are pessimistic, fear uncertainty, feel guilty, tire easily, have poor self-esteem, are shy and depressed
    h. *Recurrent abdominal pain*— with no organic cause, common in children who grow up in families with multiple illnesses
   3. The Role of Stress and Trauma
    a. Disorder triggered by personal conflict or stressor
    b. Physical symptoms convey emotional distress for children
    c. Exposure to stressors, increased physiological reactivity
G. Treatment of Somatoform Disorders
  1. Clients typically resist psychological interpretations of their problems
  2. Goals of treatment in general medical care system
    a. Help patients cope better with stressor that trigger
    b. Wean them from chronic dependence on medical providers
    c. Teach alternative ways of communicating emotional needs
    d. Gently encourage to seek personal counseling
  3. Conversion disorder treatment
    a. Hypnosis and behavioral interventions
    b. Psychotherapy
  4. Body dysmorphic disorder treated with medication
  5. Pain disorder treatment (medical setting)
    a. Biofeedback and relaxation techniques
    b. Rehabilitation programs to increase physical activity
    c. Cognitive behavioral therapy to help patient and family members better understand how cognitions and emotions affect physical behaviors
    d. Family or marital therapy to help patients and family member see how pain behaviors can serve as a dysfunctional form of communication

8 Dissociative and Somatoform Disorders

LECTURE MAKER 8.1

Purpose To introduce simplified biofeedback techniques to reduce anxiety and assist in relaxation. (pp. 278-279)

Lecture Introduction Define biofeedback and explore possible uses for this technique. Automatic processes, not generally under cognitive control, are part of the basic fight/flight or arousal response to real or perceived danger. With biofeed back training, the autonomic arousal can be reduced, thereby attenuating the unpleasant physical sensations associated with anxiety.

Demonstration A hand held biofeedback monitor can be purchased for under $20 at Radio Shack. Ask for a volunteer and wrap the Velcro finger cuffs on two fingers. Set the ticking noise with the reostat down to a relatively fast clicking. Tell the volunteer to imagine a peaceful scene and concentrate on that image. Continue talking through the lecture introduction, no longer focusing on the volunteer. Within a few minutes, the noise from the biofeedback monitor should be slowed to a hesitant tick. Casually motion the class' attention to the volunteer but wait a minute or two before commenting. The volunteer should be demonstrating a physiological relaxation response. When you call attention to the slowed ticking, that may again "arouse" the volunteer. Note that with training, most people can stop the "ticking" indicating a reduction in arousal.

Lecture Capsule Gaining conscious control over autonomic processes can be demonstrated readily with this technique. Learning to relax can be an integral aspect of therapy.

LECTURE MAKER 8.2

Purpose To demonstrate a relaxation technique useful in reducing anxiety. (pp. 282-283)

Lecture Introduction Relaxation can be used in the therapeutic treatment of anxiety. Dissociative and somatoform disorders are suggested to have a traumatic incident or anxiety based etiology. Discuss relaxation as a possible technique in the overall treatment plan for these disorders.

Lecture Demonstration Have students take a moment to jot down their current feeling and take their own pulse. Ask the students to get comfortable in their chairs and relax. Tell them you want them to focus on your words and the images you create. Read the relaxation demonstration.

Relaxation Instructions

Take a few seconds to relax and get comfortable. Close your eyes. Concentrate on your breathing. Try to push all other thoughts out of your mind. Breathe in through your nose, hold it for a few seconds and exhale slowly through your mouth. Inhale, hold, exhale. Think only about your breathing. To re-orient, concentrate on your sensations and feelings. Wait five seconds. Now open your eyes.

More than once, a student has fallen asleep during this exercise. When it is completed, and the students have mentally returned to class, (it is an enjoyable interlude) ask them to make a few notes of how they feel and take their pulse. It is best to do this in the last portion of the class so they walk away feeling relaxed.

Lecture Capsule This is a positive experience for the students. It helps them define relaxation and feel it.

Post Script If at all possible, invite a hypnotist to class for a demonstration. Students are fascinated!

LECTURE MAKER 8.3

Purpose To illustrate the relative ease of producing a false memory. (pp. 266-268)

Lecture Introduction Discuss the theory and research regarding False Memory Syndrome. Since memory tends to be "constructive" evaluate the suggestion that everyone probably has some false memories. Relate suggestibility, therapeutic encouragement, and normal memory processes to false memory syndrome.

Demonstration Instruct students to listen to the words as they are read. They will be tested on recall later. Read one of the lists. Wait five seconds. Now ask the students to write as many of the words as they can remember. Proceed in the same fashion with two more lists. Next, read five words from each list including the "association word," asking for a show of hands for each word if the students remember it to be one that was read previously. The false alarm rate should be fairly high for the association words. This is an associative false memory.

Lecture Capsule This is a dramatic demonstration. While students are willing to admit that others may have false memories, it is insightful as they experience their own. Discuss dissociative memory and errors in recall.

Resource Roediger III, Henry L. And McDermott, Kathleen B. Creating False Memories: Remembering Words Not Presented in Lists Journal of Experimental Psychology: Learning, Memory, and Cognition 1995, Vol.21, No. 4, 803-814

List 1	List 2	List 3
Bread	**Needle**	**Sleep**
butter	thread	bed
food	pin	rest
eat	eye	awake
sandwich	sewing	tired
rye	sharp	dream
jam	point	wake
milk	prick	snooze
flour	thimble	blanket
jelly	haystack	doze
dough	thorn	slumber
crust	hurt	snore
slice	injection	nap
wine	syringe	peace
loaf	cloth	yawn
toast	knitting	drowsy

Resources

General

Society For Personality Assessment
750 First Street N.E.
Washington, DC 20002
Phone 202-336-6192
Fax   202-336-6158

Multiple-Personality Disorder
International Society for the Study of Multiple Personality
and Dissociation (ISSMP&D)
5700 Old Orchard Road
Skokie, IL 60077
708-965-2776

This group will respond both to professionals and sufferers
of MPD. Ask about study groups in your area.
Many Voices (Newsletter)
P.O. Box 2639
Cincinnati, Ohio 45201-2639
For and by People with MPD

Post Traumatic Stress Disorder
Society for Traumatic Stress Studies
P.O. Box 1564
Lanacaster, Pennsylvania 17603-1564

Media

Hysteria: Language of the Body (Bouch, 43 min, color 1967)
Examines the phenomenon of conversion disorders which result in the physical expression of pain that is actually of mental origin. Usually associated with a suppressed conflict or with traumatic memories, it is considered by professionals to be the physical manifestation of an unbearable idea. The patient himself has no clue to its meaning. Examines several individual cases, strangest of which is a traveling patient who has managed to convince twenty different surgeons that he might be helped by surgery.

Hypochondreasis and Health Care: A Tug of War (Workshop Films, 38 min, color 1978) A lecture illustrated with simulated interviews on hypochondriacs and ways of dealing with them. "Most fascinating...very interesting...very informative" (Mental Health Materials Center review)

Case Study of a Multiple Personality (PCR-2049k, 30 min, 1957
Interesting case study of dissociative reaction in a woman (Eve White, Eve Black, and Jane.) A mimeographed transcript may be ordered; the sound is poor in some instances.

The Three Faces of Eve (FI, 95 min). The classic film depicting the course of Eve's struggles with multiple personalities.

Breathing Away Stress (Beyond Stress, 30 min, color) Eli Bay leads the class in a series of deep-breathing exercises designed to manage stress and promote relaxation. One of the students is profiled. In another class, students learn to use breathing and massage to release emotions causing stress.

Relaxing Muscle Tension (Beyond Stress, 30 min, color) The class is taught exercises for recognizing and relaxing muscle tension, and a student explains how the technique has helped her. Shiatsu, a Japanese massage technique for relaxing the body and mind is also examined.

The Relaxation Response (Beyond Stress, 30 min, color) The relaxation response is explained and students are guided through exercises designed to trigger the response; a student who has been cured of insomnia with relaxation is profiled; and flotation tanks are discussed.

For additional video resource materials, please contact your Allyn & Bacon representative.

Nietzel et al., *Abnormal Psychology*, Transparencies

Chapter Eight

	Text Figure Number	Text Page Number
42. Criteria for Dissociative Identity Disorder		256
43. Diathesis-Stress Model of Dissociative Disorders	8.1	265
44. Dissociation-Trauma Model of Dissociative Identity Disorder	8.2	266
45. Criteria for Somatization Disorder		274
46. Criteria for Hypochondriasis		277
47. Glove Anesthesia	8.3	278
48. Diathesis-Stress Model of Somatoform Disorders		280

9 Mood Disorders and Suicide

CHAPTER OUTLINE

I. Depressive Disorders (pp. 289-294)
   A. Mood Disorders
      1. Also known as *affective disorders*
      2. Emotional disturbances
         a. Persistent difficulty maintaining even, productive emotional state
         b. Interfere with work, relationships, family life, good physical health
         c. *Depression*—low, miserably unhappy mood (*unipolar*)
         d. *Mania*—person feels excessively, *unrealistically* positive
         e. *Manic depressive or bipolar disorder* (both depression and mania)
         f. Are mood disorders and creativity linked?
      3. Depressive Disorders
         a. What differentiates it from "the blues"
            (1) Mood not temporary; persists for weeks, months, years
            (2) Impairs one's ability to work, interact with friends or family
            (3) Reduced appetite, sleep disturbance, no interest in pursuits
         b. Depression accompanied by comorbid problems
            (1) Depressed person abuses alcohol or drugs
            (2) *Negative affect*—combination of depression and anxiety
            (3) *Double depression*—depressive and dysthymic disorder
   B. Major Depressive Disorder
      1. Most severe form of depression
         a. At any one time 5-9 % of women, 2-3% of men in U.S.
         b. Key indicator—*major depressive episode*
         c. Two most common symptoms
            (1) Depressed mood
            (2) *Anhedonia*—loss of ability to enjoy activities central to life
         d. Predominant emotions
            (1) Dull despair, constant sadness (nothing is worthwhile)
            (2) May have bitterness, short temper, guilt
         e. Physical symptoms
            (1) Loss of appetite; variety of aches and pains
            (2) Persistent fatigue (near immobility)
            (3) Impairment in immune system functioning
         f. Cognitive symptoms
            (1) Sense of guilt and worthlessness
            (2) Difficulty concentrating even on simple things
            (3) Postpone decisions for fear of making mistakes
            (4) Self-critical, pessimistic about future, unforgiving of past
            (5) Most severely depressed experience psychotic symptoms
            (6) Delusions, hallucinations, *mood congruent*
            (7) *Mood incongruent* delusions

2. Course and Recurrence
   a. Most clear up even without treatment in matter of months
   b. Greater concern whether person will repeat episodes (high chance)
   c. Typical onset mid-twenties; three-quarters cases are recurrent
   d. Full recovery of double depression less likely than just depression
   e. Relapse much more common in double depression
3. Subgroups of Major Depressive Disorder
   a. DSM-IV diagnoses include *specifiers*
      (1) *Chronic* (2 years)
      (2) *With atypical features*—sleep and eat more than usual, intense sensitivity to rejection that disrupts relationships
      (3) *With melancholic features* (formerly called *endogenous depression*) display severe anhedonia
      (4) *With catatonic features* extreme psychomotor disturbances; stay immobile; fixed bizarre postures; *waxy flexibility*; agitated, purposeless behavior; *echopraxia; echolalia*
      (5) *With seasonal pattern (seasonal affective disorder)* only winter months—low energy, extreme fatigue, greater amount of sleeping; often craving carbohydrates
      (6) *With postpartum onset:* begins birth of child; frequent severe anxiety; obsessive worries about harm befalling the baby; shame and guilt because no joy as taught to expect

C. Dysthymic Disorder and Other Types of Depression
   1. Dysthymic disorder must have difficulties for at least 2 years
   2. In children irritability rather than depression
   3. People feel inadequate and brood about the past
   4. If not sufficiently severe *depressive disorder not otherwise specified*
   5. *Bereavement* not disorder
   6. *Pathological grief reaction*: thoughts of suicide, clinging to deceased person's belongings, strong reaction to anniversary of death

II. Bipolar Disorder (pp. 294-298)
   A. Mania and/or Depression
      1. Periods of depression as well as mania
         a. Mixed episodes (manic-depressive);can have both in same day
         b. Major depressive more common in women; bipolar equal
         c. Bipolar starts in teens; earlier than major depressive
         d. More frequent in higher socioeconomic; greater genetic basis
         e. Bipolar less often triggered by social stressors
      2. Characteristics of Bipolar Disorder
         a. Women depression first; men manic stage first
         b. More than one major depressive episode goes on to bipolar
         c. Recurring disorder
         d. Episode must last a week to be officially defined as manic
         e. Person abnormally elevated, expansive or irritable
         f. Unlimited energy and enthusiasm, unrealistic goals

        g.   Invincible and omnipotent one minute; utter despair the next
        h.   Go for days with only few hours sleep each night
        i.   Speech rapid and "pressured"; goes on and on and on
        j.   Attention and conversation shift rapidly
        k.   Inflated sense of self-esteem (*grandiosity*)
        l.   Confusion, memory loss, fear of death frequent
        m.   Psychotic features make psychiatric hospitalization necessary
        n.   Last couple of days to about 3 months
        o.   May occur from 2 to 30 times in lifetime (median 9)
  B.   Classification of Bipolar Disorders
      1.   Bipolar I and Bipolar II
          a.   Bipolar I severe, full-blown manic symptoms usually accompanied by one or more periods of major depression (2/3 patients)
          b.   Major depressive episode occurred in addition to period in which manic episodes are mild *(hypomanic)* not serious enough to interfere with social functioning or require hospitalization
          c.   Two specifiers
              (1)   *With rapid cycling*: four or more discrete, full-blown mood episodes experienced in 1-year period
              (2)   *With/without full enterepisode recovery*: between episodes patients experience periods of relatively normal mood; 1/3
      2.   Cyclothymic Disorder
          a.   2 or more years in adults; 1 or more in children and adolescents
          b.   Neither manic nor depressive mood is as severe as Bipolar I and II

III.   Biological Causes of Mood Disorders (pp. 298-302)
  A.   Medical conditions
      1.   Strokes, vitamin deficiencies, infections
      2.   Secondarily to abuse of drugs or alcohol
  B.   Genetic Influences on Mood Disorders
      1.   *Linkage analysis* done on Amish citizens
      2.   Genes play role in *predisposition* to mood disorders
      3.   Major depressive disorder 4 times more likely in identical twins
      4.   Genetic factor stronger in bipolar than unipolar
  C.   Neurobiological Influences on Mood Disorders
      1.   Neurotransmitters and Depression
          a.   Abnormalities in central nervous system
              (1)   Production of *neurotransmitters*
              (2)   Production and impact of stress hormones
          b.   *Catecholamine theory* (norepinephrine and epinephrine)
              (1)   Low levels of norepinephrine lead to depression
              (2)   Increased norepinephrine levels trigger mania
          c.   Mood-related neural activity affected
              (1)   Amount of a neurotransmitter at a synapse
              (2)   Neurotransmitter's effect on other neurotransmitters
              (3)   Number and receptivity of receptor sites

    d. Dysregulation of serotonin, dopamine, and norepinephrine
     (1) Low levels of serotonin allow others out of control
     (2) Antidepressants—inhibited uptake of serotonin or dopamine
     (3) Subtypes according to serotonin, norepinephrine, dopamine
    e. MRI and PET scans explore differences in brain activity
     (1) Blood flow increased in frontal cortex
     (2) Decreased blood flow parietal and posterior temporal lobes
     (3) Increased blood flow in amygdala and thalamus
   2. Neurotransmitters and Bipolar Disorder
    a. Lithium lowers norepinephrine activity in brain
    b. Both depression and mania—low levels of serotonin
    c. May be neurons themselves not working properly
     (1) Neurons fire too quickly—mania
     (2) Neurons fire too sluggish—depression
   3. Depression and the Endocrine System
    a. Hypothalamus (sleep and appetite) Pituitary gland (growth) Adrenal glands
    b. Key part—*hypothalamic-pituitary-adrenal*(HYPAC) *axis*
    c. Adrenal glands respond to hypothalamic-pituitary ; increase cortisol and adrenaline
    d. Disruption in HYPAC axis leads to depression
    e. Hypothalamus strongly influenced by catecholamines
IV. Psychological Causes of Mood Disorders (pp. 302-311)
 A. Intimate Relationships and Depression
   1. Psychoanalytic Theories (Freud)
    a. Person prone to depression harbors unresolved conflicts
    b. Childhood overindulged, suffered loss of care giver, disappointed
    c. Result: abnormally dependent; prone to anger when needs not met; feel worthless, fragile self-esteem
    d. After death of loved one, *introject* lost person
    e. Maintain *ego-ideals*, fail to live up to them
   2. Attachment Theories
    a. Social and cognitive factors
     (1) Impaired self-esteem
     (2) Needs for external gratification
     (3) Distorted cognitive processing
    b. John Bowlby—insecure attachments basis for depression
   3. Interpersonal Theories
    a. Social, cultural, and family causes of psychopathology
    b. Deterioration in social support potential triggers
    c. People who interact with depressed person become depressed
    d. Decreased support contributor *and* consequence of depression
 B. Learning, Cognition, and Depression
   1. The Role of Reinforcement

  a. One stops receiving reinforcement; has "punishing" experiences
  b. Individual lacks skills to obtain positive results or cope with negative consequences
  c. Interprets events way that minimizes positive, accentuates negative
 2. The Importance of Self-Control
  a. Lynn Rehm's *self-control model*—depressed people
   (1) Establish excessively high standards their own performance
   (2) Concentrate on negative events, immediate consequences
   (3) Too little self-reinforcement; too much self-punishment
  b. Never take pleasure in what they *do* accomplish
 3. Learned Helplessness and Depression
  a. Person feels unable to control life events; learns helplessness
  b. Martin Seligman—learned helplessness
   (1) Interferes with ability to learn responses to solve or cope
   (2) Causes them to give up even trying
   (3) Eventually impairs motivation, mood, and self-efficacy
  c. *Negative attributional style*
   (1) Attribute success to luck or external factors
   (2) Attribute failures to lack of intelligence or internal factors
  d. Lynn Abramson—*hopelessness*
   (1) Negative events inevitable, positive events unlikely
   (2) No prospect for changing this pattern
   (3) Three factors
    (a) Attribute negative outcomes to enduring causes
    (b) Focus on the most negative consequences
    (c) Draw negative inferences about overall self-worth
 4. Beck's Cognitive Triad
  a. Aaron Beck's cognitive theory
   (1) vulnerability to depression develops during childhood
    (a) *Self-schemas*—basic beliefs about the self
    (b) Great importance on interpersonal relationships or independence and achievement
    (c) Negative schemas produce "automatic thoughts"
   (2) *Primitive thinking*—judgement absolute, irreversible
    (a) *Cognitive triad*—automatic, repetitive, negative thoughts about self, world, and future
    (b) Self is inadequate and worthless; world's demands overwhelming; dread future will be more of same
 5. Self-Awareness
  a. *Self-awareness theory* focuses on two psychological processes
   (1) *Self-focused attention*: concentrate attention on internal
   (2) *Self-regulation*: actions that result from this reflection
  b. People trapped in ongoing, unresolved self-reflective process
   (1) Negative affect and self-criticism increase
   (2) Leads to *depressive self-focusing style*

6. Does Realism Produce Depression?
   a. Relentlessly accurate appraising abilities, accomplishments
   b. Unforgivingly accurate pattern of self-judgment
C. Stressors as Triggers of Depression
   1. Theorists View Depression From Diathesis-Stress Perspective
      a. Symptoms do not emerge until genetic risk or disturbances in early parent-child relationships combine with stressful events
      b. Onset and relapse associated with significant negative life event
         (1) Since 1940 higher prevalence of mood disorders, suicide
         (2) Onset of mood disorders occurring at younger ages
         (3) Greater number of stressors; greater chance depression
         (4) Onset or relapse more likely following major loss
         (5) Triggering function most obvious for initial episodes
D. Coping Style, Personality, and Depression
   1. Coping Style
      a. *Distraction* (with others) allows relief and positive feedback
      b. *Rumination* amplifies and prolongs
      c. Usually men employ distraction; women rumination
   2. Personality
      a. *Dependent; sociotropic personality*
      b. *Achievement; autonomy-oriented personality*
E. Psychological Theories of Bipolar Disorder
   1. Little empirical evidence psychological factors major role in causation
   2. Repeated or chronic stressors lead to biological changes

V. Treatment of Mood Disorders (pp. 311-327)
   A. Drug Treatments for Depressive Disorders
      1. Antidepressant Medications
         a. Adults—improved sleep, brighter mood, increased energy
         b. Not as effective in adolescents or children
      2. Monoamine Oxidase (MAO) Inhibitors
         a. Block monoamine oxidase, enzyme breaks down neurotransmitters
         b. Greater availability of neurotransmitters at synapses
      3. Tricylics
         a. Increase levels of neurotransmitters
         b. Block the reuptake of norepinephrine and serotonin
      4. Selective Serotonin Reuptake Inhibitors (SSRIs)
         a. Slow the reabsorption of serotonin by neurons that secrete it
         b. Keep more of it in the synapse longer
   B. Drug Treatment for Bipolar Disorder
      1. Lithium Carbonate
         a. Brings symptoms of acute manic episode under control
         b. Can be toxic to kidneys and thyroid
         c. Blood levels must be watched closely
         d. After manic episode "breaks"; antidepressants started
      2. *Carbamazepine* fewer side effects; can be used for long periods

                3.   *Valproate* acts rapidly to reduce manic symptoms
        C.   Other Biological Treatments for Mood Disorders
                1.   ECT *electroconvulsive therapy* purposely induce brief seizures
                        a.   Clinicians noted remission of symptoms in patients with seizures
                        b.   Now, only *unilateral ECT* accompanied by medication, oxygen
                        c.   Effective for severe patients not responding to antidepressants
                        d.   Most controversial treatment currently in use
                2.   Light Therapy
                        a.   Treats depressive disorders with seasonal pattern
                        b.   Person develops phase delay in circadian rhythms
                        c.   Exposes patient to bright light source in early morning hours
        D.   Psychotherapy for Mood Disorders
                1.   Psychodynamic Approaches
                        a.   Traditional: alter patient's personality structure
                        b.   Contemporary
                                (1)   *Time-limited dynamic psychotherapy*
                                (2)   *Short-term dynamic psychotherapy*
                                (3)   *Supportive-expressive therapy*
                2.   Behavioral Approaches
                        a.   Teaching skills needed to experience support
                        b.   Training in relaxation and assertiveness
                3.   Cognitive-Behavioral Therapy
                        a.   Client and therapist together change maladaptive thinking patterns
                        b.   Identify and test validity of "automatic thoughts"
                        c.   Effects equaled or exceeded those of behavioral treatments
                4.   Interpersonal Therapy
                        a.   Focuses on current social support system
                        b.   Four possible interpersonal problems
                                (1)   Severe or prolonged grief reactions
                                (2)   Role conflicts in interpersonal relationships
                                (3)   Role transitions
                                (4)   Deficits in interpersonal skills
                        c.   Goal—reduce dependency; increase self-esteem
        E.   Combining Treatments
                1.   Optimal Treatment Program for Depression
                        a.   Antidepressants and cognitive or interpersonal psychotherapy
                        b.   Drugs relieve physical symptoms; therapy relieves patterns
                        c.   *Life charting*, for bipolar patients, and medication
                        d.   Family therapy for bipolar patients
VI.   Suicide (pp. 325-331)
        A.   Who Is Suicidal?
                1.   A Profile of Suicide Attempts
                        a.   Approximately 300,000 attempts yearly in U.S.
                        b.   More frequent among females (ratio—3 to 1)
                        c.   More common in younger people

    d. 70-90% involve drug overdoses
    e. *Risk/rescue ratio* suggests person hoped to be saved
    f. *Parasuicidal behaviors* common in early trauma
   2. Completed Suicides—Who Is at Risk?
    a. Completed suicides gunshot, hanging, carbon monoxide
    b. Strongly associated with mental disorder
    c. *Psychological autopsies*—depression or alcoholism
    d. Schizophrenic symptoms, especially among young men
    e. Cluster suicides common among Native American youth
    f. Being male, being older, European American, stressful life
 B. Adolescent Suicide
   1. 2,000 teenagers per year; many more boys than girls
   2. Respond impulsively to an acute stressor
   3. Cluster suicides—one youth's death leads to another
   4. 80% long standing mental health problems
   5. 50% had relative who attempted or did commit suicide
 C. Causes of Suicide
   1. Biological Factors in Suicide
    a. Impossible to determine if genetic loading is related
    b. Unusually low concentration of 5-HIAA
    c. Low CSF concentrations of *homovanillic acid* (HVCA)
   2. Environmental Factors in Suicide
    a. Japanese *kamikaze* pilots (honorable death)
    b. *Egoistic suicide*—lonely, isolated people
    c. *Altruistic suicide*—person places social goal ahead of survival
    d. *Anomic suicide*— people feel lost or abandoned by society
    e. *Fatalistic suicide*— prisoner or slave; severe social isolation
   3. Developmental Factors in Suicide
    a. Traditional psychoanalysts—intense, unresolved, internalized anger at primary parent figure; unable to maintain self-worth, self-caring
    b. Object-relations and interpersonal theories—role of disturbed family relationships; dysfunction early in life hampers ability to cope
    c. Cognitive perspective—early negative experiences increase tendency to feel hopelessness; one of best predictors of suicide
 D. Suicide Prevention
   1. Three Basic Components
    a. Assessing the risk of suicide
    b. Helping the person cope with immediate crisis
    c. Treating any behavior disorders that increase risk of later attempts
    d. Crisis intervention
   2. Treating Suicidal Tendencies
    a. Antianxiety and antipsychotic medications
    b. Psychotherapy sessions: help to feel more hopeful and connected
    c. *Suicide contract*—client to seek help if urges overwhelming

9 Mood Disorders and Suicide

LECTURE MAKER 9.1

Purpose To illustrate a subtype of dependent personality, using a checklist for codependency. (pp. 302-303)

Lecture Introduction Discuss dependency as a primary personality feature. This person requires others' approval for their sense of well-being. The nature of this needy relationship to others can breed resentment, fear, and depression. Highlight the features of the codependent person.

Demonstration Duplicate the codependency characteristics checklist or read aloud. Discuss the personality features suggested to represent the codependent. Critique the checklist with students for usefulness and weaknesses.

Lecture Capsule Having completed the checklist, students are curious about the evolution of these qualities and relate well to the lecture discussion. Read or duplicate the fourteen questions of Adult Children of Alcoholics and discuss.

LECTURE MAKER 9.2

Purpose To evaluate perceived need for approval using the Social Desirability Scale. (pp. 304-305)

Lecture Introduction Dependency on other's for approval or validation creates a fragility to the personality. Discuss dependent personality features and characteristic behavior. Link dependency to possible depression and reduced self-efficacy.

Demonstration Duplicate the Social Desirability Scale, scoring, and interpretation ranges for students to complete anonymously. Review the interpretation and implication of high and low scores. Review the limitations of true/false personality survey.

Lecture Capsule As the old saying goes: At twenty I was sure everyone was looking at me. At sixty, I realized nobody was looking. Younger students are somewhat more sensitive to the imaginary audience and approval from others. Be aware that their scores might be more approval-dependent because of youth.

CODEPENDENT CHARACTERISTICS 9.1

Caretaking

Codependents may

- think and feel responsible for other people—for other people's feelings, thoughts, actions, choices, wants, needs, well-being, lack of well-being, and ultimate destiny
- feel anxiety, pity, and guilt when other people have a problem
- feel compelled—almost forced—to help that person solve the problem, such as offering unwanted advice, giving a rapid-fire series of suggestions, or fixing feelings
- feel angry when their help isn't effective
- anticipate other people's needs
- wonder why others don't do the same for them
- find themselves saying yes when they mean no, doing things they don't really want to be doing, doing more than their fair share of the work, and doing things other people are capable of doing for themselves
- not knowing what they want and need or, if they do, tell themselves what they want and need is not important
- try to please others instead of themselves
- find it easier to feel and express anger about injustices done to others, rather than injustices done to themselves
- feel safest when giving
- feel insecure and guilty when somebody gives to them
- feel sad because they spend their whole lives giving to other people and nobody wants to give to them
- find themselves attracted to needy people
- find needy people attracted to them
- feel bored, empty, and worthless if they don't have a crisis in their lives, a problem to solve, or someone to help
- abandon their routine to respond to or do something for somebody else
- overcommit themselves
- feel harried and pressured
- believe deep inside other people are somehow responsible for them
- blame others for the spot the codependents are in
- say other people make the codependents feel the way they do
- believe other people are making them crazy
- feel angry, victimized, unappreciated, and used
- find other people become impatient or angry with them for all the preceding characteristics

Low Self-Worth

Codependents tend to:

- come from troubled, repressed, or dysfunctional families
- deny their family was troubled, repressed, or dysfunctional
- blame themselves for everything
- pick on themselves for everything, including the way they think, feel, look, act, and behave
- get angry, defensive, self-righteous, and indignant when others blame and criticize the codependents—something codependents regularly do to themselves
- reject compliments or praise
- get depressed from a lack of compliments and praise (stroke deprivation)
- feel different from the rest of the world
- think they're not quite good enough
- feel guilty about spending money on themselves or doing unnecessary or fun things for themselves
- fear rejection
- take things personally
- have been victims of sexual, physical, or emotional abuse, neglect, abandonment, or alcoholism
- feel like victims
- tell themselves they can't do anything right
- be afraid of making mistakes
- wonder why they have a tough time making decisions
- expect themselves to do everything perfectly
- wonder why they can't get anything done to their satisfaction
- have a lot of "shoulds"
- feel a lot of guilt
- feel ashamed of who they are
- think their lives aren't worth living
- try to help other people live their lives instead
- get artificial feeling of self-worth from helping others
- get strong feelings of low self-worth—embarrassment, failure, etc—from other people's failures and problems
- wish good things would happen to them
- believe good things never will happen
- believe they don't deserve good things and happiness
- wish other people would like and love them
- believe other people couldn't possibly like and love them
- try to prove they're good enough for other people
- settle for being needed

Repression

Many codependents:

- push their thoughts and feelings out of their awareness because of fear and guilt
- become afraid to let themselves be who they are
- appear rigid and controlled

Obsession

Codependents tend to:

- feel terribly anxious about problems and people
- worry about the silliest things
- think and talk a lot about other people
- lose sleep over problems or other people's behavior
- worry
- never find answers
- check on people
- try to catch people in acts of misbehavior
- feel unable to quit talking, thinking, and worrying about other people or problems
- abandon their routine because they are so upset about somebody or something
- focus all their energy on other people and problems
- wonder why they never have any energy
- wonder why they can't get things done

Controlling

Many codependents:

- have lived through events and with people that were out of control, causing the codependents sorrow and disappointment
- become afraid to let other people be who they are and allow events to happen naturally
- don't see or deal with their fear of loss of control
- think they know best how things should turn out and how people should behave
- try to control events and people through helplessness, guilt, coercion, threats, advice-giving, manipulation, or domination
- eventually fail in their efforts or provoke people's anger
- get frustrated and angry
- feel controlled by events and people

Denial

Codependents tend to:

- ignore problems or pretend they aren't happening
- pretend circumstances aren't as bad as they are
- tell themselves things will be better tomorrow
- stay busy so they don't have to think about things
- get confused
- get depressed or sick
- go to doctors and get tranquilizers
- become workaholics
- spend money compulsively
- overeat
- pretend those things aren't happening, either
- watch problems get worse
- believe lies
- lie to themselves
- wonder why they feel like they're going crazy

Dependency

Many codependents:

- don't feel happy, content, or peaceful with themselves
- look for happiness outside themselves
- latch onto whoever or whatever they think can provide happiness
- feel terribly threatened by the loss of any thing or person they think provides their happiness
- didn't feel love and approval from their parents
- don't love themselves
- believe other people can't or don't love them
- desperately seek love and approval
- often seek love from people incapable of loving
- believe other people are never there for them
- equate love with pain
- feel they need people more than they want them
- try to prove they're good enough to be loved
- don't take time to see if other people are good for them
- worry whether other people love or like them
- don't take time to figure out if they love or like other people
- center their lives around other people
- look to relationships to provide all their good feelings
- lose interest in their own lives when they love

- worry other people will leave them
- don't believe they can take care of themselves
- stay in relationships that don't work
- tolerate abuse to keep people loving them
- feel trapped in relationships
- leave bad relationships and form new ones that don't work either
- wonder if they will ever find love

Poor Communication

Codependents frequently:

- blame
- threaten
- coerce
- beg
- bribe
- advise
- don't say what they mean
- don't mean what they say
- don't know what they mean
- don't take themselves seriously
- think other people don't take the codependents seriously
- take themselves too serioulsy
- ask for what they want and need indirectly—sighing, for example
- find it difficult to get to the point
- aren't sure what the point is
- gauge their words carefully to achieve a desired effect
- try to say what they think will please people
- try to say what they think will provoke people
- try to say what they hope will make people do what they want them to do
- eliminate the word *no* from their vocabulary
- talk too much
- talk about other people
- avoid talking about themselves, their problems, feelings, and thoughts
- say everything is their fault
- say nothing is their fault
- believe their opinions don't matter
- wait to express their opinions until they know other people's opinions
- lie to protect and cover up for people they love
- lie to protect themselves
- have a difficult time expressing their emotions honestly, openly, and appropriately
- think most of what they have to say is unimportant
- begin to talk in cynical, self-degrading, or hostile ways
- apologize for bothering people

Weak Boundaries

Codependents frequently:

- say they won't tolerate certain behaviors from other people
- gradually increase their tolerance until they can tolerate and do things they said they never would
- let others hurt them
- keep letting people hurt them
- wonder why they hurt so badly
- complain, blame, and try to control while they continue to stand there
- finally get angry
- become totally intolerant

Lack of Trust

Codependents:

- don't trust themselves
- don't trust their feelings
- don't trust their decisions
- don't trust other people
- try to trust untrustworthy people
- think God has abandoned them
- lose faith and trust in God

Anger

Many codependents:

- feel very scared, hurt, and angry
- live with people who are very scared, hurt, and angry
- are afraid of their own anger
- are frightened of other people's anger
- think people will go away if anger enters the picture
- think other people make them feel angry
- are afraid to make other people feel anger
- feel controlled by other people's anger
- repress their angry feelings
- cry a lot, get depressed, overeat, get sick, do mean and nasty things to get even, act hostile, or have violent temper outbursts
- punish other people for making the codependents angry
- have been shamed for feeling angry
- place guilt and shame on themselves for feeling angry
- feel increasing amounts of anger, resentment, and bitterness
- feel safer with their anger than with hurt feelings
- wonder if they'll ever *not* be angry

Sex Problems

Some codependents:

- are caretakers in the bedroom
- have sex when they don't want to
- have sex when they'd rather be held, nurtured, and loved
- try to have sex when they're angry or hurt
- refuse to enjoy sex because they're so angry at their partner
- are afraid of losing control
- have a difficult time asking for what they need in bed
- withdraw emotionally from their partner
- feel sexual revulsion toward their partner
- don't talk about it
- force themselves to have sex, anyway
- reduce sex to a technical act
- wonder why they don't enjoy sex
- lose interest in sex
- make up reasons to abstain
- wish their sex partner would die, go away, or sense the codependent's feelings
- have strong sexual fantasies about other people
- consider or have an extramarital affair

Miscellaneous

Codependents tend to:

- be extremely responsible
- be extremely irresponsible
- become martyrs, sacrificing their happiness and that ot others for causes that don't require sacrifice
- find it difficult to feel close to people
- find it difficult to have fun and be spontaneous
- have an overall passive response to codependency—crying, hurt, helplessness
- have an overall aggressive response to codependency—violence, anger, dominance
- combine passive and aggressive responses
- vacillate in decisions and emotions
- laugh when they feel like crying
- stay loyal to their compulsions and people even when it hurts
- be ashamed about family, personal, or relationship problems
- be confused about the nature of the problem
- cover up, lie, and protect the problem
- not seek help because they tell themselves the problem isn't bad enough, or they aren't important enough
- wonder why the problem doesn't go away

Progessive

In the later stages of codependency, codependent may:

- feel lethargic
- feel depressed
- become withdrawn and isolated
- experience a complete loss of daily routine and structure
- abuse or neglect their children and other responsibilities
- feel hopeless
- begin to plan their escape from a relationship they feel trapped in
- think about suicide
- become violent
- become seriously emotionally, mentally, or physically ill
- experience an eating disorder (over- or undereating)
- become addicted to alcohol and other drugs

The preceding checklist is long but not all-inclusive. Like other people, codependents do, feel, and think many things. There are not a certain number of traits that guarantees whether a person is or isn't codependent.

ADULT CHILDREN OF ALCOHOLICS

1. Do I often feel isolated and afraid of people, especially authority figures?
2. Have I observed myself to be an approval seeker, losing my own identity in the process?
3. Do I feel overly frightened of angry people and personal criticism?
4. Do I often feel I'm a victim in personal and career relationships?
5. Do I sometimes feel I have an overdeveloped sense of responsibility, which makes it easier to be concerned with others rather than myself?
6. Do I find it hard to look at my own faults and my own responsibilities?
7. Do I get guilt feeling when I stand up for myself instead of giving in to others?
8. Do I feel addicted to excitement?
9. Do I confuse love with pity and tend to love people I can pity and rescue?
10. Do I find it hard to feel or express feelings, including feelings such as joy or happiness?
11. Do I find I judge myself harshly?
12. Do I have a low sense of self-esteem?
13. Do I often feel abandoned in the course of my relationships?
14. Do I tend to be a reactor, instead of an actor?

From *"Codependent No More"* by Melody Beattie. Reprinted with permission.

Social Desirability Scale 9.2
by Douglas P. Crowne and David Marlowe

Listed below are a number of statements concerning personal attitudes and traits. Read each item and decide whether the statement is true (T) or false(F) as it pertains to you personally. It's best to go with your first judgement and not spend too long mulling over any one question. Place a mark in the space next to each question.

T or F

1. Before voting I thoroughly investigate the qualifications of all the candidates.   1. _____
2. I never hesitate to go out of my way to help someone in trouble   2. _____
3. It is sometimes hard for me to go on with my work if I am not encouraged.   3. _____
4. I have never intensely disliked anyone.   4. _____
5. On occasions I have had doubts about my ability to succeed in life.   5. _____
6. I sometimes feel resentful when I don't get my way.   6. _____
7. I am always careful about my manner of dress.   7. _____
8. My table manners at home are as good as when I eat out in a restaurant.   8. _____
9. If I could get into a movie without paying and be sure I was not seen I would probably do it.   9. _____
10. On a few occasions, I have given up something because I thought too little of my ability.   10. _____
11. I like to gossip at times.   11. _____
12. There have been times when I felt like rebelling against people in authority even though I knew they were right.   12. _____
13. No matter who I'm talking to, I'm always a good listener.   13. _____
14. I can remember "playing sick" to get out of something.   14. _____
15. There have been occasions when I have taken advantage of someone.   15. _____
16. I'm always willing to admit it when I make a mistake.   16. _____
17. I always try to practice what I preach.   17. _____
18. I don't find it particularly difficult to get along with loudmouthed, obnoxious people.   18. _____
19. I sometimes try to get even rather than forgive and forget.   19. _____
20. When I don't know something I don't mind at all admitting it.   20. _____
21. I am always courteous, even to people who are disagreeable.   21. _____
22. At times I have really insisted on having things my way.   22. _____
23. There have been occasions when I felt like smashing things.   23. _____
24. I would never think of letting someone else be punished for my wrong-doings.   24. _____
25. I never resent being asked to return a favor.   25. _____
26. I have never been irked when people expressed ideas very different from my own.   26. _____
27. I never make a long trip without checking the safety of my car.   27. _____
28. There have been times when I was quite jealous of the good fortune of others   28. _____
29. I have almost never felt the urge to tell someone off.   29. _____
30. I am sometimes irritated by people who ask favors of me.   30. _____
31. I have never felt that I was punished without cause.   31. _____
32. I sometimes think when people have a misfortune they only get what they deserve.   32. _____
33. I have never deliberately said something that hurt someone's feelings.   33. _____

Douglas Crowne and David Marlowe, "A new scale of social desirability independent of pathology." *Journal of Consulting Psychology*, 1960, 24, Table 1, p. 351. Copyright 1960 by the American Psychological Association. Reprinted by permission.

SCORING THE SCALE

To find your score, compare your answers to those listed on the Scoring Key. Count the number of times the answers you marked agree with the ones listed on the Scoring Key and write that number in the box below. Your total score can range from a low of zero agreement to a high of 33.

SCORING KEY

1. T _____
2. T _____
3. F _____
4. T _____
5. F _____
6. F _____
7. T _____
8. T _____
9. F _____
10. F _____
11. F _____
12. F _____
13. T _____
14. F _____
15. F _____
16. T _____
17. T _____
18. T _____
19. F _____
20. T _____
21. T _____
22. F _____
23. F _____
24. T _____
25. T _____
26. T _____
27. T _____
28. F _____
29. T _____
30. F _____
31. T _____
32. F _____
33. T _____

TOTAL SCORE

SOCIAL DESIRABILITY SCALE 9.2 INTERPRETING YOUR SCORE

Low Scorers (0-8)—If you scored in this range, you (a) answered most of the questions in socially *undesirable* direction, but (b) answered them in a way more honest and true to real life than most people. You are very comfortable with who you are. You do not feel discomfort when other people view you as behaving in a socially undesirable way or you want to be seen by others as a social rebel, someone who is different.

Average Scorers (9-19)—If you scored in this range, you are scoring as two out of three people do when taking the test. Scores here represent a combination of socially desirable and socially undesirable responses.

High Scorers (20-33)— Your score in this range suggests that being seen as socially acceptable is very important to you. (Of course, you have to consider where you scored within this range to decide how much these statements are true for you.) Perhaps your score indicates what Drs. Crowne and Marlowe see as a need for approval from others. If a high need for approval describes you, you may feel frequent social insecurity, or anxiety about doing what others expect.

RESOURCES

General

Co-dependents Anonymous
Box 33577
Phoenix, Arizona 85067-3577

Society for the Right to Die
250 West 57 Street
New York, NY 10107
212-246-6973

American Association of Suicidology
2459 S. Ash
Denver, CO 80222
303-692-0985

FBI, U.S. Dept of Justice
National Crime Information Center
9th St. & Pennsylvania Avenue
Washington, DC 20535
202-324-2606

International Association for Suicide Prevention
Suicide Prevention and Crisis Center
1811 Trousdale Dr
Burlingame, CA 94010
415-877-5604

American Suicide Foundation (ASF)
1045 Park Ave
New York, NY 10028-1030
Herbert Hendin, M.D. Exec. Dir.
Phone 212-410-1111
Fax 212-410-0352

Depression and Related Affective Disorders Association
John Hopkins Hospital Meyer 3-181
600 N. Wolfe Street
Baltimore, MD 21287-7381

Media

Depression: Beating the Blues (CBC; FML;28 min, color, 16mm/video, 1983)
Investigates the nature of clinical depression, the most common form of mental illness. Examines its biochemical basis and the theory of genetic causation, and discusses treatments: chemical therapy, psychotherapy, and electroconvulsive therapy. Considers the role of the family and other support system in helping victims of depression.

Psychopathology: Diagnostic Vignettes, No. 1--Dysthymic Disorders and Major Affective Disorders (Case Numbers 1-4) (INURTS; INUAVC; 38 min, color, video, 1984)
Portrays a group of depressed patients exhibiting a range of symptoms and levels of severity. The cases can be used to illustrate both contemporary and traditional ways in which the affective disorders have been subdivided. The differences between the first and second cases, for example, can be used to emphasize the distinction between minor and major depressions. Similar comparisons can be drawn between psychotic and non-psychotic, primary and secondary, and unipolar and bepolar affective disorders.

Biochemistry of Depression. (CM, 29 min, color) the biogenic amine theory, the catecholamine hypothesis, indolamine, permissive and two-disease hypothesis, neurotransmitters, the endocrine theory, and the electrolyte theory. Discusses and negates the hormone imbalance, increased cortisol, and oral contraceptives theories of depression. Explains sex differences in the incidence of depression by showing the correlation between sex hormone levels and mood disorders.

Depression: Recognizing It, Treating It. (HRM, 42 min, 1980
Presents biochemical theories, cognitive and psychoanalytic viewpoints, and treatment of depression.

Depression: A Study in Abnormal Behavior (CRM, 27 min) Follows a 29-year-old teacher through severe depression and her treatment with a variety of methods, including chemotherapy, electro-convulsive therapy, and group therapy. The value of the film is that it serves as a model of abnormal behavior, enabling the narrator to explain the variety of approaches to the understanding and treatment of abnormal behavior.

One Man's Madness (TL, 31 min) The first-hand account of a writer who becomes a manic depressive. Footage of the subject's hospital treatment is included, and, with a hidden camera, some unnerving scenes unfold. Guaranteed to stimulate discussion among your students.

Depression and Manic Depression: Depression affects over 17 million Americans each year, and it's been estimated that only one-third of this group gets any treatment, largely because of stigma and fear. The lack of treatment results in a high number of suicides, making this illness as fatal as any other illness and a public epidemic. This program explains the disease through the experiences of people. (28 minutes, color)

Depression: Back from the Bottom: This program explains the symptoms of depression and the range of treatment options, from antidepressant medication to electroconvulsive therapy (ECT). It also explains the differences between the old and new ECT procedures, showing how ECT is thought to stimulate the brain's neurotransmitters, restoring the brain's chemical balance. Two patients, both suffering from severe depression, explain what it feels like to be severely depressed and how they manage to go on. (17 minutes, color)

Unmasking Depression: This program follows the lives of four adults in their prime years. We hear about their fears and emotional pain and their thoughts of suicide. The best part of the program comes when they explain how they overcame depression in ways that others can learn from. (28 minutes, color)

Serious Depression: This program explains that women are twice as likely as men to be diagnosed with serious depression, and interviews experts on causes and treatment. Psychotherapy is explained, as are new drug treatments and the revised form of electroconvulsive therapy. People in a national depression support group talk about their lives and how to live with a depressed person. (28 minutes, color)

Understanding Depression: Through the Darkness: This program explores clinical depression, explaining the symptoms, various treatment options, and the need to erase the negative stigma that this illness carries. The program features three patients who suffer from clinical depression, examining the devastating effect of the illness on them, how they dealt with the social stigma, the roles of their families and friends during their illness. (27 minutes, color)

Everything to Live For: This documentary features the stories of four young people: two attempted and two committed suicide. The families and the two surviving teens talk about the causes or presumed causes of the catastrophic actions taken, the cries for help that went unheard, and the warning signals to which peers, parents, teachers, and counselors must be alert and responsive. (52 minutes, color)

Teenage Suicide: This documentary explores some of the reasons teens commit suicide and describes some of the the behavior patterns to which family and friends should be alerted. A young man who attempted suicide describes his calls for help and how he hoped they would be heeded. (19 minutes, color)

Dying to Be Heard...Is Anybody Listening? This program offers specific advice on how to recognize teens in danger of committing suicide and successfully intervene. It talks to teens who have attempted suicide about their reasons for trying and about their lives after treatment, and it profiles a Texas community that banned together to stop a rash of teen suicides, showing how it turned tragedy into triumph. (25 minutes, color)

The Suicide Clinic: A Cry for Help (IU, 28 min) Indicates that the suicide attemp is a cry for help, sympathy, and understanding. Links most suicides with long-term depression involving love, work, or physical illness.

Suicide: But Jack Was a Good Driver (CRM, 14 min) "Two friends of a boy who was killed in a car accident reflect upon his activities and conversations during the month before his death. Their reflections provide insight into the causes of suicide and the subtle communication of intentions to commit suicide.

Suicide: It Doesn't Have to Happen (UCEMC, 20 min) The story of a teacher who prevents a student's suicide by referring the student to a suicide prevention center. Discusses the symptoms of suicide and ways to deal with them

Mood Disorders American Psychiatric Press and Allyn & Bacon
This series of three clinical programs reveals additions and changes from DSM-III-R to DSM-IV for mood, psychotic, and anxiety disorders. Each videotape focuses on one particular area of psychiatric diagnosis and contains enactments of three outstanding clinician's actual patient interviews. Each videotape begins with an introductory discussion between the clinician and the moderator. The clinician then conducts three 10-minute psychiatric diagnostic interviews. Following each interview, the clinician and the moderator discuss the taped segments and comment on issues illustrated during the interviews. The interviews utilize reference data to examine conclusion reached during the interview. Each tape also demonstrates good interviewing relationship. A printed list of relevant issues highlighted in interviews and elaborated in the clinical discussions is enclosed.

For additional video resource materials, please contact your Allyn & Bacon representative.

Nietzel et al., *Abnormal Psychology,* Transparencies

Chapter Nine

	Text Figure Number	Text Page Number
49. Criteria for Major Depressive Episode		290
50. Criteria for Dysthymic Disorder		294
51. Criteria for Manic Episode		296
52. Overview of DSM-IV Major Mood Disorders	9.1	297
53. Psychological Mechanisms Involved in Depression	9.4	305
54. A Diathesis-Stress Perspective on Depression	9.6	310
55. A Diathesis-Stress Model of Suicide	9.8	324

10 Schizoprenia

CHAPTER OUTLINE

I. What Is Schizophrenia? (pp. 332-343)
    A. A Psychosis
        1. Can impair almost all aspects of psychological functioning
        2. Includes
            a. *Hallucinations*—sensory experiences that seem real to person; are not based on any external stimulation of relevant organ
            b. *Delusions*—false beliefs about reality so firmly held no evidence or argument can convince person to give them up
    B. A Fragmentation
        1. Basic psychological functioning is fragmented
        2. Attention, perception, thought, emotion, and behavior involved
        3. Person sees and hears things that are not there
    C. The Evolving Concept of Schizophrenia
        1. Emil Kraepelin—subtype of *dementia praecox*
        2. Eugen Bleuler (Swiss psychiatrist) gave name
            a. Split ("schizen") in the mind's ("phren") equals *schizophrenia*
            b. Four primary symptoms
                (1) Loosening of associations (thoughts and ideas not linked)
                (2) Ambivalence—wants 2 contradictory things, unable to choose
                (3) Autism—self-centeredness; reality replaced with fantasy
                (4) Affective disturbance—emotional responses inconsistent
        3. Kurt Schneider—delusions and hallucinations "first rank" of schizophrenia
        4. Synthesis of all three achieved in DSM-III; remain in DSM-IV
    D. Schizophrenia According to the DSM-IV
        1. No specific symptoms that must *always* be present
        2. Any one single symptom not enough to diagnose
        3. Symptoms classified as positive or negative
    E. Positive Symptoms of Schizophrenia
        1. Delusions
            a. Misinterpretations of normal perceptual experiences
            b. Attempted explanations for experiences suffered
        2. Classified by Specific Content
            a. *Somatic delusions*—something is wrong with body
            b. *Delusions of persecution*—tormented or harassed
            c. *Delusions of reference*—sounds, stimuli special reference to person
                Delusions of control—foreign entity is controlling person
            d. *Thought withdrawal*—thoughts are being stolen
            e. *Thought insertion*—thoughts forced into head
            f. *Thought broadcasting*—thoughts being transmitted to others
            g. *Delusions of grandeur*—belief person is famous or important

3. Hallucinations
   a. *S*ensory experiences that seem real to person; are not based on any external stimulation of relevant organ
   b. Person acts as if experiences real, unable to stop them, reports that they persist no matter what person does
   c. About 60% report *auditory hallucinations*
   d. About 40% report *tactile hallucinations*
      (1) Sensation of being electrically shocked
      (2) *Formication*—bugs or creatures under skin
   e. *Visual hallucinations* in about 33%
   f. *Gustatory* (taste), *olfactory* (smell) less common
4. Disordered Thought Processes
   a. Disturbances in *form* of thought—how thoughts are organized, controlled, and processed
   b. Called *formal thought disorder* evidenced by disorganized speech
      (1) Present in up to 85% of hospitalized schizophrenics
      (2) Speech called *derailment, word salad, cognitive slippage*
      (3) *Neologisms*, the creation of words
      (4) *Preseveration*—repeats word or concept over and over
5. Disorders of Behavior
   a. Peculiar motor behavior
      (1) Odd muscular movements
      (2) Hold themselves in contorted postures
      (3) *Catatonia*—maintain awkward body position for hours
      (4) Opposite end—excitement, extreme motor activity, violence
   b. *Disorganized behavior*—giggle, sob inappropriately; uncontrollably

F. Negative Symptoms of Schizophrenia
   1. *Deficit schizophrenia*—flat affect, alogia, and avolation
      a. Flat affect—2/3 patients, emotionless masks, robotic voices
      b. Alogia—failure to say anything in response to questions, comments
      c. Avolation—sit for hours on end; if activity, wander off in middle
      d. Avolation may be accompanied by anhedonia
   2. Schizophrenics do not find pain as aversive as other people do

G. Distinguishing Schizophrenia from Other Psychotic Disorders
   1. Psychotic Disorder Due to a General Medical Condition
      a. Alcohol, drugs, tumors, epilepsy, migraine, CNS infections
      b. Endocrine disorders, metabolic disorders
   2. Brief Psychotic Disorder
      a. Reaction to severe stressor (death of loved one, etc)
      b. Can follow childbirth (*postpartum onset*)
   3. Schizophreniform Disorder
      a. Impaired social or occupational functioning not required
      b. Symptoms present for at least 1 but not more than 6 months

H. Schizoaffective Disorder
   1. Hallucinations or delusions and also mood disorder symptoms
   2. More often diagnosed in females than males

    I.   Delusional Disorder
           1.   Presence of at least one *nonbizarre* delusional belief
           2.   Person organizes much of his or her life around the belief
    J.   Shared Psychotic Disorder
           1.   *Inducer* develops psychotic disorder
           2.   Influences another person *(receiver)* to act on it
           3.   Whole families, groups, religious cults form systems
    K.   Substance-Induced Psychotic Disorder
           1.   Hallucinations and delusions result from
                 a.   Drugs of abuse (cocaine)
                 b.   Medications (corticosteroids)
                 c.   Toxins (organophosphate insecticides)
           2.   Not aware substances are producing hallucination or delusion
II.   Life with Schizophrenia: Patterns and Variations (pp. 343-349)
    A.   The Course of Schizophrenia
           1.   Males diagnosed earlier age than females
           2.   Two important differences between childhood schizophrenia and autism
                 a.   Hallucinations and delusions *not* prominent in autism disorder
                 b.   Speech absent or limited in autistic disorder
           3.   Schizophrenia starts with *prodromal phase* (insidious onset)
           4.   Prodromal phase progresses to *active phase*, usually following crisis
           5.   Following, *residual phase*—psychotic symptoms subside
    B.   Who Is Affected by Schizophrenia?
           1.   Worldwide-about 20 million people
           2.   1.2 million in U.S.
           3.   Cultural Background
                 a.   Studies done by WHO;
                         (1)   International Pilot Study on Schizophrenia
                         (2)   Determinants of Outcome of Severe Mental Disorders
                 b.   Symptoms identical in all countries studied
                 c.   Very low (0.3 cases per 1,000) in Amish in U.S.
                 d.   Unusually low rates in Ghana and New Guinea
                 e.   Unusually high rates in Ireland and former Yugoslavia
                 f.   Third World patients show *higher* rates of improvement
           4.   Social Background
                 a.   Risk for person in lowest quartile, 8 times higher in U.S.
                 b.   Urban living, lower social classes, England, Sweden, Germany
           5.   Gender and Morbidity Risk
                 a.   Equal for males and females, 5 years earlier for males
                 b.   Men hospitalized more often; prognosis poorer
    C.   DSM-IV Subtypes and Other Classifications
           1.   Five types
                 a.   Paranoid Type
                         (1)   Prominent, persistent, and elaborate delusions
                         (2)   Intellectual and cognitive functions generally well preserved

        b. Disorganized Type
           (1) Grossly inappropriate, disorganized speech, behavior, affect
           (2) Emotional responses flat or flagrantly inappropriate
           (3) Involves serious intellectual incapacities
        c. Catatonic Type
           (1) Extremely disordered, odd motor movements
           (2) Relentless activity ; catatonic stupor, may develop *catalepsy*
           (3) May involve *waxy flexibility, mutism, echopraxia, echolalia*
        d. Undifferentiated Type
           (1) Do not satisfy specific criteria for first three kinds
           (2) Reclassified here when symptoms become less distinct
        e. Residual Type
           (1) At least one prior episode
           (2) Do not display major *positive* symptoms
           (3) Transition from active to marked improvement or remission
        f. Future—*simple deteriorative disorder*
           (1) Noticeable decline in occupational or academic functioning
           (2) Gradual appearance and worsening of negative symptoms
    2. Other Classifications of Schizophrenia
        a. *Process-reactive dimension*
           (1) Onset at early age; *poor premorbid adjustment*
           (2) Progressive deterioration in functioning
        b. *Reactive schizophrenia*
           (1) Symptoms come suddenly, reaction to traumatic situation
           (2) *Good premorbid adjustment*; better chance of recovery
        c. Type-I
           (1) Positive symptoms, good premorbid functioning
           (2) Acute onset of symptoms, responsive to psychotropic drugs
        d. Type-II
           (1) Negative symptoms, poor premorbid functioning, insidious
           (2) Intellectual problems, less responsive to psychotropic drugs
III. Biological Causes of Schizophrenia (pp. 349-360)
    A. Genetic Factors and Schizophrenia
        1. Schizophrenia "runs" or aggregates in families
           a. Found in family, adoption, twin studies; all countries
           b. Vulnerability that predisposes is genetically transmitted
           c. Genes alone not sufficient to account for development
        2. Family Aggregation Studies
           a. Studies begin with *proband* or *index cases*
           b. Closer genetic relationship to schizophrenic, higher risk
        3. Twin Studies
           a. Concordance rate: 48% for MZ twins; 17% for DZ twins
           b. Even though pairs do not exhibit; they still carry, pass on
        4. Adoption Studies
           a. Children born to schizophrenic parents; adopted by normal
           b. Among 144 adoptees; 9% became psychotic

       5. A Model of Genetic Influence
          a. No single dominant, no two recessive genes determine
          b. Linkage analyses have not produced well-replicated findings
          c. Meehl; single schizogene conveys vulnerability *(schizotaxia)*
          d. People *(schizotypes)* subjected to physical, social, or familial stressors, ultimately decompensate into schizophrenia

B. Early Physical Trauma
    1. Decreased brain density, volume, or function
       a. Physical trauma to brain prenatally, during birth process, after
       b. Prenatal exposure to a viral infection as influenza
       c. *Season of birth* (children born in winter or early spring)
    2. Complication during pregnancy and birth
       a. Prolonged delivery, hypoxia, breech delivery
       b. Forceps delivery, excessive bleeding

C. Brain Structures and Functions
    1. Enlarged *ventricles*, cavities in center of brain filled with cerebral spinal fluid
    2. Abnormal neurological development or pathological brain deterioration
    3. Evidence of Hypofrontality
       a. Decreased frontal lobe volume
       b. Diminished neuronal and blood flow activity
       c. Lowered performance neuropsychological, problem-solving tests
       d. Frontal lobe involved in problem solving, planning, and thinking
    4. Temporal Lobe and Limbic System
       a. Greater temporal abnormalities in left hemisphere of schizophrenics
       b. Blood flow abnormalities in basal ganglia, limbic system
       c. Limbic system regulates emotions, aggressions, social behavior
       d. Hippocampus, amygdala abnormalities—auditory hallucinations
       e. Thalamus linked to limbic system; information relay station
       f. Thalamus most diminished for schizophrenic group
    5. Some Preliminary Conclusions
       a. Differences do not appear in all schizophrenic patients
       b. Neuroleptic drugs may account for abnormalities
       c. Deficits occur also in mood disorders and medical diseases

D. The Role of Biochemical Processes
    1. Role of Dopamine
       a. Tissues and fluids of patients higher levels of dopamine by-products
       b. Drugs that increase dopamine activity intensify symptoms
       c. Drugs that block dopamine relieve symptoms, especially positive
       d. Degree to which neuroleptics block directly correlated to reduction
       e. Clinical effects of drugs do not occur for days or weeks
       f. Limbic system shows excess dopamine (Type I)
       g. Frontal lobes deficiencies (Type II)

    E.   Evidence From High-Risk Studies
        1.   Employ Prospective Designs
            a.   Focus on children born to schizophrenic parent
            b.   10-18 years old; none were schizophrenic
            c.   High risk sample, 207 ; low risk sample, 104
            d.   Recent follow-up revealed
                (1)   Morbidity risk 17.1% for high risk group
                (2)   Morbidity risk 2.9% for low risk group
                (3)   42.1% of HR group carried diagnosis of schizophrenia, related psychosis, personality disorder; 7.8% LR
            e.   High risk group more generalized cortical brain deficits
            f.   Behavioral and academic differences; high risk children
                (1)   Show poorer coordination, lower IQ scores
                (2)   More difficulty concentrating and paying attention
                (3)   More problems interacting with other children
            g.   Psychological and environmental
                (1)   Greater levels of family conflict or instability (positive)
                (2)   Complications during gestation or delivery (negative)
IV.   Psychological and Sociocultural Causes of Schizophrenia (pp. 360-371)
    A.   The Role of Social Class and Urbanicity
        1.   Prevalence of schizophrenia in U.S. highly correlated with
            a.   Living in an urban setting
            b.   Being a member of a lower social class
        2.   Social Drift
            a.   As people develop symptoms; cannot maintain occupation
            b.   Social drift links lower socioeconomic class as consequence
        3.   Social Residue
            a.   Urban areas decay, people more ocupationally able move away
            b.   Less able, including severe mental disorders left behind
        4.   Breeder or Social Causation
            a.   Chronic psychological and social stressors
            b.   Lower socioeconomic groups exposed to higher rates of crime, unemployment, deterioration of neighborhoods, medical illnesses
    B.   The Role of Family Environments
        1.   Past Theories
            a.   *Schizophrenogenic mother*—domineering, overprotective, cold
            b.   *Double-bind hypothesis*—incompatible messages from parent
            c.   Paradoxical communications wreak havoc on development
        2.   Erroneous Beliefs
            a.   Casts blame and guilt on family members
            b.   Families strive valiantly to cope with difficulties, guilt
    C.   The Role of Expressed Emotion
        1.   Expressed emotion factor in relapse; not related to original onset
        2.   Family's emotional overinvolvement
            a.   Criticism ("You watch too much TV.")

    b. Hostility ("I'm sick and tired of your craziness.")
    c. Overinvolvement ("I'll do something with you.")
   3. Patient's compliance for taking antipsychotic drugs helps protect
   4. Relapse rate high EE families 48%; low EE relapse rate 21%
   5. Crtitcism may drive up level of psychophysiological arousal
   6. Crucial feature of high EE families, *how* they respond to disruption

V. Treatments of Schizophrenia (pp. 376-381)
 A. Past—Victims of Neglect; Recipients of Aggressive Treatments
   1. Confinement in mental hospitals
   2. Barbaric and crude experimental therapies
    a. Psychosurgery; prefrontal lobotomies; tooth extraction
    b. Electro-convulsive shock
    c. Prolonged isolation, restraint
   3. Patient became almost totally dependent on institution
 B. Present—Biological Treatments
   1. Drugs Primary Treatment
   2. *Antipsychotics* (neuroleptics)
    a. Within hours patients are calmed
    b. After few weeks, conversing calmly, much more normally
    c. Most symptoms thought disorder relieved
   3. The Phenothiazines
    a. Chlorpromazine (Thorazine)
    b. Trifluoperazine (Stelazine)
    c. Thioridazine (Mellaril)
    d. Fluphenazine (Prolixin)
   4. Block the action of neurotransmitter dopamine (D_2 receptor found in limbic system, basal ganglia, and cortex)
   5. Cause serious side effects
    a. Dry mouth, hypersensitivity to sun, constipation, sleepiness
    b. *Extrapyramidal symptoms*:
     (1) Parkinsonism: hand tremors, shuffling gait, blank stare, muscular rigidity, slowness of movement
     (2) *Acute dystonia*—uncontrollale muscle contractions, spasms
     (3) *Acute akathesia*—constantly restless and agitated
     (4) *Tardive dyskinesia*—grotesque, uncontrollable spasmodic jerks, ticks, and twitches of the face, tongue, trunk, limbs; lips make smacking and sucking sounds, jaws grind, limbs may writhe uncontrollably, speech is progressively impaired
     (5) *Neurolyptic malignant syndrome*—can be fatal; involves extremely high fever, muscle rigidity, irregular heart rate, blood pressureAtypical Antipsychotic Drugs
    c. *Clozapine* (Clozaril) act stongly on D_4; weakly on D_2
    d. Effective in reducing both positive and negative symptoms
    e. Can cause *agranulocytosis* (loss of white blood cells)

6. Conclusions
   a. Complete treatment must include psychosocial interventions
   b. Drugs do not teach how to interact; how to handle stress
C. Psychosocial Treatments
   1. Psychoanalytic treatment not the treatment of choice
   2. Two important changes
      a. *Milieu programs* to resocialize patients in the hospital
         (1) Help to develop self-help skills lost in hospitalization
         (2) Reward patients for resuming independent, skilled living
         (3) Priciples of operant conditioning
      b. Community based *therapeutic communities or group homes*
   3. Self-Management and Social Skills Training
      a. Self-management
         (1) Shopping, cooking, managing money, administering, monitoring medications
         (2) Help patient to become independent as possible
      b. Social Skills Training
         (1) Carrying on conversations, expressing needs clearly, refusing unreasonable demands by others, interacting appropriately
         (2) Takes place in structured groups
   4. Family Therapy
      a. Families taught to avoid harsh criticisms, overinvolved reactions
      b. Treatment focused on decreasing family guilt, stressors
      c. None of patients in *combined* treatments relapsed
   5. Psychosocial Rehabilitation
      a. Aims
         (1) Prevent unnecessary hospitalizations
         (2) Reduce impairments that interfere with daily functioning
         (3) Strengthen independent living skills necessary to resume normal social roles
         (4) Modify environments to make more supportive
   6. Implementation of programs in U.S. influenced by 3 groups
      a. Relatives of people with severe mental illnesses (National Alliance for the Mentally Ill)
      b. Self-help groups of people suffering from mental illness
      c. Mental health professionals who believe that treatment of the severely mentally ill should take place in community settings whenever possible
      d. Programs important in preventing relapses

10   Schizophrenia

LECTURE MAKER   10.1

Purpose   To illustrate and define delusional content. (pp. 235-236)

Lecture Introduction   Discuss the meaning of psychosis and define hallucination and delusion. Delusions are considered positive symptoms of schizophrenia. Discuss the misinterpretation of perceptual experiences and the attempt at explanation that delusions provide.

Demonstration   Use brief case history representations and ask students to identify the type (content) of the delusion.

1. Son of Sam—the serial murderer who believed the neighbor's dog told him to kill.

    Type of delusion?

2. Charles Manson—cult leader directing members to kill, emphasized revolution and political harassment.

    Type of delusion?

3. Jim Jones—leader of the People's Temple movement, self-proclaimed god-like figure, convinced more than 900 followers to commit suicide.

    Type of delusion?

4. Heaven's Gate—Religious group/cult that believed an alien space craft was traveling in the tail of the Hale-Bopp Comet and they would join the aliens by dying. They committed suicide.

    Type of delusion?

Lecture Capsule   You can expand this activity with flourishes from the history of these people/groups or with the addition of other groups. For extra credit, I sometimes have my students search and document a case.

LECTURE MAKER 10.2

Purpose   To familiarize students with the impact of schizophrenia on the entire family, to broaden their understanding of the complexity of schizophrenia, and to encourage understanding. (pp. 362-365)

Lecture Introduction   Review the nature, symptoms and types of schizophrenia. Discuss positive and negative symptoms, and prognosis. Define premorbid adjustment. Explore treatment alternatives.

Demonstration   Instructor should request recent newsletters called *"Living With Schizophrenia."* The source is listed in the resource section for this chapter. Read articles and news information aloud. There are touching and revealing articles as well as fascinating information available. It provides:

> News on new treatments and medications on Schizophrenia—as they are announced.
>
> News on events for families, researchers, and care-givers around the world.
>
> Updates on the state of the art in the ongoing research into the causes.
>
> Reviews of other Web sites with information on Schizophrenia.
>
> Offers for participation in ongoing research into the causes.

Lecture Capsule   This newsletter personalizes this tragedy of human malfunctioning. Students gain a greater sense of humanity when exposed to this type of information.

Resources

General

Software:
Title: *Psychopathology*
Source: PsychWorld
McGraw-Hill Publishing Company
1221 Avenue of the Americas
New York, NY 10020
Type of Software: Simulation
Content: Students attempt to answer fake symptoms so they can be admitted to a psychiatric facility

The "Living with Schizophrenia" Newsletter is a periodic newsletter covering new developments in Schizophrenia that is FREE to ALL subscribers. By subscribing to this newsletter you'll get:
> News on new treatments and medications on Schizophrenia-as they are announced
> News on events for families, researchers, and care-givers around the world
> Updates on the state of the art in the ongoing research into the causes of Schizophrenia.
> Reviews of other Web sites with information on Schizophrenia
> Offers for participation in ongoing research into the causes of Schizophrenia
> For your free subscription Living with Schizophrenia please send an e-mail with your EXACT E-Mail address in the body of the message to
> **Brianc@informaniac.com.www.schizophrenia.com**

Schizophrenic Anonymous
1209 California Road
Eastchester, NY 10709
914-337-2252

Schizophrenia
Look into this unmoderated discussion list devoted to schizophrenia research. This is a place for researcher and medical professionals to explore this mental illness, facilitate collaborations between investigators, and foster discussion on published and unpublished findings and ideas.
Listserv Mailing Address
List Address schiz-1@umab.bitnet
Subscription Address: listserv@umab.bitnet

Media

Psychopathology: Diagnostic Vignettes, No. 3--Schizophrenic Disorders (Case Numbers 9-12) (INURTS; INUAVC, 35 min, color video, 1984) Represents 'classic' patterns of schizophrenia, rather than difficult or ambiguous cases, emphasizing the heterogeneity of this general diagnostic category. The patients exhibit various signs of formal thought disorder, including derailment, tangentiality, neologisms, poverty of content of speech, and illogicality. In some cases, these problems are intermittent, but the last patient is almost entirely incoherent. The cases reveal a variety of affective states as well as a number of different types and combinations of hallucinations and delusions.

Full of Sound and Fury--Living with Schizophrenia (TVONT; FML, 54 min, color, 16mm, video, 1985 This program explores the lives of three individuals who have been profoundly affected by this illusive mental disorder. A fifty-year-old schizophrenic talks of the isolation and personal despair which are the result of his perception of reality. Another, who is able to maintain a part-time job, speaks of the daily struggle to control her illness through medication. For the families of those suffering from schizophrenia, the experience can be tragic. The mother of a young schizophrenic recounts the mental torment that drove her son to suicide. This documentary is hosted by Dr. Vivian Rakoff of the Clarke Institute of Psychiatry.

Victorian Flower Paintings: Pictorial Record of a Schizophrenic Episode. (UCEMC-7641, 7 MIN, 1968) "Rare, breathtaking clinical history of schizophrenia as manifested in a folio of floral watercolors painted by an unknown person between 1863 and 1868. The first seven paintings give way to grotesqueries; at the climax of the illness, the paintings are wild, chaotic; then the mood gradually subsides, violence disappears, and the last few paintings are as gentle and tranquil as the first. Modern commentary points out distortions and explains them."

Schizophrenia: This specially adapted Phil Donahue program is widely regarded as one of the most helpful programs on schizophrenia. The program offers basic information about this illness that affects nearly one million Americans, usually striking 17- to 25-year olds. Dr. E. Fuller Torrey, author of *Surviving Schizophrenia: A Family Manual*, reviews the suspected causes, the symptoms, the prognosis for recovery, and the steps to be taken by supportive family members. (28 minutes, color)

Schizophrenia and the Family: A Stranger in the House Why are families living with schizophrenia hiding behind a curtain of silence? How can we change this unhealthy situation? This program examines how two families are coping with the devastating and debilitating disease; how they deal with the pain, denial, and grief to arrive at acceptance, renewal and —ultimately—hope. It is also a guide to tapping onto the community's most important resource: the family. (24 minutes, color)

Schizophrenia: Out of Mind This program enters into the world of the schizophrenic, showing patients, their families, and mental health care professionals who deal with schizophrenics. Patients range from eager to please, to indifferent or negative; doctors and nurses are hopeful; and families are perplexed, hurt, and often guilt-ridden. (52 minutes, color)

Schizophrenia: The Voices Within, the Community Without This program discusses the nature, symptoms, and psychotropic medications used to control hallucinations, paranoia, and other evidences of schizophrenia; it focuses on the deinstitutionalization of patients, explaining the problems of releasing patients with mental disorders into communities with insufficient resources to deal with them. (19 minutes, color)

Multiple Personality Disorder: In the Shadows Multiple Personality Disorder (MPD) is a completely preventable medical condition. Studies show that the average MPD patient spends seven years and receives three incorrect diagnoses before receiving an accurate diagnosis and appropriate treatment. It is now recognized that MPD is the result of severe childhood trauma, usually sexual and physical abuse—and it develops as a coping mechanism in young children who develop other personalities to deal with pain, fear, and danger. As the child grows older, this dissociation ceases to be a coping mechanism and becomes a block to normal functioning. This program shows how therapy can integrate the multiple personalities and make a patient "whole" again. Following two MPD patients and health care professionals, the program traces the struggles and triumphs in treating the disorder. (24 minures, color)

Repulsion (SW, 105 minutes) Catherine Deneuve stars in this Polanski film depicting a young woman experiencing a schizophrenic episode. Polanski's filming of visual hallucinations is excellent.

Schizophrenia: The Shattered Mirror (IU, 60 min) One of the three or four best films you could show. Follows a real schizophrenic patient. Shows institutional care and current research on schizophrenia. Often hard to believe that the folks in the film are not actors.

Pharmacotherapy of Schizophrenia
American Psychiatric Press and Allyn & Bacon
These new and richly comprehensive videotapes are based on material recently presented by the distinguished faculty at West and East Coast conferences on treatments of psychiatric disorders, sponsored by the American Psychiatric Association. For those who did not attend these conferences, these videotapes present the unusual opportunity to listen and watch these clinicians discuss four of the most critically important psychiatric disorders.

John M. Kane, M.D. is Chair of the Department of Psychiatry at Hillside Hospital, a division of Long Island Jewish Medical Center, and Professor of Psychiatry at the Albert Einstein College of Medicine. He currently directs the NIMH-funded clinical Research Center for the Study of Schizophrenia at the Hillside Hospital division of Long Island Jewish Medical Center, Glen Oaks, New York.

Ian Alger, M.D., is Executive Producer of the Treatments of Psychiatric disorders Videotape Series; Clinical Professor of Psychiatry, the new York Hospital-Cornell Medical Center; Multimedia Consultant to the American Psychiatric Association's Psychiatric Services; and Editor of the American Psychiatric Press Video Series.

For additional video resource materials, please contact your Allyn & Bacon representative.

Case Video to accompany Nietzel et al., *Abnormal Psychology (A&B)*
Includes an interview with former Green Bay Packer Lionel Aldridge, diagnosed with schizophrenia, conducted by author Michael Nietzel.

Nietzel et al., *Abnormal Psychology*, Transparencies

Chapter Ten

	Text Figure Number	Text Page Number

56. Criteria for Schizophrenia..335

57. Lifetime Risk for Developing Schizophrenia..350

58. Diathesis-Stress Model of Schizophrenia................................10.7............365

11 Cognitive Disorders

CHAPTER OUTLINE

I. Aging
    A. Normal Aging (pp. 379-383)
        1. *Ageism*
            a. Form of prejudice against the elderly
            b. Stereotypes rely on misinformation
        2. Keys to successful aging
            a. Staying physically and mentally active
            b. Maintaining some type of religious or spiritual values
            c. Controlling stress by focusing on relationships, commitments that person finds most fulfilling or pleasing
        3. Sensory and motor function loss
            a. Body flexibility, muscular strength and speed
            b. Hearing, vision, sensitivity to taste and smell, balance
        4. Metabolic changes
            a. Decreases in respiratory, cardiac, liver, kidney function
            b. Older persons metabolize drugs more slowly
                (1) Sensitivity of brain's receptors increases
                (2) Drugs more effective at lower dose
                (3) Elderly prone to using prescribed drugs incorrectly
                (4) Likelihood of drug-induced brain disorder increases
        5. Cognitive functioning
            a. Average IQ scores tend to decline a bit in late 50s, early 60s
            b. Performance on tasks that require motor speed, rapid information processing, or fine motor control decreases
            c. Older persons complain of memory loss
                (1) For some, when tested, memory is fine
                (2) May be by-product of depression
                (3) May be side effect of medications
                (4) Result of inefficient information storage at time of learning
                (5) Distractibility is problem in inefficient storage as people age
    B. Cognitive Disorders and Aging
        1. Biologically caused impairment in processes of memory, language, consciousness, perception, intelligence
            a. *Amnestic disorders*: memory loss without other impairment
                (1) Inability to learn new information
                (2) Inability to recall previously acquired information
            b. *Delirium*—individual loses ability to focus, sustain, or shift attention
            c. *Dementia* (senility)
                (1) Always involves memory loss plus one or more of following
                (2) *Aphasia*—disturbance in language

(3) *Agnosia*—inability to recognize or interpret objects
(4) *Apraxia*—inability to carry out motor activities
(5) *Executive functioning*—loss of ability to plan or organize

II. Amnestic Disorders and Delirium (pp. 383-388)
    A. Amnestic Disorders
        1. *Amnesia* involves *pure memory loss*
            a. If other cognitive failures; delirium or dementia usually diagnosed
            b. Direct effects of general medical condition or effects of substance
        2. DSM-IV diagnosis
            a. Serious enough to cause problems social, occupational functioning
            b. Marked decline from previous levels of functioning
            c. Must *not* occur only during delirium or dementia
        3. *Anterograde amnesia*—inability to learn new information
        4. *Retrograde amnesia*—inability to recall information previously learned
        5. If damage to medial temporal structures, disturbance may be permanent
        6. Persons with severe amnestic disorders deny them, remain apathetic
            a. Disoriented to time and place, not own identity
            b. *Confabulation,* (making up material to fill in gaps), occurs
        7. Long-term alcohol abusers develop because vitamin deficiencies
        8. Important to distinguish from factitious disorder, malingering
    B. Delirium
        1. An altered or clouded awareness of environment
            a. Difficulty sustaining, focusing, or shifting attention
            b. Memory deficits, perceptual, language disturbances, disorientation
        2. Course, Characteristics, Prevalence
            a. Course
                (1) In children, onset typically rapid, usually with high fever
                (2) In elderly, awareness fluctuates days, deteriorates at night
                (3) During delirium, memory impaired for recent events
                (4) After delusion, memory absent or false memory
            b. Characteristics
                (1) Warning signs similar to migraine
                (2) Some especially sensitive to smells or sounds
                (3) Mild perceptual distortions, changes in moods
                (4) May swing rapidly from one emotional extreme to another
                (5) Cannot judge passing time, maintain concentration
                (6) Autonomic nervous system arousal
                (7) Visual hallucinations, paranoid delusions common
                (8) Engage in *perseveration* (same answer, different questions)
                (9) *Capgras syndrome*—delusion impostors posing as family
                (10) ICD-10 emotional disturbances, disturbances in sleep-wake cycle, psychomotor (restlessness, lethargy, stupor)
                (11) DSM-IV classifies these as associated features, not core criteria; lists no time limit
                (12) Complete recovery common once underlying cause treated

        c.   Prevalence
             (1)   High as 25% for elderly in hospital
             (2)   About 80% of elderly open-heart surgery patients
    3.   Assessment of Delirium
        a.   Patient's reports often unreliable
             (1)   Relatives, neighbors, friends asked to provide information
             (2)   If information not available, home is examined
        b.   *Mini-Mental State Examination* (MMSE)
             (1)   Attention, memory, language, concentration, figure copying
             (2)   Orientation to place and time ("draw a clock test")
             (3)   EEG recordings show wide-spread slow waves
             (4)   EEG alone not enough
    4.   Causes of Delirium
        a.   Many physical causes
             (1)   Head trauma
             (2)   Postoperative states
             (3)   Using or withdrawal from drugs
             (4)   Exposure to toxins
             (5)   Epilepsy
             (6)   Metabolic disturbances
             (7)   Dehydration
             (8)   Infections
        b.   Among elderly—infectious disease plus medication—induced side effects
    5.   Treatment of Delirium
        a.   Most important goal—identify and correct underlying causes
        b.   Critical treatment delivered in supportive environment
        c.   Some require treatment for posttraumatic stress disorder
        d.   Education of care givers so institutionalization not done too soon
        e.   Physical restraints avoided if possible
        f.   Rooms well lighted, familiar objects brought from home
        g.   Lowest effective doses of antipsychotics, sedatives, tranquilizers
        h.   Most important, dignity of patient appreciated, protected
        i.   *Looping*—humiliation—negative reaction—more humiliating treatments

III.   Dementia (pp. 383-393)
    A.   Most Common Causes
        1.   Alzheimer's disease
        2.   Vascular illness; primarily strokes (loss of blood flow and oxygen to brain)
        3.   Multiple conditions (infections, drug reactions, tumors, head injuries, vitamin deficiencies, metabolic disturbances)
        4.   If arises from cardiovascular problems, certain types of infection, side effects of drugs; disorder arrested, reversed if underlying cause treated
    B.   Vascular Dementia
        1.   Caused by cardiovascular conditions (strokes, arterial diseases)

2. Second most common form; often progressive disorder
3. 1800s called "softening of the brain"; destruction of "higher centers"
4. 1900s tendency to blame on arteriosclerosis
5. Can appear abruptly; impairments progress step-wise (not gradual) fashion
6. No consistent pattern of symptoms
7. Palsy and paralysis in one extremity common, personality unaffected
8. Period of delirium or confusion typical after each stroke
9. Risk factors
   a. Age, chronic use of tobacco and alcohol, high blood pressure
   b. High cholesterol, diabetes, lack of exercise, previous stroke
10. Prevention more effective than treatment

C. Other Medical Conditions Causing Dementia
1. Pick's disease
   a. Brain atrophy restricted frontal lobes; ballooned neurons common
   b. Neurons contain protein deposits *(Pick bodies)*
   c. Early, memory remains intact, changes in personality
   d. Tactless behavior, uninhibited mood, emotional reactivity
2. Lewy body dementia
   a. Abnormal protein deposits (*lewy bodies*)
   b. Bodies cause degeneration of neurons of cortex, deep in brain stem
   c. Motor signs found: muscular rigidity, slow movements, immobility
   d. Prominent hallucinations produce strong paranoia
3. Dementia due to Parkinson's disease
   a. Lewy bodies also found here
   b. Motor symptoms similar to Lewy body disease
   c. One of first symptoms tremors in one or both hands
   d. Reduced production of neurotransmitter dopamine
   e. Symptoms fairly well controlled with medication
4. Dementia due to Huntington's disease
   a. Progressive subcortical degeneration, motor disturbances
   b. Primary symptoms facial grimaces, twitches, *chorea*, changes in personality, memory loss, depression early stages
   c. Later stages, progressive intellectual deterioration, memory problems, disorganized speech, psychotic behavior
   d. Hereditary; caused by dominant gene on chromosome 4
5. Dementia due to Creutzfeldt-Jakob disease
   a. Infectious disease transmitted through eating diseased tissue
   b. "Mad cow disease" is variant; transmitted by infected beef
   c. Progression is rapid; death usually within a year
   d. Other infectious agents—HIV; Syphilis
6. Dementia due to head trauma
   a. Persistent memory impairment
   b. Young males at elevated risk due to risk-taking behavior
7. Other causes
   (1) Hypothyroidism; tumors; subdural hematoma; vitamin

deficiencies (thiamine, niacin, vitamin B_{12}) lung, kidney, or liver disease, neurological disorders (multiple sclerosis)

IV. Alzheimer's Disease (pp 393-403)
    A. Stages of Alzheimer's Disease
        1. Early Stages
            a. Increased forgetfulness, especially for emotionally neutral events
            b. Loss of ability to cope with changes in environment, routine
        2. Middle Stages
            a. Increasing problems language, understanding, perception
            b. Great difficulty learning new information
        3. Later Stages
            a. Language becomes increasingly simple until stops altogether
            b. Patients cannot find their way even to familiar places
            c. May become hostile, striking out physically or verbally
            d. Emotionally unstable, running away in tears for no known reason
            e. Paranoia common, may complicate care
            f. Eventually deteriorate to the point unable to care for themselves
            g. Impossible to eat, dress, use the bathroom alone
        4. Life expectancy 3-20 years with average of 8-12 years
    B. Neuropathology of Alzheimer's Disease
        1. Brain Shows Atrophy
            a. Form of neuron and synapse loss
            b. "Hardest hit" areas that mediate language, learning, and memory, association cortex of frontal and parietal lobes; the limbic cortex, hippocampus, amygdala
            c. Primary sensory and motor cortex spared
        2. Disease Identified
            a. German Alois Alzheimer discovered two features now recognized as most distinctive signs of the disease; tangles and plaques
                (1) *Neurofibrillary tangles*—clumps of protein fibers
                (2) *Neuritic plaques*—residue of dead neurons, cellular garbage
            b. Death of brain cells caused by *beta-amyloid-4* (abnormal protein)
    C. Genetic Factors and Alzheimer's
        1. Gene on Chromosome 21
            a. People with Down syndrome carry three copies of chromosome 21
            b. Extremely likely to develop Alzheimer's disease usually by age 40
            c. Brains develop large numbers *amyloid* (senile) *plaques* almost 50 years before seen in large numbers in normal persons
            d. Abnormal derivative of *amyloid precursor protein (APP)* produced by a gene on chromosome 21
            e. Persons with early onset Alzheimer's have amyloid plaques caused by mutation of APP-producing gene on chromosome 21
        2. Gene on Chromosome 19
            a. Linked to much more common late-onset variety Alzheimer's
            b. Gene produces *apolipoprotein E (ApoE)* transports cholesterol

        c.   ApoE gene three variants (2,3,4) ApoE-3 most common form
        d.   ApoE-4 appears to increase risk of Alzheimer's disease
        e.   ApoE-2 may protect against disease
        f.   90% of persons with 2 copies of ApoE-4 gene (one from each parent) develop Alzheimer's
        g.   Comparison: 50% of persons with one copy ApoE-4 gene
        h.   Less than 20% of persons with no ApoE-4 gene develops

D.   Other Risk Factors for Alzheimer's Disease
    1.   Head Trauma
        a.   *Dementia puglistica,* seen in boxers suffering repeated head blows
        b.   Milder and less frequent as even single concussion now linked
        c.   American Psychological Association 1995: hitting soccer balls with one's head leads to impaired performance on neuropsychological tests of cognitive flexibility, attention, concentration, intellect
    2.   Coronary Artery Disease, myocardial infarctions especially in women
    3.   Environmental Toxins
        a.   Aluminum, mercury found in high concentrations
        b.   Aluminum highly concentrated in hippocampal neurons of patients who developed dementia in course of chronic blood dialysis due to kidney failure
    4.   Acetylcholine (ACh) dramatically reduced in Alzheimer's patients
    5.   Low Levels of Education
        a.   Better educated person; better levels of health care
        b.   Better able to avoid head trauma, heart disease, exposure to toxins
        c.   Higher levels of mental activity early in life offers protection
        d.   Higher education levels; more cognitive ability to begin with

E.   Medical Treatments of Alzheimer's Disease
    1.   *Tacrine* (COGNEX) only drug approved by FDA for treatment in U.S.
        a.   Slows breakdown of ACh
        b.   Useful only in mild to moderately severe cases
    2.   Estrogen
        a.   Promotes synapse formation; increases ACh synthesis
        b.   Improves mood, cognition in postmenstrual women with disease
    3.   Deprenyl (ELDEPRYL)
        a.   Inhibits monoamine oxidaseB (MAO-B) which destroys dopamine, norepinephrine, and serotonin
        b.   Level of these neurotransmitters raised to more normal levels
    4.   Vitamin E (alpha-tocopherol)
        a.   Antioxidant inactivates oxygen free radicals (damage to neurons)
        b.   Given alone or in combination with deprenyl
    5.   Nimodipine
        a.   Calcium channel blocker
        b.   Calcium involved in neuronal degeneration
    6.   Propentofylline
        a.   Enhances blood flow, energy metabolism in brain

    b. Improves function in Alzheimer's or vascular dementia
  7. Prednisone—inflammatory response may be involved
F. Psychosocial Interventions for Alzheimer's Disease
  1. Long period of time in which symptoms not yet obvious or manageable
    a. Interventions may delay onset or slow its progress
      (1) Reducing head injuries
      (2) Preventing cardiovascular disease
      (3) Control of blood pressure and stress
      (4) Improving education; staying mentally active
  2. Cure not available
    a. Treatment of symptoms
      (1) Medication used sparingly for agitation, depression
      (2) Medication monitored carefully for short-, long-term effects
    b. Management of behavior; training of care givers
      (1) Frequent gentle reminders or lists to prop up memory
      (2) Sewing labels on clothing
      (3) Maintaining familiar schedules
      (4) Keeping personal possessions in the same locations
      (5) Adhering to daily routines
      (6) Provide loose-fitting clothing; *few* buttons, snaps, zippers
      (7) Maintaining well-lighted environments
      (8) Radio tuned to familiar, favorite music
      (9) Night lights reduce *sundowning* (wandering or agitation)
      (10) Hugs, gentle touch, hand holding reduces paranoid thoughts
      (11) Conversation direct, concrete, matter of fact
    c. Care givers often need special help themselves
      (1) Rate of clinical depression extremely high
      (2) Resentment and anger toward patient
      (3) Anger may boil over into physical abuse
      (4) Care givers need time to lead their own lives
      (5) Need to know feelings of resentment are normal
      (6) When necessary; taught how to control aggressiveness
      (7) Self-help groups and special agencies provide needed assistance to care givers
      (8) Primary aim of programs—help care givers deal with the almost constant stress imposed by caring for loved one

11 Cognitive Disorders

LECTURE MAKER 11.1

Purpose
To explore internal vs. external locus of control as it applies to health. (pp. 378-380)

Lecture Introduction
Staying mentally and physically healthy generally requires some effort and vigilance. However, attitude toward health and illness also plays a role in that vigilance. Discuss heathy living and coping.

Demonstration
Read the statements aloud for the students to rate from strongly agree to strongly disagree. Read the scoring and interpretation.

Lecture Capsule
Emphasize attitude and perceived internal locus of control as variables contributing to mental physical health.

LECTURE MAKER 11.2

Purpose
To personalize the idea of aging and identify prejudicial attitudes toward the elderly. (pp. 380-382)

Lecture Introduction
Define and present the scope of ageism. Present the reality of losses (physically and cognitively) with aging. Highlight positive adjustment and healthful aging.

Demonstration
Present the brief open-ended survey on aging to your students. Each question could be a discussion topic. However, you may wish to ask more global questions about student expectations for themselves as they age. In our culture, the elderly are not valued very highly and that reality (along with the idea they **will** get old someday) is vividly apparent from this exercise.

Lecture Capsule
Remind the students that although aging is inevitable, **how** they approach it and what **they** do will determine the quality of their later years.

HEALTH LOCUS OF CONTROL SCALE 11.1

Check Whether You Agree or Disagree With The Following Statements:

	Strongly Disagree	Disagree	Strongly Agree	Agree
1. If I take care of myself, I can avoid illness.				
2. Good health is largely a matter of good fortune.				
3. Whenever I get, sick it is because of something I've done or not done.				
4. No matter what I do, if I am going to get sick, I will get sick.				
5. People's ill health results from their own carelessness.				
6. Most people do not realize the extent to which their illnesses are controlled by accidental happenings.				
7. I am directly responsible for my health.				
8. People who never get sick are just plain lucky.				

Theses statements come from the Health Locus of Control Scale (Wallston, Wallston, Kaplan, & Maides, 1976). People who agree with statements 1, 3, 5, and 7 tend to have an internal locus of control regarding their health. They take responsibility for their health by seeking information about and engaging in good health practices. People who agree with statements 2, 4, 6, and 8 tend to have an external locus of control regarding their health. They don't recognize the value of preventive health, and they underestimate their responsibility for maintain good health.

TEST YOUR BELIEFS 11.2

What physical problem do you fear most with old age?

What mental problem do you fear most with old age?

What are some beliefs you've heard about the elderly? Add to this list.

>All old people drive poorly.

>The reason why women over 55 shouldn't have babies is that they can't remember where they left their keys.

>Old people get fat, like the chubby grandmother.

>If you can't get around or remember anything,
>What's the point of living?

>Old people can't remember what happened five minutes ago.

Would you like to work with the elderly, say, in a nursing home? Why or why not?

How old were your grandparents or parents when they died (if they have)?

RESOURCES

General

Foundation Aiding The Elderly (FATE)
P.O. Box 254849
Sacramento, CA 95865-4849
Phone 916-481-8558
Fax   916-364-0948

American Association of Retired Persons
1908 K Street, N.W.
Washington, DC 20049
Phone 202-728-4200

American Geriatrics Society
770 Lexington Ave. Suite 400
New York, NY 10021
Phone 212-308-1414

Gerontological Society of America
1411 K Street, N.W.
Washington, DC 20005
Phone 212-393-1411

Hospice Education Institute
5 Essex Square, Suite 3-B
P.O. Box 713
Essex, CT 06426

National Hospice Organization, Inc
1901 N. Moore St. Suite 901
Arlington, VA 22209
703-243-5900 or 800-658-8898

International Association for Near-Death Experiences
Department of Psychiatry
University of Connecticut Health Center
Farmington, CT 06032
Phone 203-679-2000

Survival Research Foundation
P.O. Box 8365
Pembroke Pines, FL 33084
Phone 305-435-2730

National Association for Widowed People, Inc.
P.O. Box 3564
Springfield, IL 62708
217-787-0886

Widowed Persons Services
1909 K Street
Washington, DC 20049
Phone 202-728-4370

ALCOR Life Extension Foundation
12327 Doherty
Riverside, CA 92503
Phone 714-736-1703

American Cryonics Society
1098 Euclid Ave
Berkeley, CA 94708
Phone 415-397-3386

Cryogenic society of America c/o Laurie Huget
Huget Advertising
1033 South Blvd
Oak Park, IL 60302
Phone 312-383-7053

Immortalist Society c/o Mae Junod
24443 Roanoke
Oak Park, MI 48237
Phone 313-548-9549

Association for Death Education and Counseling
2211 Arthur Ave.
Lakewood, OH 44107
Phone 216-228-0034

Center for Death Education and Research
1167 Social Science Building
267 19th Avenue, South
University of Minnesota
Minneapolis, MN 55455
Phone 612-624-1895

Foundation of Thanatology
630 West 168th Street
New York, NY 10032
Phone 212-928-2066

Media

Nobody Ever Died of Old Age. (Films Inc., 55 min, color, 1976) A series of interviews with older people on the subject of what it is like to age in America. "Beautifully acted, well-written, and expertly crafted." (Mental Health Materials Center review.)

Aging. (McGraw-Hill films, 22 min, color, 1975) "A diversified, up-beat film essay on aging that effectively flouts stereotypes ...lots of excellent discussion material" (Mental Health Materials Center review.)

Make a Wish. (PSU, 5 min, color 1973) Attempts to give some insight into the problems sensory impairments create for the aged by using audio and visual techniques to simulate a 75-year-old's view of her 5-year-old granddaughter's birthday party.

The Last of Life. (Filmakers Library, 27 min, color 1978) "...this nicely produced documentary turns out to be an excellent review of the process of aging and its effects upon humans." Considers both biological and emotional aspects of aging. (Mental Health Materials Center review.)

See No Evil. (Filmakers Library, 15 min, b & w, 1977) A compressed tale of an elderly romance. "This intimate and detailed picture of what older people need and what they actually get...especially useful for opening up discussion on the sexual and emotional needs of the aging." (Mental Health Materials Center review.)

Never Trust Anyone Under 60. (USNAC, 60 min, color, 1971) "Describes graphically problems of aging, such as isolation, housing, and other problems.

Learning About Stroke. (EBEC, 19 min, color) The film explores the three kinds of stroke, cerebral hemorrhage, cerebral embolism, and cerebral thrombosis, and their effects. Risk factors involved with stroke are discussed, including hypertension, obesity, heart disease, stress, and high cholesterol.

Old Age. (TL, 45 min, color) This film from the *Family of Man* series explores aging as it occurs in five cultures.

Designing the Physical Environment for Persons with Dementia. (UMI, 22 min, color, video, 1987) Examines the ways in which a carefully designed physical environment can offer support and help to compensate for deficits of persons with Alzheimer's disease or related dementias, based on a two-year demonstration project in a special living area named Wesley Hall. Presents interventions in the physical environment which can help compensate for problems of orientations, sensory loss, and spatial problems. Includes safety features that still ensure the patients' freedom of movement, ideas for providing visual stimulation and maintaining continuity with a patient's earlier life. Describes several changes that were made in the physical environment to reduce agitation and other problem behaviors. User's manual included.

The Man Who Mistook His Wife for a Hat. (FFHS, 75 min, color, video, 1986 By incorporating interviews with Oliver Sacks and with a neurological surgeon, the program investigates problems of perception and Alzheimer's Disease. The patient in this famous case of Oliver Sacks is diagnosed with visual agnosia, a condition in which he can see but cannot make sense of what he see. Chamber opera by Michael Nyman.

The Mind, No. 3—Aging (WNET; PBS, 60 min, color, video, 1988 Examines what happens to the brain and mind during the aging process, questioning some long-held stereotypes about the elderly. Explores if mental decline is inevitable, or does the brain continue to learn from experience.

The Gift of Aging. Longevity has increased by thirty years in the 20th century, and most of us enjoy better health in those later years. How five individuals are spending their later years is the subject of this inspiring program. (28 minutes, color)

The Aging Process. Part of the aging process in inevitable— but only part. This program explains the effects of aging on the mind and body, explores the "damage" and the "cell clock" theories about why cells wear out, and examines habits that affect both longevity and the quality of life: exercise, regular checkups, proper diet, moderate drinking, and no smoking. (19 minutes, color)

Aging. This program covers the physical process of aging, examining the various body systems to see how and why they change as they age. It also shows that not all the changes in older people are inevitable and that some changes in the body can be slowed down or reversed. (26 minutes, color)
Factors in Health Aging. A half-century study that examined the mental health of Harvard graduates over their lifetimes is used to illuminate the predictors of healthy aging. The impacts of diet, smoking, drinking, family history, and personality are discussed. New research highlights the possibility of altering our genetic structure to enable us to live longer and in better healt. (28 minutes, color)

Aging Well. This program explains how people are living longer than their parents did and why they are staying healthier. The program examines medical advances that continue to boost our life expectancy rate, and the role that lifestyle changes play. The program also explores what seniors can do to motivate themselves to keep their mental powers sharp, and the effects of aging on mental skills. Finally the program loooks at the emotional issues of aging, such as the death of one's spouse, and explores how seniors can be helped to overcome feelings of loneliness and uselessness. (18 minutes, color)

Symptoms of Aging. Some symptoms of age can be cloaked, and others can be postponed, but the process of aging is inevitable. This program covers some of the symptoms of aging—loss of muscular strength, reduced visual capability, arteriosclerosis—and shows both how fitness can be maintained and how seniors may have the edge over younger people. (28 minutes, color)

Alzheimer's: Effects on Patients and their Families. This program explains what is now known about the mechanisms of Alzheimer's, what remains unknown about brain changes in the disease, and the use of drugs and other strategies to preserve memory. It also shows how Alzheimer's affects the lives of a patient's family.

Caring for the Elderly. An overview of the various methods of care available for the aging, from day-care centers and group housing to respite care and nursing homes. This program profiles a middle-aged couple and talks to social workers, senior citizen advocates, and nursing home administrators to clarify the issues and options. (19 minutes, color)

For additional video resource materials, please contact your Allyn & Bacon representative.

Nietzel et al., *Abnormal Psychology*, Transparencies

Chapter Eleven

	Text Figure Number	Text Page Number
59. Brain-Behavior Relationships	11.1	379
60. Multiple Causes of Brain Dysfunctions in the Aged	11.2	381
61. Differential Diagnosis of Delirium and Dementia		382
62. Criteria for Amnestic Disorder		383

12 Personality Disorders

CHAPTER OUTLINE

I. Fateful Patterns: An Overview of Personality Disorders (pp. 409-414)
    A. Defining Characteristics and Prevalence of Personality Disorders
        1. Personality
            a. Unique pattern of consistency in behavior that distinguishes each person from every other
            b. French novelist, Andre Malreaux, "character is fate."
            c. *Personality trait*—psychological attribute relatively stable over time, across different situations
        2. Personality Disorder
            a. Enduring pattern of inner experience, behavior extremely inflexible, deviates markedly from expectations of a person's culture
            b. Important features
                (1) *Ego-syntonic*—people do not see themselves as troubled
                (2) Clients believe their problems due to actions of others, reluctant to seek or co-operate in own treatment
                (3) More distressing for others; severe disorder can leave trail of disaster (Ted Bundy's case illustrates)
                (4) 25-85% of people with one disorder have another one
                (5) 27-65% comorbidity rate with Axis I mental disorders
        3. Prevalence
            a. Antisocial personality disorder 3-4% in U.S.
            b. Histrionic, schizotypal as many as 4%
            c. 10-13% of population met criteria sometime in life
            d. Paranoid, narcissistic, antisocial far more often in men
            e. Borderline personality disorder about 3 times more often in women
    B. Diagnosing Personality Disorders
        1. Personality Disorders and Axis I Disorders
            a. DSM-IV places on Axis II, encourages clinicians to diagnose personality disorder in addition to Axis I disorder
            b. Clinicians find difficult to distinguish Axis I and Axis II disorders
            c. Axis I disorder and personality disorder may simply coexist
            d. One disorder likely to aggravate the other
            e. One disorder predisposes person to develop another
            f. Antisocial personality and substance abuse are similar
            g. Avoidant personality and social phobia are similar
        2. Other Diagnostic Difficulties
            a. Criteria used to define disorders overlap considerably
            b. Accurate social history may be difficult to obtain
            c. DSM-IV requires clinician to assign diagnosis if client meets particular number out of fixed set of criteria

                (1) No evidence to support a cutoff (five out of nine)
                (2) Two people diagnosed same; only one feature shared
                (3) Two people not diagnosed same; do not share fifth
    C. Dimensional Description of Personality Disorders
        1. Big Five Model of Personality
            a. *Neuroticism*—tendency to experience negative emotions (anxiety, anger, depression) accompanied by disruptions of behavior, distressed thinking (contrasted with emotional stability)
            b. *Extroversion*—preference for social interaction, tendency to be active, talkative, optimistic, affectionate (contrast with introvert)
            c. *Openness*—interest in new experiences, receptivity to new activities, ideas for their own sake; creative, curious, untraditional
            d. *Agreeable*—compassionate interest in others; high scorers trusting, tender-hearted; sometimes putting other's needs above own
            e. *Conscientiousness*—well-organized dedication to work; ambitious, persistently strive to be achievers
            f. Extreme scores sufficient to describe maladaptiveness
        2. Interpersonal Circumplex
            a. More elaborate description of extroversion and agreeableness
            b. Two basic dimensions: *dominance/submission; love/hate*
            c. Interaction of two dimensions produces eight personality styles
II. Types of Personality Disorders (pp. 414-425)
    A. Odd/Eccentric Personality Disorders
        1. Paranoid Personality Disorder
            a. Persons habitually suspicious, constantly on guard, mistrustful
            b. Prone to anger and intense jealousy
            c. Air of moral superiority, condescension (others are corrupt)
        2. Schizoid Personality Disorder
            a. Indifference to social relationships; pervasive emotional blandness
            b. Lack close friends, no pleasure positive events, no unhappiness after setbacks; prefer solitary activities and occupations
            c. Emotional color has been bleached from their lives
        3. Schizotypal Personality Disorder
            a. Socially isolated; tend to shun close relationships
            b. Act, dress, talk in odd ways (sometimes frighten other people)
            c. Socially anxious, apprehensive; react stiffly in social situations
            d. Ideas of reference; paranoia, suspiciousness
            e. Report talking to dead relatives; spirits inhabiting rooms
    B. Dramatic/Emotional/Erratic Personality Disorders
        1. Histrionic Personality Disorder
            a. Attention-getting behaviors; seductiveness, demands for reassurance and praise, exaggerated displays of emotions
            b. All actions, even manner of dress, to make others notice them
            c. May develop attention-getting physical complaints
            d. Drawn to strong authority figures whose admiration they desire

2. Narcissistic Personality Disorder
   a. Overinflated sense of importance, worth; leading to a sense of entitlement to special privileges; exemptions to rules
   b. Prone to feelings of rage or humiliation if overlooked, criticized
   c. Preoccupied with own status; lack empathy for others; exploit
   d. Poor candidates for psychotherapy
3. Borderline Personality Disorder
   a. Frequent disorder; involves potentially destructive behavior
   b. Impulsivity; instability in mood, self-image, relationships, behavior
   c. During periods of increased stress display psychotic symptoms
   d. Particularly unable to tolerate negative emotions
      (1) Unable to say "I'll get over it"
      (2) One negative emotion leads to another
      (3) Prone to getting into physical fights
      (4) Go on sprees eating, drinking, spending, sex
   e. Considered one of most severe disorders due to intensity, range, unpredictability of its symptoms
4. Antisocial Personality Disorder (APD)
   a. People chronically callous and manipulative
   b. Trample on rights of others, ignore social rules and laws
   c. Behave impulsively, dishonestly, irresponsibly
   d. Fail to learn from punishment
   e. Lack remorse or guilt over crimes, misdeeds
   f. Examples—Ted Bundy, Charles Manson, Jeffrey Dahmer
   g. Psychopathy and antisocial personality disorder not synonymous
   h. Begins prior to age 15 as symptoms of conduct disorder

C. Anxious/Fearful Personality Disorders
   1. Avoidant Personality Disorder
      a. Constant feeling of inadequacy, ineptitude especially socially
      b. Afraid of being embarrassed, criticized, ridiculed by others
      c. Avoid social situations when possible
      d. Avoid occupations requiring social interaction
      e. Long for affection, social acceptance; distressed by its absence
      f. Inhibited, overly cautious; avoid situations to act spontaneously
   2. Dependent Personality Disorder
      a. Unable to make decisions without exorbitant advice, reassurance
      b. Cling to others, make excessive self-sacrifices for appreciation
      c. Dread being alone; excessive dependency drives people away
   3. Obsessive-Compulsive Personality Disorder
      a. People preoccupied with rules, details, organization
      b. Tenaciously manage by trying to make predictable, safe
      c. Stubbornly perfectionistic; make little or no progress
      d. Unwilling to delegate tasks to others; fear standards not met
      e. Inflexible about moral and ethical matters
      f. Controlling, aloof in personal, romantic relationships

III. Causes of Personality Disorders (pp. 425-434)
    A. Theoretical Perspectives on Personality Disorders
        1. Genetics and Personality Differences
            a. Minnesota Study of Twins Reared Apart
                (1) Reared apart or together had little effect
                (2) Identical twin reared apart had greater within-pair similarity
                (3) About 50% of difference due to genetic influence
            b. *Non-shared environment* less important than genetics
            c. Parents' income, education less impact than birth order, friends
        2. Genetics and Personality Disorders
            a. Few family, twin, or adoption studies published
            b. Odd/eccentric
                (1) Paranoid, schizoid higher among relatives of individuals diagnosed with schizophrenia than among normal controls
                (2) No direct evidence of genetic risk established
                (3) Genetic contribution to schizotypal stronger
                (4) Found 33% concordance rate for identical twins
            c. Dramatic/emotional/erratic
                (1) Many studies support role of genetics in antisocial personality disorder
                (2) Role not strong in borderline, narcissistic, histrionic
            d. Anxious/fearful
                (1) Very little research conducted
                (2) Has not supported a genetic vulnerability
                (3) Possible genetic influence for obsessive-compulsive
        3. Psychodynamic Theories of Personality Disorders
            a. Freud: "character" arose from fixations during passage through psychosexual stages of development
                (1) Three stages (oral, anal, phallic) involved concentration of energy and anxiety on certain areas of the body
                (2) Few clinicians see psychoanalysis as viable method of explanation
            b. More recent—object relations theory
                (1) nature and quality of early attachments infants, caretakers
                (2) colors all other close relationships, determines person's strongest needs and vulnerabilities; form the core of personality disorders
        4. Interpersonal Learning Theories
            a. People desire to be with others who reinforce their typical ways of behaving
            b. Personalities shaped by experiences people prefer and seek out
            c. Disorders result when individual relies too heavily on extreme
            d. Encounters will follow rule of *complementarity* which is *reciprocal*

        e.   Dominant behavior by one invites submissive behavior in other
        f.   Love/hate: form of *correspondence*; love for love; hate for hate
    5.   Evolutionary Theory
        a.   Theodore Millon—three fundamental *polarities* underlie biological structures, psychological processes constituting personality
            (1)   *Minimization of pain and the maximization of pleasure*
            (2)   *Passive accommodation or active modification*
            (3)   *Advancing the self and/or caring for others*

B.   Causes of Borderline Personality Disorder
    1.   Biological Contributions
        a.   Neurologically impaired children show hyperactivity, poor attention, unstable moods, fussiness, impulsivity
        b.   Translate into interpersonal problems, academic difficulties, troubles with parents; ultimately lead to poorly regulated emotions, impulsive behavior, identity confusion that typify borderline
        c.   High prevalence of affective disorders among relatives of borderlines
            (1)   Indicates basic similarity borderline, affective disturbances
            (2)   Possible genetic diathesis for both disorders
            (3)   Two disorders tend to co-occur
    2.   Psychoanalytic Factors
        a.   Seeds sown in first 2 years of life
            (1)   Excessively aggressive impulses in child, inadequacies in parenting impair child's ability to form self-identity
            (2)   Stem from a lack of bonding between infants, care givers
        b.   Desire for independence undercut by fear of abandonment
        c.   Desire for closeness brings fear of being engulfed
        d.   Relationship between borderline and occurrence of mistreatment
    3.   Early Childhood Trauma
        a.   Childhood neglect and abuse
            (1)   Separation from parents (death or divorce)
            (2)   Physical and sexual abuse
            (3)   Observation of domestic violence
        b.   As many as 80% suffered early history of physical, sexual abuse
            (1)   Evidence from adult borderlines' reports
            (2)   Reliability and validity of reports unknown

C.   Causes 0f Antisocial Personality Disorder
    1.   Men who engage in repeated antisocial behavior tended in early childhood
        a.   More hyperactive, physically clumsy, impulsive
        b.   Had more trouble regulating emotions
        c.   Had more learning disabilities, speech problems
        d.   Prone to break rules at home and school
        e.   Academic failures, early school dropouts
    2.   Biological Predispositions
        a.   Genetic factors contribute to risk

      (1) Adopted children of criminal parents raised by normal parents arrested for antisocial conduct
      (2) Highest risk—adopted children born of criminal parents, raised in criminal families
    b. Tendency to be underaroused
      (1) Occurs in central nervous system, autonomic nervous system
      (2) Related to difficult temperament, attention deficits, hyperactivity, oppositional-defiant and conduct disorders
    c. Portions of cerebral cortex slow to develop
      (1) Show low levels of high frequency brain waves
      (2) High levels of low frequency brain waves (*theta waves*)
      (3) Psychopaths suffer "immature cortex"
    d. Unusually low anxiety level
      (1) Less strongly affected by adverse stimuli (social rejection, electric shocks)
      (2) Difficulty learning to inhibit behavior in response to cues
      (3) Heightened sensitivity to rewards
      (4) High need for stimulation
    e. Biologically predisposed to have difficulty developing classical conditioned fear responses to emotional stimuli
    f. Unable to learn from punishment or delay gratification
    g. Development of conscience depends on ability to learn fear and avoidance responses through classical conditioning
   3. Family and Childrearing Practices
    a. Specific family variables associated with antisocial behavior
      (1) History of parental criminality
      (2) Chronic parental uninvolvement, erratic discipline, physical abuse, poor supervision of children
      (3) Early loss of a parent (if due to bitter divorce or angry separation more traumatic impact than parental death)
      (4) Social and health handicaps in family; lower SES, poverty, educational underattainment, higher rates physical illness youngster feels alienated, hostile toward social expectations
      (5) Exposure to deviant peers
IV. Treatment of Personality Disorders (pp. 434-439)
  A. Treatment of Narcissistic Personality Disorder
   1. Heinz Kohut pioneered therapeutic approach *self-psychology*
    a. Narcissists' parents failed to meet their normal needs
    b. Result: children developed incomplete selves
   2. In self-defense, exaggerated beliefs about own power, importance
    a. Task for therapist—provide relationship in which needs unmet during infancy can be recognized, even gratified;
    b. Person can enjoy a more realistic, healthy sense of self-worth

B. Treatment of Avoidant Personality Disorder
   1. Cognitive-behavioral treatments; techniques used to treat social phobias
   2. Systematic desensitization; training to develop improved social skills
C. Treatment of Borderline Personality Disorder
   1. Particularly difficult to treat
      a. Clients vacillate between loving and hating their therapists
      b. Cross boundaries other clients honor
      c. Intrude into therapist's personal life
      d. Engage in dramatic, even dangerous behavior for attention
      e. Call therapist; show up at therapist's home, demand to be seen
   2. Approaches developed by interpersonal, analytic, cognitive therapists
   3. Lithium, antidepressants, antipsychotic medications shown some success
   4. Therapists often combine psychotherapy with drug treatment
   5. Psychodynamic therapy based on object relations model prominent
   6. *Expressive psychotherapy* of Otto Kernberg
      a. Concentrates on analyzing the *transference*
      b. Client transfers to therapist feelings tied to person from past
      c. Example—*splitting*, client unable to see negative, positive qualities are just different aspects of same person
      d. Client sees therapist as all good or all bad
      e. Treatment sessions to help clients maintain firmer controls
   7. Most effective by Marsha Linehan, *dialectical behavior therapy* (DBT)
      a. Diathesis-stress model; sees children raised in *invalidating environments*, all emotions tightly controlled, ignored, punished or trivialized; person never learns to cope with intense emotions
      b. DBT helps clients develop basic skills in containing erratic behaviors; reduce suicidal preoccupations, substance abuse
      c. Gradually develop greater tolerance for painful emotions
      d. Therapist helps client confront traumatizing experiences that took place in those invalidating environments
         (1) Recovering memories of past trauma
         (2) Eliminating self-blame associated with trauma
         (3) Reducing posttraumatic stress symptoms
         (4) Resolving question of whom to blame for trauma
D. Treatment of Antisocial Personality Disorder
   1. Treatment should be controlled environment, preferably residential center
   2. Treatment staff must maintain strict limits on antisocial behavior
   3. Personalities must be taught
      a. Substitute less deviant mean of gaining stimulation
      b. Value cooperation as a basic moral principle
   4. So difficult to alter, most clinicians regard essentially untreatable
   5. Persons seldom motivated to change; there through legal coercion
   6. No form of psychotherapy, no drugs, no biological treatment useful
   7. *Burnout* occurs after about age 40; reason for burnout unknown

CHAPTER TWELVE
LECTURE MAKER 12.1

Purpose To expand students' understanding of personality disorders. (pp. 414-422)

Lecture Introduction Introduce and describe types of personality disorders with symptomology. Students usually find this material fascinating. As homework, have students each write a brief character sketch of a personality disorder. You can compose your own but I have found students to be very creative with this.

Demonstration With a collection of character sketches in hand, read one at a time, aloud. You can do this for points, as jeopardy game, or just for fun. Play: Name the Diagnosis!

For Example:
Del is a 28-year-old female with a history of cocaine abuse, three hospitalizations, and currently living with her elderly parents (65M and 68F). She has heard voices that tell her to hurt herself. The voices tell her she is bad and needs to be punished. After her first hospitalization at age 22, she has been alcohol and drug free. Del is about 75 pounds overweight. She hates her life, her dependence on her parents, her size, and her lack of finances. She is on disability and doesn't think she can deal with the pressure of a job. Her parents have taken her credit cards because of reckless spending and they keep her on an allowance. Although she never hit her parents, she has been combative in her other relationships.

Del is most likely to be diagnosed as _____(Borderline)

Lecture Capsule Many students have family members with diagnosed disorders. Do not make light of a diagnosis or character sketch. Point out that a single diagnosis may be "the best we have" based on the sketch only.

LECTURE MAKER 12.2

Purpose — To illustrate possible adult behaviors that might evolve from incest trauma.

Lecture Introduction — Discuss sexual abuse and incest with ramifications for the survivor. Note that many survivors develop healthy lifestyles. Focus on the childhood feelings that might be engendered by this intimate violation and how these could become translated into odd or destructive adult tendencies. Most of the aftereffects are listed in the checklist survey.

Demonstration — This survey can be read aloud and discussed item by item. Note that any single behavioral item (or group) could result from most any severe trauma.

Lecture Capsule — Review incest statistics for male and females. If a student should be an incest survivor, it is a comfort to know they are not alone. Also note that many survivors lead healthy lives. This survey was reprinted form a popular book, available in bookstores. Using the checklist in class stimulates discussion, understanding, and compassion.

Reference — E. Sue Blume, CSW, DCSW. As adapted in *Secret Survivors: Uncovering Incest and its Aftereffects in Women*. Reprints may be obtained by sending a business-sized, self-addressed envelope with two stamps to:
Checklist
P.O. Box 7167
Garden City, NY 11530

Could incest have happened to you?

"POST-INCEST SYNDROME" IN WOMEN": THE INCEST SURVIVORS' AFTEREFFECTS CHECKLIST

by E. Sue Blume, C.S.W., Diplomate in Clinical Social Work

INCEST is such a traumatic violation that its victims often forget that it even occurred. But the emotional scars live on, confusing in their seeming meaninglessness. Ongoing problems with relationships, sex, trust, touch, addictions, paralyzing depression and guilt can, when the cause is unknown, feel crazy and out of control. This checklist can be used as a guide to help adult survivors identify themselves and know that there are real reasons for their unrelenting difficulties—that, in fact, these "problems" are actually healthy attempts to cope with an impossible situation.

Incest has traditionally been defined as sex and/or marriage between close relatives. But incest, the most common form of child sexual abuse, is, above all, *child abuse*—abuse of the child's personal and sexual boundaries by the very person(s) entrusted with her care. And sexual violation can occur through the way a child is talked or looked at, even when there is no touching at all. Incest, then, is *any use of a minor child to meet the sexual or sexual/emotional needs of one or more persons whose authority is derived through ongoing emotional bonding with that child* (parents, step-parents, babysitter, sibling, mother's boyfriend, teacher, priest, family doctor). Note that incest is an abuse of a power relationship, not a blood relationship; is the violation of trust that damages the child.

Incest is especially common in alcoholic families. On the alcoholic's part this is due to damaged judgment, a need to control others (momentarily satisfied through playing out dominant/submissive gender roles), and inability to identify with other human beings (to care about the damage he does to others). Often the alcoholic does not remember the experience(s), or applying the same defenses that surround alcoholic drinking and other alcoholic behaviors, he denies, minimized, projects blame. *But these defenses are not elusive to perpetrators who are alcoholic*—and not all alcohol-related incest is attributable to the *disease of alcoholism*. Also, families where there is incest, like alcoholic families, have denial systems, and both experience total confusion of boundaries and disregard for the legitimately dependent developing child. As you will see from this list, children of alcoholics and incest survivors share many other characteristics, along with other adults who endured such childhood trauma as battering, etc.

Do you find that you have the majority of items on this list? If so, you could be a survivor of incest. However separate from people that you might feel, *you are not alone*. Healing is possible; with help, you can break from self-blame, isolation, and the entrapment of Post-Incest Syndrome.

> *This list is based on observation and interviews with incest survivors as well as work done by New York Women Against Rape. To all those who contributed to this fact sheet, thank you; your generous sharing of your pain and experiences is a gift to all survivors.*

1. Fear of being alone in the dark, of sleeping alone; nightmares,(especially of rape, pursuit, threat, entrapment, blood), night terrors

2. Swallowing and gagging sensitivity; repugnance to water on face when bathing or swimming (suffocation feelings)

3. Alienation from the body—not at home in own body; failure to heed signals of body or take care of it; poor body image; manipulating body size to avoid sexual attention; compulsive cleanliness, including bathing in scalding water; or, total inattention to personal appearance or hygiene

4. Gastrointestinal problems; GYN disorders (including spontaneous vaginal infections); vaginal/internal scarring; headaches; arthritis or joint pain; aversion to doctors (especially gynecologists, dentists)

5. Wearing a lot of clothing, even in summer; baggy clothes; failure to remove clothing even when appropriate to do so (while swimming, bathing, sleeping); extreme requirement for privacy when using bathroom

6. Eating disorders, drug/alcohol abuse (or total abstinence); other addictions; compulsive behaviors (including compulsive busyness)

7. Self injury (cutting, burning, etc) (physical pain is manageable) (this is an addictive pattern*); self-destructiveness

8. Phobias, panic

9. Need to be invisible, perfect, or perfectly bad

10. Suicidal thoughts, attempts, obsession (including "passive suicide")

11. Depression (sometimes paralyzing); seemingly baseless crying

12. Anger issues: inability to recognize, own, or express anger; fear of actual or imagined rage; constant anger; intense hostility toward entire gender or ethnic group ("race") of the perpetrator

13. Dissociation ("splitting"); depersonalization; going into shock, shutdown in crisis (stressful situation always a crisis); psychic numbing; physical pain or numbness associated with particular memory, emotion (e.g., anger), or situation (e.g., sex)

14. Rigid control of thought process; humorlessness or extreme solemnity

15. Childhood hiding, hanging on, cowering in corners (security-seeking behaviors); adult nervousness over being watched or surprised; feeling watched; startle response; hypervigilance
16. Trust issues; inability to trust (trust is not safe); absolute trust that turns to rage when disappointed; trusting indiscriminately

17. High risk taking ("daring the fates"); inability to take risks

18. Boundary issues; control, power, territoriality issues; fear of losing control; obsessive/compulsive behaviors (attempts to control things that don't matter, just to control something); power/sex confusion

19. Guilt/ shame/low self-esteem/feeling worthless/ high appreciation of small favors by others

20. Pattern of being a victim (victimizing oneself after being victimized by others), especially sexually; no sense of own power or right to set limits or say "no"; pattern of relationships with much older persons (onset in adolescence); OR exaggerated sense of entitlement; revictimization by others (adult sexual violence, including sexual exploitation by bosses and "helping" professionals)

21. Feeling demand to "produce and be loved"; instinctively knowing and doing what the other person needs or wants; relationships mean big tradeoffs ("love" was *taken*, not given)

22. Abandonment issues; desire for relationships with no separateness; avoidance/fear of intimacy

23. Blocking out some period of early years (especially 1-12 but may continue into adulthood), or a specific person or place

24. Feeling of carrying an awful secret; urge to tell/fear of its being revealed; certainty that no one would listen. Being generally secretive. Feeling "marked" (the "scarlet letter").

25. Feeling crazy; feeling different; feeling oneself to be unreal and everyone else to be real, or vice versa; creating fantasy worlds, relationships, or identities (especially for women: imagining/ wishing self to be male, i.e. not a victim)

26. Denial: no awareness at all; repression of memories; pretending; minimizing ("it wasn't *that* bad"); having dreams or memories ("maybe it's my imagination");(these are actually flashbacks, which is how recall begins) strong, deep, "inappropriate" negative reactions a person, place, or event; "sensory flashes" a light, a place, a physical feeling) without any sense of their meaning; remembering surroundings but not the event. Memory may start with the least threatening event or perpetrator. Actual details of abuse may never be fully remembered; however, much recovery is possible without complete recall. You inner guide will release memories *at the pace your can handle*.

27. Sexual issues: sex feels "dirty"; aversion to being touched, especially in the GYN exam; strong aversion to (or need for) particular sex acts; feeling betrayed by one's body; trouble integrating sexuality and emotionality; confusion or overlapping of affection/sex/dominance/aggression/violence; having to pursue power in sexual arena which is actually sexual acting out (self-abuse, manipulation, [especially women]; abuse of others, [especially men]; compulsively "seductive" or compulsively asexual; must be sexual aggressor or cannot be; impersonal, "promiscuous" sex with strangers concurrent with inability to have sex in intimate relationship (conflict between sex and caring); prostitute, stripper, "sex symbol", (Marilyn Monroe), porn actress; sexual "acting out" to meet anger or revenge needs; sexual addiction; avoidance; shutdown; crying after orgasm; all pursuit feels like violation; sexualizing of all meaningful relationships; erotic response to abuse or anger, sexual fantasies of dominance/real rape (results in guilt and confusion); Note: Homosexuality is *not* an "aftereffect!"

28. Pattern of ambivalent or intensely conflictual relationships (In true intimacy, issues are more likely to surface; in problem relationships, focus can be shifted from real issue of incest). Note: Partner of survivor often suffers consequences of Post-Incest Syndrome also (especially sex and relationship issues)

29. Avoidance of mirrors (connected with invisibility, shame/self-esteem issues, distorted perceptions of face or body)

30. Desire to change one's name (to disassociate from the perpetrator or to take control through self-labeling)

31. Limited tolerance for happiness; active withdrawal from happiness/reluctance to trust happiness ("ice=thin")

32. Aversion to noise-making (including during sex, crying, laughing, or other body functions); verbal hypervigilance (careful monitoring of one's words); quiet-voiced, especially when needing to be heard

33. Stealing (adults); fire-starting (children)

34. Multiple personality "disorder" (often hidden)

35. Food sensitivities/avoidance based on texture (mayonaisse) or appearance (hot dogs), which remind the survivor of abuse, the smell/sound which remind survivor of perpetrator; aversion to meat, red foods.

36. Compulsive honest or compulsive dishonest (lying)

37. Hypervigilance regarding child abuse, or inability to see child abuse, or avoidance of any awareness or mention of child abuse; tendency to develop relationships with incest perpetrators

Note to therapist and others: Many of these "aftereffects" can be the consequence of other problems that occur in early life. There are, however, some items which nearly always indicate childhood sexual abuse, and when one experiences over 25 of the items on this checklist, incest should be strongly suspected. *Proceed with caution!* (Survivors and partners, be gentle with yourselves—and each other.)

> E. Sue Blume's book based on this list,
> *Secret Survivors: Uncovering Incest and its Aftereffects in Women*
> is available as a Ballantine paperback
> (ask at your bookstore)
> or in hardcover by special order from the author.
> Your thoughts on this material are also welcome.

* For further information contact Karen Conterio, Founder,
National Program for Treatment of Self-Injury
Box 26810
Chicago, IL 60626

Copyright © 1985, 1986, 1987, 1989, 1990, 1992, 1993 by E. Sue Blume. All rights reserved

e. sue blume, csw

●

P.O. Box 7167
Garden City, N.Y. 11530

Offices in Freeport
(516) 379-4731

INCEST BACKLASH EVALUATION

The current popular perception is that most reports of remembered childhood sexual abuse are actually "false memories," part of a hysteria orchestrated by greedy therapists and authors. These and other claims of a special interest movement, or Backlash, have uncritically embraced by the media, who present them as fact to an unsuspecting and uneducated populace. Yet there is virtually no scientific substantiation for the theories of the Blacklash, while decisive evident exists to support the validity of such memories. Don't allow yourself to be manipulated. Newsletters by survivors themselves (*Many Voices* and *SurvivorShip* are two of the best) are invaluable because nothing tells the truth about incest more convincingly than the voices of those who have experienced it.

175

RESOURCES

General

National Child Rights Alliance
This organization, formed by survivors of child abuse and neglect, offers the youth bill of rights, many articles on children's rights, and a history of the NCRA.
World Wide Web:
URL: http:/www.ai.mit.edu/people/ellens/NCRA/ncra.html

National Child Rights Alliance
P.O. Box 17005
Durham, NC 27705-0005
Voting membership consist of victims and survivors of child abuse (all kinds)

Cognitive and Psychological Sciences Index
This web page is a huge index to academic programs, organizations and conferences, jounals and magazines, Usenet newsgroups, mailings lists, announcements, publishers, and many more resources relating to cognitive and psychological sciences.

Incest Survivor's Information Exchange
P.O. Box 3399
New Haven, CT 06515
Quarterly newsletter follows particular themes
Survivors of Incest Anonymous (SIA) now mergerd with the former Sexual Abuse Anonymous (SAA). 12-Step "spiritually based" (focus on a "higher power") recovery program that follows the model used by AA and Al-Anon. Meetings in most cities. Offers extensive literature list—send self-addressed stamped envelope.
World Service Office (headquarters)
P.O. Box 21817
Baltimore, MD 21222-6817 (no newsletter)

Adults Molested as Children
605 SE 39th
Portland, Oregon 97214

VOICES (Victims of Incest Can Emerge Survivors) IN ACTION, INC.
P.O. Box 148309
Chicago, IL 60614
Literature, conference, local groups and "special interest groups" that link people by mail and phone nationwide (for example, survivors who are male, and survivors who experience cult abuse).

The Incest Awareness Project, *Breaking the Silence* (newsletter)
P.O. Box 8122
Fargo, SD 58109

Survivors Newsletter Collective, *Breaking the Silence* (newsletter)
Women's Center
46 Pleasant Street
Cambridge, MA 02139
Also available from Survivors Newsletter Collective *Incest Resources* (One time only resource handbook) $3

Media

Descriptions and Interventions (CM, 17-25 min, filmstrip) One film in this series covers personality disorders; other topics in the series include origins of abnormal behavior, anxiety disorders, and schizophrenia.

Closet Narcissistic Disorders: The Masterson Approach with Dr. James F. Masterson (66 minutes, color) James Masterson is widely known for pioneering assessment and treatment approaches for borderline/narcissistic syndromes. This program shows highlights from a complete, 16-month-long, weekly course of therapy. Dr. Masterson accomplishes a diagnosis of the complex problem, and his interventions engage the patient in exploration that result in an increase in the sense of self. The program clearly demonstrates how to
- Use mirroring interpretations of narcissistic vulnerability
- Overcome repeated patient resistance
- Establish a therapeutic alliance with a patient
- Utilize transference as a tool for working through

Battered Teens (FI, 16 min, 1982) Battered and neglected adolescents (film)

Child Abuse: Breaking The Cycle (IM) Three individuals tell their stories about being abused/abusers. (video)

Generations of Violence (FML, 55 min, 1989) How abused children sometimes grow up to become abusive parents and possible solutions. (video)

Incest, the Family Secret (FML, 57 min, 1984) Women's stories of being traumatized in their youth by incestuous fathers, lack of protection by mothers, and treatment of one abusive father (video).

Integrated Treatment of Borderline Personality Disorder

Pharmacotherapy and Psychotherapy
American Psychiatric Press, Inc. and Allyn & Bacon
These new and richly comprehensive videotapes are based on material recently presented by the idstinguished faculty at West and East Coast conferences on treatments of psychiatric disorders, sponsored by the American Psychiatric Association. For those who did not attend these conferences, these videotapes prresent the unusual opportunity to listen and watch these clinicians discuss four of the most critically important psychiatric disorders.

Glen O. Gabbard, M.D., is Vice Presidetn for Adult Services at the Menninger Clinic; Director, F.F. Menninger Memorial Hospital; Training and Supervising Analyst, Topeka Institute for Psychoanalysis; and Clinical Professor of Psychiatry, University of Kansas School of Medicine, in Wichita, Kansas.

Ian Agler, M.D., is Executive Producer of the Treatments of Psychiatric Disorders Videotape Series; Clinical Professor of Psychiatry, The New York Hospital-Cornell Medical Center; Multimedia Consultant to the American Psychiatric Association's Psychiatric Services; and Editor of the American Psychiatric Press Video Series.

For additional video resource materials, please contact your Allyn & Bacon representative.

Nietzel et al., *Abnormal Psychology*, Transparencies

Chapter Twelve

	Text Figure Number	Text Page Number

63. **DSM-IV Personality Disorder Clusters**..409

64. **Overview of Personality Disorders and Their Prevalence**....................12.1.........410

65. **Criteria for Personality Disorder**..412

66. **Five-Factor Approach to Personality**..413

67. **Essential Features of Cluster A Personality Disorders**.......................................416

68. **Essential Features of Cluster B Personality Disorders**.......................................419

69. **Essential Features of Cluster C Personality Disorders**.......................................424

70. **Biological, Psychological, and Family Contributions to Early Precursors of Antisocial Personality Disorder**...12.4........433

13 Substance-Related Disorders

CHAPTER OUTLINE

I. Defining Substance-Related Disorders (pp. 445-447)
    A. Basic Terms and Concepts
        1. *Psychoactive Drugs*
            a. Affect users' thinking, emotions, and behavior
            b. Are widely available, used by many people
            c. Legally available only through prescriptions
            d. Illegal (cocaine, marijuana, and LSD)
        2. *Substance Intoxication*
            a. Temporary condition, direct result of ingesting too much substance
            b. Impaired judgment, altered thinking, pronounced mood changes, disturbed perception, impaired motor behavior
            c. Certain drugs amplify the effects of other substances
        3. *Drug Abuse*
            a. Level of use hazardous to person's health
            b. Leads to significant impairment in work, family life, school
            c. Produces personal distress
            d. Leads to legal problems
        4. *Polysubtance abuse*
            a. Abusing several substances at the same time
            b. Adverse consequences more important than number, amount drugs
        5. *Psychological Dependence*
            a. *Craving*, intense desire for drug, preoccupation with obtaining it
            b. Continue to use knowing it causes ulcers, heart trouble, etc
        6. *Physiological Dependence*
            a. *Addiction* caused by excessive, frequent consumption
            b. Leads to tolerance (larger doses required to achieve same effect)
            c. Withdrawal syndrome (physical symptoms resulting from discontinuing drug use)
                (1) Headaches, nausea, tremors, hallucinations
                (2) Can cause convulsions, even death
    B. DSM-IV Diagnosis of Substance-Related Disorders
        1. *Substance-induced disorders* involve impaired functioning as a direct result of the physiological effects of ingested psychoactive substance
            a. Person ingests alcohol—alcohol intoxication—alcohol-induced
            b. Displays slurred speech, loss of coordination, unsteady gait
        2. *Substance-use disorders* repeated, frequent use of substances
            a. Problematic behaviors
            b. Impairments in personal, social, occupational functioning
            c. *Substance Abuse*
                (1) Maladaptive pattern of substance use with repeated, significant adverse consequences

                (2) Maladaptive behavior
                    (a) Failure major obligations home, work, school
                    (b) Repeatedly using psychoactive substance in hazardous ways (driving)
                    (c) Experiencing recurrent legal problems (arrests)
                    (d) Continuing to use despite negative impact
            d. DSM-IV substance related disorders include:
                (1) Alcohol
                (2) Amphetamine (stimulants)
                (3) Caffeine
                (4) Cannabis (marijuana)
                (5) Cocaine
                (6) Hallucinogens (e.g., LSD)
                (7) Inhalants (glue or spray paint)
                (8) Nicotine
                (9) Opioids (e.g., heroin)
                (10) Phencyclidine (PCP)
                (11) Sedatives, hypnotics, anxiolytics

II. Alcohol Use and Alcohol-Induced Disorders (pp. 447- 468)
    A. Alcohol in the Body
        1. Stomach, small amount *ethanol* immediately absorbed into bloodstream
        2. Rest goes into small intestine, carried in the blood to heart, brain, liver
        3. In liver (*oxidation*), converted to *acetaldehyde* by *dehydrogenase*
        4. Acetaldehyde further *metabolized* into other products
        5. Liver can metabolize ½ to 1 ounce of alcohol per hour
        6. *Tolerance* occurs when body's capacity to metabolize increases
        7. When amount exceeds liver's capacity to metabolize it, ethanol, acetaldehyde begin to accumulate in body cells, producing problems
        8. Unmetabolized ethanol measured as *blood alcohol concentration* (BAC)
            a. *Drink*: 1 ounce of 100-proof alcohol; 12-ounce beer, 4 ounces wine
            b. 1 or 2 drinks yields BAC of 0.02 to 0.05 percent
            c. Definition of drunken driving most states 0.10 percent
            d. Consumed with food, slower absorption, lower BAC, intoxication
        9. Women metabolize alcohol less efficiently than men
            a. Higher BACs in shorter periods
            b. Higher risk for liver damage
        10. Unmetabolized alcohol devastating effect on bodily organs
            a. *Alcohol cirrhosis*
                (1) Damaged liver cells
                (2) Development of scar tissue
                (3) Eventual inability of liver to filter toxins from blood
                (4) Men at risk after 6 or more ounces; women at 1.5 ounces
            b. Cardiovascular disease
                (1) Non-drinkers at higher risk
                (2) 2 to 3 ounces per day raises HDL cholesterol
                (3) Heavy drinking risk factor for several coronary diseases
                    (a) High blood pressure

     (b) Weakening of heart muscles
     (c) Arrhythmias
     (d) Strokes
     (e) Enlarged red blood cells leading to anemia (10%)
     (f) Pancreatitis
     (g) Suppresses body's immune system
     (h) Males, suppressed testosterone levels
     (i) Females, menstrual problems
     (j) Alcohol crosses placental barrier, problems in infants

B. Effects of Alcohol on the Brain and Behavior
  1. Depressant Effects in the Brain
    a. Bloodborne alcohol reaches brain; affects neurotransmitters
     (1) *Glutamate—major excitatory* neurotransmitter (reduces)
     (2) *GABA—major inhibitory* neurotransmitter (increases)
     (3) Alcohol central nervous system *depressant*
     (4) GABA/alcohol affects two areas in brain
      (a) *Medial septal nucleus*, emotional sedation
      (b) *Cerebellum*, sensory and motor functions reduced
     (5) *Nucleus accumbens* mediate pleasure, dopamine increases Pleasure sensations, alcohol increases dopamine
     (6) Increases levels of *serotonin*
     (7) Increases levels levels of *endorphins* (chemically similar to opioid drugs such as morphine and heroin)

C. Effects on Behavior
  1. People feel less inhibited, more talkative, relaxed
  2. As BAC rises, judgment, clear thinking impaired, self-awareness reduced
  3. Unpredictable mood changes, poor attention, memory, lack of inhibition
  4. At 0.10, some become verbally, physically aggressive
  5. At 0.25, some lose consciousness, severe respiratory problems can kill
  6. Can have both sedating and agitating effects on behavior
  7. At some point, no amount of drinking will eliminate tension, agitation
  8. Can develop into brooding, ongoing hostility, directed at spouse, family

D. Prevalence of Alcohol Use Disorders
  1. 1992 survey by National Institute on Alcohol Abuse and Alcoholism
    a. 7.4% of adult population of U.S. (about 13.7 million people)
    b. Met DSM-IV criteria during one year
  2. 1993 report U.S. Department of Health and Human Services 15.3 million
  3. All reports unacceptably high levels maladaptive drinking in U.S.
  4. Same story in United Kingdom, Russia, Australia, Ireland, Korea, etc
  5. Abuse 3 times more prevalent among males than females
  6. Teenagers, male and female equally likely to drink alcohol
  7. Highest rate in 18-29 age group (college age)
  8. African-American teenages more likely to abstain than White European-American
  9. Alcohol abuse more prevalent among Hispanic-American males
  10. Lower among Asian-Americans of both genders

E. Patterns of Alcohol Abuse and Dependence
    1. *Alcoholism*: pattern of heavy drinking
        a. Worsens until person has lost control
        b. So dependent physical, mental health jeopardized
        c. Social and occupational functioning impaired
    2. Alcoholics Anonymous (AA) Jellinek, 1946 proposed 4-stage model
        a. *Prealcoholic*—drink occasionally socially or to relieve tension
        b. *Prodromal*—drinking heavier, secret, few signs intoxication
        c. *Crucial*—lose control;
            (1) One drink leads to binge drinking until blackouts result
            (2) Health affected, social lives begin to deteriorate
        d. *Chronic* phase
            (1) Daily drinking, malnutrition, physical tolerance
            (2) No alcohol—withdrawal symptoms
    3. Scientists now say
        a. Not everyone suffers blackouts, all alcoholics do not lose control
        b. Females start drinking later in life, often after crisis, less likely binge
    4. Robert Cloninger distinguished two types alcoholics
        a. Type I— late onset of problem drinking, prone to anxiety, binge drinking, unlikely to behave antisocially, develop health problems
        b. Type II— begin problem drinking in adolescence, experience little anxiety, antisocial tendencies, disruptions social, occupational functioning, fewer medical complications linked to drinking

F. Disorders Associated With Alcohol Abuse or Dependence
    1. Symptoms associated with other psychiatric conditions
        a. Mood disorders, anxiety disorders, antisocial personality disorder
        b. Psychotic symptoms—delusions, hallucinations
    2. DSM-IV lists 11 alcohol-induced disorders:
    3. Four possible explanations for comorbidity
        a. Mental disorder precedes and causes the alcohol disorder
        b. Alcohol disorder precedes and causes the mental disorder
        c. A common factor precipitates both disorders
        d. Both disorders—regardless which first—exacerbates each other

G. Causes of Alcohol Use Disorders
    1. Genetic Factors
        a. Problem drinking runs in families, risk 7 times greater 1st degree
        b. Higher concordance rate for identical twins
        c. Higher concordance rate in males
        d. Adoption studies show children born to alcoholics prone to it
    2. Neurobiological Influences
        a. EEG: sons of alcoholics higher-than-normal rates beta waves
        b. Show less EEG change after consuming alcohol
        c. Less enzyme *monoamine oxidase (MAO)* activity
        d. Neurotransmitter *serotonin* related to alcohol craving

3. Psychological Factors
   a. *Tension reduction hypothesis*
   b. *Alcohol expectancies*
   c. Alcoholics not good at detecting cues to stop (dizziness, nausea)
   d. Pattern of impulsive, reckless, hyperactive, aggressive behavior
   e. Externalizing behavior influenced drinking problems
      (1) By directly leading to more exposure to and use of
      (2) Promoting more positive alcohol expectancies
4. Sociocultural Factors
   a. England and North America—heavy drinking, loss of control
   b. France—steady drinkers (wine) who never show loss of control
   c. Muslim countries—incidence of alcoholism very low
   d. Social processes in the home; adolescents mirror parents
   e. Peer group influence
   f. Young individuals who increase their use of substances
      (1) Suffered a greater number of major life stressors
      (2) Had parents who used substances more frequently
      (3) Associated more with substance-using peers
      (4) Felt less family support
5. A Multifactor Model
   a. Neither "bad" temperament nor "bad" environment *alone*
   b. Different combinations lead to different *pathways*
      (1) High activity level and ineffective parental discipline
      (2) Low sociability and exposure to deviant peer group

H. Treatment and Prevention of Alcohol Use Disorders
   1. *Minnesota Model*
      a. Requires patients be hospitalized for 4 to 6 weeks
      b. Begins with *detoxification*, period of "drying out"
      c. Main focus on education about consequences of use and abuse
      d. Individual counseling for psychological problems
      e. Group therapy to enhance interpersonal skills
      f. Continued participation in AA at end of hospital program
   2. Alcoholics Anonymous
      a. Organized in 1935 by "Dr. Bob" and "Bill W."
      b. Based on the twelve steps to recovery
      c. Today, thousands of AA groups in countries all around world
      d. AA philosophy—disease controlled only if complete abstinence
      e. Unlimited meetings, frequent personal contact
   3. Marital and Family Therapy
      a. Patterns of abuse linked to close social relationships of abuser
      b. *Codependents* become so enmeshed they prevent changes
      c. Marital conflict stimulates bouts heavy drinking
      d. Alcoholism treatment programs involve spouse, family members
         (1) May be present as spectators

    (2) Participate in alcohol-focused counseling sessions
    (3) Marital therapy aimed at communication skills
    (4) Therapy in conflict resolution techniques
  4. Behavioral Treatments
   a. Help alcoholics associate alcohol with *unpleasant* stimuli
   b. *Aversion therapy* sight, smell, taste presented when vomiting
   c. *Community reinforcement*—arrange reinforcement reward sobriety
   d. Deal with relationship problems; vocational, financial difficulties
   e. Develop new friendships with people who discourage drinking
  5. Medication
   a. Withdrawal effects minimized by *benzodiazepines*
   b. Used in two ways to discourage drinking
    (1) *Disulfiram (Antabuse)* creates unpleasant effects if drinking
    (2) *Naltrexone* (anticraving drug) stops production opiates
  6. Controlled Drinking Treatments
   a. Teaching alcoholics to drink in moderation
   b. Most appropriate for younger drinkers not dependent on alcohol
  7. Relapse Prevention
   a. Alcoholic believes lapse in abstinence valuable learning experience
   b. Replace drinking with positive addiction like jogging
   c. Teach to focus on miserable aspects; jail for DUI, loss of family
  8. Brief Interventions
   a. Recruited through primary health care agencies
   b. Teach controlled drinking skills; self monitoring, self-reinforcement
   c. Dan Kivlahan, Alan Marlatt, et al, developed ASTP
    (1) Alcohol Skills Training Program for college-age drinkers
    (2) Emphasizes
     (a) Controlled drinking through relapse prevention skills
     (b) Avoidance of hangovers, negative consequences
     (c) Controlled drinking through BAC estimation
     (d) Nonconfrontational group discussions
  9. Patient-Treatment Matching
   a. Relapse prevention programs for severe problems
   b. "Talking" therapy for less severe impairments
   c. Individual's readiness to change
   d. Changing drinking patterns occurs in 5 stages
    (1) *Precontemplation:* aware problem, no intention to change
    (2) *Contemplation:* aware, thinking about it, no commitment
    (3) *Preparation:* making small changes, intends to make more
    (4) *Action:* substantial efforts, reached criterion for success
    (5) *Maintenance:* works to prevent relapse, keep new way life
III. Other Depressants (pp. 468-470)
 A. Barbiturates
  1. Odorless, white, crystalline derivatives of *barbituric acid*

        2. Seconal, Tuinal, Nembutal familiar examples
        3. Called "downs" or "downers" prescribed for insomnia
        4. Typically produce relaxation, mild euphoria at low doses
        5. At high doses, state similar to alcohol intoxication
        6. High doses can depress respiratory functions, lower blood pressure and body temperature to point of coma and death, especially if taken with another depressant such as alcohol; accidental death major risk

    B. Benzodeazepines
        1. Derived from *benzoic acid*
        2. Valium, Librium, Xanax
        3. Prescribed to alleviate anxiety, panic disorders, muscle spasms
        4. Safer than barbiturates, still account for tragic deaths
        5. Prolonged use can cause dependence and withdrawal

    C. Depressant Abuse and Dependence
        1. 15% Americans get prescriptions per year; 1% meet criteria for abuse
        2. "Recreational" use by adolescents, young adults
        3. Take 2 or 3 therapeutic doses to produce pleasurable high, reduce anxiety
        4. Polydrug: downers mixed with alcohol and marijuana
        5. Leads to high tolerance; soon 10 to 20 times therapeutic dose
        6. Middle class, middle age or older take prescribed then become dependent
        7. Withdrawal brings high blood pressure, accelerated heart rate, and rapid breathing, anxiety, agitation, tremulousness, insomnia

    D. Treatment of Depressant Abuse and Dependence
        1. Detoxification after prolonged abuse can require weeks of hospitalization
        2. For some, a drug agonist (*carbamazepine*) given instead of abused drug
        3. After detoxification, (*abstinence syndrome*) insomnia, head, body aches anxiety, depression
        4. Treatments include individual, group therapy; drug-specific education, peer support groups such as AA

IV. Stimulants (pp. 470-476)
    A. Amphetamines
        1. Called "uppers" or "speed"
        2. Produce temporary elevation in neurotransmitter dopamine
        3. Effect apparent in *nucleus accumbens*, major reward center in brain
        4. First used medically to control asthma, nasal congestion
        5. Stimulate sympathetic branch of autonomic nervous system
        6. Increases heart rate, blood pressure, constricts blood vessels, shrink mucous membranes; also increases alertness, reduces appetite
        7. Medical purposes, taken in tablet form
        8. Recreational users inhale nasally, inject them, or smoke them
        9. Abusers favor *dextroamphetamine* (Dexedrene), *methamphetamine* (ice)
      10. Produce alertness, focused attention; high doses exhilaration, vigor
      11. Do not produce marked euphoria associated with cocaine
      12. Very high doses: hypervigilance, restlessness; long time delirium, paranoia

13. Intoxication potentially dangerous, increased or irregular heartbeat, dilation of pupils, perspiration or chills, nausea, muscular weakness
14. *Crashing*: postintoxication fatigue, irritability, dysphoria; weeks or months
15. Three groups especially vulnerable
    a. Those who obtain prescription for disorder
    b. Obtain through illegal channels
    c. Recreational users at risk for HIV (needle sharing, high risk sex)

B. Cocaine
1. Alkaloid, from *erythroxylon coca*, from mountainous areas S.A.
2. Coca Cola contained cocaine until about 1900, replaced with caffeine
3. Rapidly increased blood pressure, irregularities in heart rhythms
4. Can cause sudden death, respiratory arrest or heart failure
5. Produces more euphoric experience than amphetamines do
6. Rush is immediate, lasts less than five minutes
7. Extreme psychological dependence in remarkably short time

C. Caffeine
1. Decreases blood flow to brain by constricting blood vessels
2. Used to treat migraine headaches, shrinks mucous membranes, widens bronchial airways; ingredient in cold medications, asthma treatments
3. Low doses—mild stimulation, improve memory, attention, problem solving
4. Moderately high—nervousness, insomnia, gastrointestinal discomfort
5. High doses muscle tremor, agitation, disorganized thinking, rapid or irregular heart beat
6. Can induce panic attacks in persons susceptible to anxiety

D. Nicotine
1. From leaves of tobacco plant, *nicotiniana tabacum*
2. In pure form nicotine deadly poison
3. Few drops on tongue can cause respiratory failure, paralysis, death
4. Tobacco smoking number one public health problem in U.S.
5. Tobacco-related cancer, heart disease, respiratory illness kills ½ million yr.
6. 40,000 deaths from heart disease, 3,000 lung cancer deaths, 26,000 childhood asthma cases attributed to "secondhand" smoke
7. Cardiovascular disease tied directly to nicotine
8. Most problems carbon monoxide and cancer-causing agents
9. DSM-IV substance abuse disorder
10. Withdrawal symptoms begin in hours, peak in few days, last a month

E. Treatment of Stimulant Abuse
1. Cocaine Anonymous, 12-step program
2. Azrin's community reinforcement model
3. Node-link mapping
4. Two medication strategies
    a. Antidepressants to offset dysphoria during withdrawal
    b. Bromocriptine mimics the dopamine-enhancing effects

F. Treatment and Prevention of Nicotine Dependence

1. Most would-be quitters fail 3 to 4 times but do succeed
2. Gradual reduction before quitting cold turkey helpful
3. Nicotine gum or patches reduce severity of withdrawal symptoms
4. New approach—combine gum or patches with drug *mecamylamine*

V. Opioids (pp. 476-478)
   A. Alkaloid Containing Opium or Derivative
      1. Derivatives—morphine, heroin, codeine, methadone
      2. From seed pods of poppy plant from Asia and Middle East
      3. Known as narcotics
      4. Prescribed for pain relief, antidiarrheals, cough suppressants
      5. Used for antidepressants in rare intractable cases of depression
      6. Body has endogenous opiates—*endorphins, enkephalins*
      7. These influence pain and appetite; produce positive moods
   B. Opioid Abuse and Dependence
      1. Heroin (derived from morphine) most commonly abused
      2. Heroic against pain; one of most addictive opioids
      3. 60% inner city users infected with HIV from sharing contaminated needles
      4. In pure form can be smoked or snorted, heavy users "mainlining" injection
      5. Intoxicated person "spacey", drunk, drowsy, disconnected for up to 6 hrs.
      6. Produce intense withdrawal syndrome, anxiety, increased sensitivity pain
      7. Excessive body excretions, pupil dilation, diarrhea, fever, insomnia
      8. Clinicians uncertain if narcotic addiction is *consequence* of antisocial pathology or vice versa
   C. Treatment of Opioid Abuse and Dependence
      1. Medications play central role
         a. Opioid antagonists (*naltrexone*) used in initial detoxification
         b. Other drugs used to reduce craving after withdrawal
         c. Most controversial, synthetic opioid *methadone*
         d. In 1990—100,000 opioid-dependent persons on methadone therapy
         e. Developed methadone substitute, *buprenorphine*, less addictive
         f. Supportive-expressive therapy, form of psychoanalysis
         g. Experts—methadone programs combined with psychological

VI. Cannabis and Hallucinogens (pp. 478-482)
   A. Cannabis
      1. Psychoactive drug derived from hemp plant, *cannabis sativa*
      2. *Marijuana* ("pot", "weed", "grass", "boo"): dried chopped leaves, tops, stem of hemp plant smokes in cigarette form ("joint")
      3. Can be taken orally by mixing it with food, brewing as tea
      4. *Hashish*, always smoked, dried resin from tops, leaves female plant
      5. Psychoactive ingredients *delta-9 tetrahydrocannabinol* (THC)cannabinoids
      6. 5.5 million people in U.S. use it weekly
      7. Young person's use increases chances experimenting more addictive drugs
      8. Effects: dilation blood vessels in eyes, dry mouth, increased appetite

("munchies") rapid heartbeat
9. Increases cerebral blood flow especially in frontal regions of brain
10. Has primarily sedating effects on central nervous system
11. Used to treat anorexia, glaucoma, cancer patients for nausea, vomiting
12. Motor performance impaired, short-term memory, reaction times
13. Tolerance, withdrawal not prominent features
14. Psychological dependence, risk-taking, conflicts, legal problems
15. 50 to 100 times the carcinogens found in tobacco

B. Hallucinogens
1. *Psychedelics*, objects shimmer, waver, halos appear, objects emit trails
2. Visual hallucinations— nonexistent people or objects
3. Users "see" sounds or "feel" colors (synesthesia)
4. Lead to depersonalization, paranoid thinking, extremely variable moods
5. Lysergic Acid Diethylamide (LSD)
   a. "Acid" synthesized or derived from ergot, a fungus
   b. "Trip" product of central nervous system excitation
   c. Also arouses sympathetic nervous system, mimics serotonin
   d. Similarity between LSD effects and symptoms of schizophrenia
   e. Can be taken in tablet form, by eating sugar cubes with drops on
   f. Produces few direct physical health risks
   g. Behavioral, emotional changes can threaten physical, psychological
   h. "Flashbacks" occur as long as five years after last usage of LSD
6. Other Hallucinogens
   a. Mescaline derived from the peyote cactus plant
      (1) Crown of cactus (peyote button)
      (2) Used in Native American religious services still today
   b. Psilocybin alkaloids found in Mexican mushrooms
   c. *Methyl-enedioxy-methamphetamine* (MDMA) "Ecstasy"
      (1) Designed by unscrupulous chemists
      (2) Not safe; raises body temperatures to danger point
      (3) Users die from hyperthermia
   d. *Phencyclidine* (PCP) "angel dust"
      (1) Originally developed as medical anesthetic
      (2) Produces analgesia, respiratory suppression, seizures, coma
      (3) PCP overdoses can be fatal
      (4) Users feel superhuman power, invulnerability
      (5) users so aggressive and violent, hurt themselves or others

C. Treatment of Cannabis and Hallucinogen Abuse and Dependence
1. Marijuana part of polydrug abuse; other drugs more risk, treated first
2. Some 12-step-type support groups developed
3. LSD intoxication requires hospitalization
4. Therapies focus on curbing psychological dependence

13 Substance-Related Disorders

LECTURE MAKER 13.1

Purpose To evaluate chronic self-destructive behavioral tendencies (pp. 451-453)

Lecture Introduction Introduce the topic of addiction and the self-destructive personality aspects often associated with drug/alcohol abuse. Discuss the paradoxical nature of this behavior pattern: if it's so bad, why do it? This provides insight into the process behind the disorder.

Demonstration Duplicate the Chronic Self-Destructiveness Scale and scoring for students to complete individually and anonymously. Emphasize that this scale shows only common behavior patterns of self-destructiveness. The 73 items make up two 52-item scales, one for each gender. Discuss general interpretation for high and low scores. Students find an inventory like this interesting and informative—guaranteed to stimulate discussion.

Lecture Capsule Highlight the negative consequences coupled with addiction. Bring Elvis Presley's story from the casebook into the conversation. Everyone knows the name and can associate him with the dire consequences of addiction.

LECTURE MAKER 13.2

Purpose To examine personal drinking experiences and negative consequences associated with use. (pp. 448-451)

Lecture Introduction Denial is a major hurdle in discussing drinking/drugging history. Review the criteria for substance abuse and typical behaviors. This exercise uses some student-related examples of negative results from drinking and can be used to illustrate how the abuser might minimize or deny their problem.

Demonstration Have the students create two lists. One list is negative consequences of drinking and drugging. The other list is their definition of abnormal drinking and drugging behavior. Combine these lists into a checklist. Present the checklist for students to complete and keep. This instrument may or may not evaluate quantity or frequency of substance used, but it will present consequences and feelings. It makes an excellent starting place for discussion. Remind them that any assessment tool would be used in conjunction with a clinical interview and formal assessment procedures.

Lecture Capsule This chapter, perhaps more than any other, strikes cords with students. There is a high probability that your students know someone personally with a substance abuse problem—it may be a family member or themselves. Bring to light the study of Betty Ford, whose center has by now become known to all. Be sure to offer suggestions at the end of this exercise for more information and help.

LECTURE MAKER 13.3

Purpose To explore ways of detecting substance abuse, as a teacher or parent. (pp. 457-459)

Lecture Introduction Substance abuse in the United States is a terrible epidemic and waste of lives. We all need to be educated—parents, teachers, children, youth. This exercise simplistically offers suggestions to increase sensitivity and awareness of potential use/abuse. "How do I *begin* to make a difference," can be answered with this brief discussion.

Demonstration Introduce the material from this hand-out. Review other awareness behaviors not listed here.

Lecture Capsule This exercise is offered as reassurance for your students. After focusing on the problem, it helps to translate DSM-IV information into practical, useful suggestions. These are not earth-shattering revelations but they are easily learnable and do-able. It provides a positive approach to begin learning how to be aware.

CHRONIC SELF-DESTRUCTIVENESS SCALE 13.1

For each of the following statements, indicate the degree to which the statement describes you. Record you responses in the space provided by writing in a letter from A to E, using the following scale:

    A expresses *strongest agreement*
    B expresses *moderate agreement*
    C indicates that you're *unsure* or *undecided* or that it's a *toss-up*
    D expresses *moderate disagreement*
    E expresses *strongest disagreement*

_____ 1. I like to listen to music with the volume turned up as loud as possible.
_____ 2. Life can be pretty boring.
_____ 3. When I was a kid, I was suspended from school.
_____ 4. I usually eat breakfast.
_____ 5. I do not stay late at school functions when I must get up early.
_____ 6. I use or have used street drugs.
_____ 7. I like to spend my free time "messing around."
_____ 8. As a rule, I do not put off doing chores.
_____ 9. Riding fast in a car is thrilling.
_____ 10. I tend to defy people in authority.
_____ 11. I have a complete physical examination once a year.
_____ 12. I have done dangerous things just for the thrill of it.
_____ 13. I am the kind of person who would stand up on a roller coaster.
_____ 14. I do not believe in gambling.
_____ 15. I find it necessary to plan my finances and keep a budget.
_____ 16. I let people take advantage of me.
_____ 17. I hate any kind of schedule or routine.
_____ 18. I usually meet deadlines with no trouble.
_____ 19. I am familiar with basic first-aid practices.
_____ 20. Even when I have to get up early, I like to stay up late.
_____ 21. I insist on traveling safely rather than quickly.
_____ 22. I have my car serviced regularly.
_____ 23. People tell me I am disorganized.
_____ 24. It is important to get revenge when someone does you wrong.
_____ 25. Sometimes I don't seem to care what happens to me.
_____ 26. I like to play poker for high stakes.
_____ 27. I smoke over a pack of cigarettes a day.
_____ 28. I have frequently fallen in love with the wrong person.
_____ 29. I just don't know where my money goes.
_____ 30. Wearing a helmet ruins the fun of a motorcycle ride.
_____ 31. I take care to eat a balanced diet.
_____ 32. Lots of laws seem made to be broken.
_____ 33. I am almost always on time.
_____ 34. I like jobs with an element of danger.
_____ 35. I often walk out in the middle of an argument.
_____ 36. Often I don't take very good care of myself.

_____ 37. I rarely put things off.
_____ 38. I speak my mind even when it's not in my best interest.
_____ 39. I usually follow through on projects.
_____ 40. I've made positive contributions to my community.
_____ 41. I make promises that I don't keep.
_____ 42. An occasional fight makes a guy more of a man.
_____ 43. I always do what my doctor or dentist recommends.
_____ 44. I know the various warning signs of cancer.
_____ 45. I usually call a doctor when I'm sure I'm becoming ill.
_____ 46. I maintain an up-to-date address/phone book.
_____ 47. I sometimes forget important appointments I wanted to keep.
_____ 48. I drink two or fewer cups of coffee a day.
_____ 49. It's easy to get a raw deal from life.
_____ 50. I eat too much.
_____ 51. I often skip meals.
_____ 52. I don't usually lock my house or apartment door.
_____ 53. I know who to call in an emergency.
_____ 54. I can drink more alcohol than most of my friends.
_____ 55. The dangers from using contraceptives are greater than the dangers of not using them.
_____ 56. I seem to keep making the same mistakes.
_____ 57. I have my eyes examined at least once a year.
_____ 58. I lose often when I gamble for money.
_____ 59. I leave on an outdoor light when I know I'll be coming home late.
_____ 60. Using contraceptives is too much trouble.
_____ 61. I often use nonprescription medicines (aspirin, laxatives, etc.).
_____ 62. I do things I know will turn out badly.
_____ 63. When I was in high school, I was considered a good student.
_____ 64. I have trouble keeping up with bills and paperwork.
_____ 65. I rarely misplace even small sums of money.
_____ 66. I am frequently late for important things.
_____ 67. I frequently don't do boring things I'm supposed to do.
_____ 68. I feel really good when I'm drinking alcohol.
_____ 69. Sometimes when I don't have anything to drink, I think about how good some booze would taste.
_____ 70. It's really satisfying to inhale a cigarette.
_____ 71. I like to smoke.
_____ 72. I believe that saving money gives a person a real sense of accomplishment.
_____ 73. I like to exercise

From "Chronic Self-Destructiveness: Conceptualization, Measurement and Initial Validation of the Construct," by K. Kelley, D. Byrne, P.J. Przbyla, C. Eberly, B. Eberly, V. Greendinger, C.K. Wan, and J. Gorsky, 1985. *Motivation and Emotion,* 9, pp 135-151. Copyright 1985 by Plenum Publishing Corp. Reprinted by permission

CHRONIC SELF-DESTRUCTIVENESS SCALE 13.1

The 73 items actually make up two 52-item scales, one for each gender. Scoring instructions for each gender follow:

FEMALES

Score A = 1, B = 2, C = 3, D = 4, E = 5 for the following items:
5, 8, 11, 15, 18, 19, 21, 22, 31, 33, 37, 39, 40, 43, 44, 45, 46, 53, 63

Score A = 5, B = 5, C = 3, D = 2, E = 1 for the following items: 1, 2, 6, 7, 9, 10, 12, 16, 17, 20, 23, 24, 25, 26, 28, 29, 30, 32, 36, 38, 41, 47, 49, 54, 56, 58, 60, 61, 62, 64, 66, 67, 69

MALES

Score A = 1, B = 2, C = 3, D = 4, E = 5 for the following items:
4, 14, 18, 21, 22, 39, 40, 45, 48, 53, 57, 59, 63, 65, 72, 73

Score A = 5, B = 4, C = 3, D = 2, E = 1 for the following items: 2, 3, 10, 12, 13, 17, 25, 26, 27, 28, 29, 30, 32, 34, 35, 36, 41, 42, 47, 49, 50, 51, 52, 54, 55, 56, 58, 60, 62, 64, 66, 67, 68, 69, 70, 71

Both genders should have 52 items with numbers recorded in place of a letter. The score on the CSDS is simply the sum of those numbers. The following norms are from Kelley et al.:

Females Males

High score   157— 260   158—260
Intermediate score 105—156   97—157
Low score   52—104   52— 96

From "Chronic Self-Destructiveness: Conceptualization, Measurement and Initial Validation of the Construct," by K. Kelley, D. Byrne, P.J. Przbyla, C. Eberly, B. Eberly, V. Greendinger, C.K. Wan, and J. Gorsky, 1985. *Motivation and Emotion,* 9, pp 135-151. Copyright 1985 by Plenum Publishing Corp. Reprinted by permission

PARENT-CHILD COMMUNICATION TIPS 13.3

Tips for Communicating Effectively

Children and adults have different communication styles and different ways of responding in conversation. Therefore effective communication between parents and children is not always easy to achieve.

Listening

- Pay attention
- Don't interrupt
- Don't prepare what you will say while your child is speaking
- Reserve judgment until you child is finished and has asked you for a response

Looking

- Be aware of your child's facial expression and body language. Is your child nervous or uncomfortable—frowning, drumming fingers, tapping a foot, looking at the clock? Or does your child seem relaxed—smiling, looking you in the eyes? Reading these signs will help parents know how the child is feeling.
- During the conversation, acknowledge what your child is saying—move your body forward if you are sitting, touch a shoulder if your are walking, or nod your head and make eye contact.

Responding

- "I am very concerned about..." or " I understand that it is sometimes difficult..." are better ways to respond to your child than beginning sentences with "You should," or "If I were you," or "When I was your age we didn't..." Speaking for oneself sounds thoughtful and is likely to be considered a lecture or an automatic response.
- If your child tells you something you don't want to hear, don't ignore the statement.
- Don't offer advice in response to every statement your child makes. It is better to listen carefully to what is being said and try to understand the real feelings behind the words.
- Make sure you understand what your child means. Repeat things to your child for confirmation.

Reprinted for non-profit, educational use from: National Clearinghouse for Alcohol and Drug Information, Department CPI, Box 2345, Rockville, MD 20852. Printed by the Department of Education. Learning to Live Drug Free—A Curriculum Model for Prevention. Section VI.

Signs of Drug Use 13.3

Changing patterns of performance, appearance, and behavior may signal use of drugs. The items in the first category listed below provide direct evidence of drug use; the items in the other categories offer signs that may indicate drug use. For this reason, adults should look for extreme changes in children's behavior, changes that together form a pattern associated with drug use. (Note: Many of these sign may also be exhibited by a child who is not using drugs but who may be having other problems at school or in the family.)

Signs of drugs and drug paraphernalia

- Possession of drug-related paraphernalia such as pipes, rolling papers, small decongestant bottles, or small butane torches.
- Possession of drugs or evidence of drugs, peculiar plants, or butts, seeds, or leaves in ashtrays or clothing pockets.
- Odor of drugs, smell of incense or other "cover-up" scents.

Identification with drug culture

- Drug-related magazines, slogans on clothing.
- Conversation and jokes that are preoccupied with drugs.
- Hostility in discussing drugs.

Signs of physical deterioration

- Memory lapses, short attention span, difficulty in concentration.
- Poor physical coordination, slurred or incoherent speech.
- Unhealthy appearance, indifference to hygiene and grooming.
- Bloodshot eyes, dilated pupils.

Dramatic changes in school performance

- Distinct downward turn in student's grades—not just from C's to F's, but A's to B's and C's. Assignments not completed.
- Increased absenteeism or tardiness

Changes in behavior

- Chronic dishonesty (lying, stealing, cheating). Trouble with the police.
- Changes in friends, evasiveness in talking about new ones.
- Possession of large amounts of money.
- Increasing and inappropriate anger, hostility, irritability, secretiveness.
- Reduced motivation, energy, self-discipline, self-esteem.
- Diminished interest in extracurricular activities and hobbies.
- Association with drug-using friends.

Reprinted for non-profit, educational use from: National Clearinghouse for Alcohol and Drug Information, Department CPI, Box 2345, Rockville, MD 20852. Printed by the Department of Education. Learning to Live Drug Free—A Curriculum Model for Prevention. Section VI.

RESOURCES

General

Self Help Clearinghouse. This national organization is an resource for names of groups or individuals that support emotional and physical needs, support groups for special populations, and concrete services regarding poverty, education, unwed mothers, and so forth. Many local affiliates publish a directory of community services. For information on starting or finding self-help groups, and for listing of many local affiliates, a guidebook called *The Self Help Sourcebook* is available.
Self Help Clearinghouse Attention: Sourcebook
St. Clares-Riverside Medical Center
Pocono Road,
Denville, New Jersey 07834

The National Council on Alcoholism and Drug Dependence (NCADD) This organization has a national phone number 1-800-475 HOPE. Call for your local affiliate, which may be listed in your local phone book under NCA or the name of the region. Local chapters can give you information about a variety of resources for alcoholism and other addictive problems.

ACTION Drug Prevention Program. ACTION, the Federal volunteer agency, works at the local, State, and national levels, to encourage and help fund the growth of youth, parents, and senior citizen groups and networks committed to helping youth remain drug free. ACTION can provide *Kids and Drugs: A Youth Leaders' Handbook* and a brochure called *Idea Exchange*, which outlines 32 drug-free activities for children and teens, including ideas for speakers, publicity community involvement and projects.
806 Connecticut Ave. N.W. Suite M-606
Washington, DC 20525
(202) 634-9292

American Council for Drug Education (ACDE). ACDE organizes conferences; develops media campaigns; reviews scientific findings; publishes books, a quarterly newsletter, and education kits for physicians, schools, and libraries; and produces films.
204 Monroe St., Suite 110
Rockville, MD 20852
(301) 294-0600

Committees of Correspondence. This organization provides a newsletter and bulletins on issues, ideas and contacts. Publishes a resource list and pamphlets. Membership is $15.00.
57 Conant ST., Room 113
Danvers, MA 09123
(617) 774-2641

Drug-Free Schools and Communities—Regional Centers Program, U.S. Department of Education. This program is designed to help local school districts, State education agencies, and institutions of higher education to develop alcohol and drug education and prevention programs. Five regional centers provide training and technical assistance. For further information on center services, contact the center in your region:

Northeast Regional Center for Drug-Free School and Communities
12 Overton Ave
Sayville, NY 11782-0403
(516) 589-7022
Connecticut, Delaware, Maine, Maryland, Massachusetts, New Hampshire, New Jersey, New York, Ohio, Pennsylvania, Rhode Island, Vermont

Southeast Regional Center for Drug-Free Schools and Communities
100 Edgewood Avenue
Suite 1110
Atlanta, GA 30303
(404) 688-9227
Alabama, District of Columbia, Florida, Georgia, Kentucky, North Carolina, South Carolina, Tennessee, Virginia, West Virginia, Virgin Islands, and Puerto Rico

Midwest Regional Center for Drug-Free Schools and Communities
2001 N. Clybourn
Suite 302
Chicago, IL 60614
(312) 883-8888
Indiana, Illinois, Iowa, Michigan, Minnesota, Missouri, Nebraska, North Dakota, South Dakota, Wisconsin

Southwest Regional Center for Drug-Free School and Communities
555 Constitution Ave.
Norman, OK 73037
(405) 325-1454
Arizona, Arkansas, Colorado, Kansas, Louisiana, Mississippi, New Mexico, Oklahoma, Texas, Utah

Western Regional Center for Communities
101 SW Main St., Suite 500
Portland, OR 97204
(503) 275-9476
(800) 547-6339 (outside Oregon)
Alaska, California, Hawaii, Idaho, Montana, Nevada, Oregon, Washington, Wyoming, American Samoa, Guam, Northern Mariana Islands

Drug-Free School and Communities—State and Local Programs, U.S. Department of Education. This program provides each state educational agency and Governor's office with funds for alcohol and drug education and prevention programs in local school and communities. For information on contact persons in you state, contact the U.S. Department of Education, Drug-Free Schools Staff
400 Maryland Avenue, SW
Washington, DC 20202-6151
(202) 732-4599

Families in Action. This organization maintains a drug information center with more than 200,000 documents. Publishes *Drug Abuse Update*, a quarterly journal containing abstracts of articles and published in medical and academic journals and newspapers. $25 for four issues.
1196 Henderson Mill Rd., Suite 204
Atlanta, GA 30345
(404) 934-6364

"Just Say No" Clubs. These nationwide clubs provide support and positive peer reinforcement to youngsters through workshops, seminars, newsletters, walk-a-thons, and a variety of other activities. Clubs are organized by schools, communities, and parent groups.
"Just Say No" Foundation
1777 N. California Blvd., Suite 211
Walnut Creek, CA 94596
(800) 258-2766 or (415) 939-6666

Narcotics Education, Inc. This organization publishes pamphlets, books, teaching aids, and prevention magazines designed for classroom use: *WINNER* for preteens and *LISTEN* for teens.
6830 Laurel St. NW
Washington, DC 20012
(800) 548-8700 or in the Washington, DC area, call (202) 722-76740

Parents' Resource Institute for Drug Education Inc. (PRIDE) This national resource and information center offers consultant services to parent groups, school personnel, and youth groups, and provides a drug-use survey service. It conducts an annual conference; publishes a newsletter, a youth group handbook, and other publications; and sells and rents books, films, videos, and slide programs. Membership is $20.
Woodruff Bldg., Suite 1002
100 Edgewood Ave.
Atlanta, GA 30303
(800) 241-9746

TARGET. Conducted by the National Federation of State High School Associations, an organization of interscholastic activities associations, TARGET offers workshops, training seminars, and information bank on chemical use and prevention. It has a computerized referral service to substance abuse literature and prevention programs.
National Federation of State High School Associations
11724 Plaza Circle
P.O. Box 20626
Kansas City, MO 64195
(816) 464-5400

Toughlove. This national self-help group for parents, children, and communities emphasizes cooperation, personal initiative, avoidance of blame, and action. It publishes a newsletter, brochures, and books and holds workshops.
P.O. Box 1069
Doylestown, PA 18901
(215) 348-7090

U.S. Clearinghouse. (A publication list is available on request, along with placement on a mailing list for new publications. Single copies are free.)
National Clearinghouse for Alcohol and Drug Information
P.O. Box 2345
Rockville, MD 20852
(800) SAY-NOTO
This organization (NCADI) combines the clearinghouse activities previously administered by the National Institute on Alcoholism and Alcohol Abuse (NIAAA) and the National Institute on Drug Abuse (NIDA)

The Department of Education does not endorse private or commercial products or services, or products or services not affiliated with the Federal government. The sources of information listed on this and the following pages are intended only as a partial listing of the resources that are available to readers of this publication. Readers are encouraged to research and inform themselves of the products or services, relating to drug and alcohol abuse, that are available to them. Readers are encouraged to visit their public libraries to find out more about the dangers of drug and alcohol abuse, or to call local, state, or national hotlines for further information, advice, or assistance.

Toll-Free Information

1-800-COCAINE—Cocaine Helpline
A round-the-clock information and referral service. Recovering cocaine addict counselors answer the phones, offer guidance, and refer drug users and parents to local public and private treatment centers and family learning centers.

l-800-NCA-CALL—National Council on Alcoholism Information Line
The National Council on Alcoholism, Inc., is the national nonprofit organization combating alcoholism, other drug addictions, and related problems. Provides information about NCA's State and local affiliates' activities in their areas. Also provides referral services to families and individuals seeking help with an alcohol or other drug problem.

1-800-662-HELP—NIDA Hotline
NIDA Hotline, operated by the National Institute on Drug Abuse, is a confidential information and referral line that directs callers to cocaine abuse treatment centers in the local community. Free materials on drug use also are distributed in response to inquiries.

1-800-241-9746—PRIDE Drug Information Hotline
A national resource and information center, Parents' Resource Institute for Drug Education (PRIDE), refers concerned parents to parent groups in their state or local area, gives information on how parents can form a group in their community, provides telephone consultation and referrals to emergency health centers, and maintains a series of drug information tapes that callers can listen to, free of charge, by calling after 5:00 p.m.

Sources of Free Catalogs of Alcohol and Other Drug Use Publications

Comp Care Publications. A source for pamphlets, books, and charts on drug and alcohol use, chemical awareness, and self-help.
1-800-328-3330 or (612) 559-4800

Hazelden Educational Materials. A source for pamphlets and books on drug use and alcoholism and curriculum materials for drug prevention.
1-800-328-9000. In Minnesota, call 612-257-4010 or 1- 800-257-0070

National Council on Alcoholism. A source for pamphlets, booklets, and fact sheets on alcoholism and drug use.
(212) 206-6770

Johnson Institute. A source for audio cassettes, films, video cassettes, pamphlets, and books on alcoholism and drug use. Offers books and pamphlets on prevention and intervention for children, teens, parents, and teachers.
1-800-231-5165. In Minnesota, 1-800-247-0484 and in Minneapolis/St. Paul area, 944-0511.

National Association for Children of Alcoholics. A source for books, pamphlets, and handbooks for children of alcoholics. Conducts regional workshops and provides a directory of local members and meetings.
(714) 499-3889

Internet

Drug Information Resources on the Net
This web page offers links to many drug-related resources on the Internet, including ftp sites, gophers, mailing lists, newsgroups, IRC bots, and organizations.
Word Wide Web:
URL;http://stein1.u.washington.edu:2012/pharm/misc/resources.html

Drug Use History
A brief history of drug use and prohibition beginning around 5000 B.C.
Anonymous FTP:
Address:**ftp.spies.com**
Path:**/Library/Fringe/Pharm/drug.use**

Gopher:
Name: Internet Wiretap
Address: **wiretap.spies.com**
Choose:**Wiretap Online Library**
  | **Fringes of Reason**
  | **Pharmacological Cornucopia**
  | **A brief history of drug use**

Drug Web Servers
These web pages offer all kinds of interesting items about drug tests, medical information, drug humor, politics,programs, and information on specific types of drugs.
World Wide Web:
URL: **http://akebono.stanford.edu/yahoo/Entertainment/Drugs/**
URL: **http://cyborganic.com/drugz/**
URL: **http://www.pitt.edu/~mbtst3/druginfo.html**
URL: **http://www.ramp.com/misc/drugs**

Ecstasy
Contrary to what most people believe, Ecstasy (or MDMA) is not a new drug. Read about the history, effects, dangers, and usage of Ecstasy.
World Wide Web:
URL: **http://stein1.u.washington.edu:2012/pharm/e4x-ht/**

General Drug Information
A directory containing subdirectories, each of which deals with a different drug and the issues surrounding its use, including LSD, peyote (mescaline), marijuana, opiates, stimulants, and others. Some nested subdirectories contain medical and legal information and one is devoted solely to drug-oriented humor.

Anonymous FTP:
    Address: **ftp.hmc.edu**
    Path: **/pub/drugs/***

Nootropics (Intelligence-Enhancing Drugs)
A subdirectory containing compressed text files that deal with nootropics, the so-called intelligence-enhancing drugs.
Anonymous FTP:
    Address:**ftp.hmc.edu**
    Path: **/pub/drugs/nootropics/***

Addictions
A mailing list for mature discussion of addictions, including food disorders, sex, codependency, nicotine, and other addictions.
Listerv Mailing List:
    List Address:**addict-1@kentvm.kent.edu**
    Subscription address:**listserv@kentvm.kent.edu**

Drug and Alcohol Information
Detailed documents and guides about the risks involved with drug and alcohol use, blood alcohol concentration statistics, state laws, and other related facts.

Gopher:
    Name: University of Montana Healthline Gopher Server
    Address:**selway.umt.edu**
    Port: **700**
    Choose: **Drug & Alcohol Information**

Listserv Mailing List:
    List Address: **alcohol@muacad.bitnet**
    Subscription Address: **listserv@lmuacad.bitnet**

Telnet:
Address:**selway.umt.edu**
Login: **health**

Readings *Publications listed below are free unless otherwise noted.*

Adolescent Drug Abuse: Analyses of Treatment Research, by Elizabeth R. Rahdert and John Grabowski, 1988. This 139-page book assesses the adolescent drug users and offers theories, techniques, and findings about treatment and prevention. It also discusses family-based approaches. National Clearinghouse for Alcohol and Drug Information, P.O. Box 2345, Rockville, MD 20852

Adolescent Peer Pressure Theory, Correlates, and Program Implications for Drug Abuse Prevention, by the U.S. Department of Health and Human Services, 1988. This 115-page book focuses on constructive ways of channeling peer pressure. This volume was developed to help parents and professionals understand the pressures associated with adolescence, the factors associated with drug use, and other forms of problem behavior. Different peer program approaches, ways in which peer programs can be implemented, and research suggestions are included. National Clearinghouse for Alcohol and Drug Information. P.O. Box 2345, Rockville, MD 20852

The Challenge newsletter highlights successful school-based programs, provides suggestions on effective prevention techniques, and the latest research on drugs and their effects. Published bimonthly by the U.S. Department of Education and available from the National Clearinghouse for Alcohol and Drug Information, P.O. Box 2345, Rockville, MD 20852

Courtwatch Manual. A 111-page manual explaining the court system, the criminal justice process, Courtwatch activities, and what can be done before and after a criminal is sentenced. Washington Legal Foundation, 1705 N Street, NW, Washington, DC 20036. Enclose $5 for postage and handling. (202) 857-0240.

Drug Prevention Curricula: A Guide to Selection and Implementation, by the U.S. Department of Education, 1988. Written with the help of a distinguished advisory panel, this 76-page handbook represents the best current thinking about drug prevention education. It shows what to look for when adopting or adapting ready-made curricula, and suggests important lessons that ought to be part of any prevention education sequence. National Clearinghouse for Alcohol and Drug Information, P.O. Box 2345, Rockville, MD 20852

National Trends in Drug Use and Related Factors Among American High School Students, 1975-1986, by Jerald G. Bachman, Lloyd D. Johnston, and Patrick M. O'Malley, 1987. A 265-page book reporting on trends in drug use and attitudes of high school seniors, based on an annual survey conducted since 1975. National Clearinghouse for Alcohol and Drug Information, P.O. Box 2345, Rockville, MD 20852

Gone Way Down: Teenage Drug-Use Is a Disease, by Miller Newton, 1981, revised 1987. This 72-page book describes the stages of adolescent drug use. American Studies Press, paperback, $3.95 (813) 961-7200

Growing Up Drug Free: A Parent's Guide to Prevention, U.S. Department of Education, 1990. A 56-page booklet featuring information on what children should know at key stages of development, suggested activities to reinforce an anti-drug message in the home, effects of drugs, and available resources. National Clearinghouse for Alcohol and Drug Information, P.O. Box 2345, Rockville, MD 20852. 1-800-SAY-NOTO or 1-800-624-0100 for the Department of Education.

Kids and Drugs: A Handbook for Parents and Professionals, by Joyce Tobias, 1986, reprinted 1987. A 96-page handbook about adolescent drug and alcohol use, the effects of drugs and the drug culture, stages of chemical use, the formation of parent groups, and available resources. PAANDA Press, 4111 Watkins Trail, Annandale, VA 22003, paperback, $4.95 (volume discounts. (703) 750-9285.

Parents, Peers, and Pot II: Parent in Action, by Marsha Manatt, 1983, reprinted 1988. A 160-page book that describes the formation of parent groups in rural, suburban, and urban communities. National Clearinghouse for Alcohol and Drug Information, P.O. Box 2345, Rockville, MD 20852

Team Up for Drug Prevention With America's Young Athletes A free booklet for coaches that includes information about alcohol and other drugs, reasons why athletes use drugs, suggested activities for coaches, a prevention program, a survey for athletes and coaches, and sample letters to parents. Drug Enforcement Administration, Demand Reduction Section
1406 I St., NW, Washington, DC 20537 (202) 786-4096

The Fact Is...You Can Prevent Alcohol and Other Drug Problems Among

What Works: Schools Without Drugs, U.S. Department of Education, 1986, revised 1989. A handbook for developing a comprehensive antidrug program involving parents, students, schools, and communities. National Clearinghouse for Alcohol and Drug Information, P.O. Box 2345, Rockville, MD 20852. 1-800-SAY-NOTO or 1-800-624-0100 for the Department of Education

Media

The following drug prevention videos were developed by the U.S. Department of Education. They are available for loan through the Department's Regional Centers and National Clearinghouse for Alcohol and Drug Information, P.O. Box 2345, Rockville, MD 20852. 1-800-SAY-NOTO

Hard Facts About Alcohol, Marijuana, and Crack. Offers factual information about the dangers of drug use in a series of dramatic vignettes.

Speak Up, Speak Out: Learning to Say No to Drugs. Gives students specific techniques they can use to resist peer pressure and say no to drug use.

Dare to Be Different. Uses the friendship of two athletes in their last year of high school to illustrate the importance of goals and values in resisting pressures to use drugs.

Downfall: Sports and Drugs. Shows how drugs affect athletic performance and examines the consequences of drug use, including steroid use, on every aspect of an athlete's life—career, family, friends, sense of accomplishment, and self-esteem.

Private Victories. Illustrates the effects of drug and alcohol use on students and the value of positive peer influences in resisting peer pressure to use drugs.

Say No! To Drugs. A videotape that offers a practical, easy-to-follow approach to improve family communications, particularly on the subject of adolescent drug and alcohol use. It includes interviews with experts in the field. NIMCO, P.O. Box 009-GAM, Calhoun, KY 42327. 1-800-962-6662 $64.95

Alcoholism (DA, 26 min). This film discusses the difference between the use and the abuse of alcohol. Interviews with young people accentuate the growing problem of alcoholism with this age-group.

Alcoholism: A Model of Drug Dependency (CRM, 20 min). Examines the problem of alcohol in our society. Illustrates how insecure people turn to alcohol to relieve tension and soon become addicted.

An Ounce of Prevention (HR, 20 min). Examines the causes of alcoholism, the damage it inflicts upon the individuals and their families, and the newest treatment and prevention programs.

Last Call: Alcoholism and Co-dependency Alcoholism affects not only the person suffering from the disease but the alcoholic's family as well. This program takes an in-depth look at the effects of alcoholism on both the individual and the family. The program provides a broad insight into alcoholism and how it effects those on its periphery. (24 min. Color)

HALLUCINOGENS

LSD and Ergot. A dozen substances, all based on lysergic acid, have been developed from ergot to synthesize compounds to treat migraine and a variety of psycho-behavioral symptoms. The most notorious substance synthesized from lysergic acid is, of course, LSD, and the program shows the use of LSD and other psychedelic drugs by medical researchers and by a shaman in a healing ceremony. (26 minutes, color)

INHALANTS

Inhalant Abuse: Breathing Easy Inhalant abuse is a particularly sinister form of substance abuse because these substances are relatively easy to access, the "high" is reached quickly, abusers can become addicted in a very short time—and unless caught very early, it almost certainly leads to permanent damage to the brain and other vital organs. This program focuses on the causes of and prevention of inhalant abuse, looking at the psychological and physiological aspects of addiction. The program also shows the coordinated effort of one community to overcome this problem among its youth. (24 minutes, color)

COCAINE

Coca coca was used by Andeans for millennia to overcome hunger, thirst, cold, and fatigue. In 1855, Gaedecke isolated cocaine, which is a potent local anesthetic, temporarily blocking transmission of nerve impulses; around the same time, a beverage was developed from the cola nut. The result, of course: Coca Cola. This program traces the course of the cocaine and crack epidemics that hit worldwide proportions in the 70s, and demonstrates the difficulty of controlling a highly profitable business while simultaneously seeking to prevent abuse and keep cocaine available in the treatment of illness. (26 minutes, color)

Cracking a Craving this program explains the surge in cocaine use, research into what cocaine does to the brain, what makes the brain seek it again and again, and how cocaine and its smokable form, crack, differ in addictive potential. The program also explores ways to treat cocaine addiction. (26 minutes, color) **Recommended by** *Video Rating Guide for Libraries*

Cocaine: The End Of The Line This program explains the origin of cocaine, how it works, and how cocaine use is dangerous; shows how cocaine kills and injures otherwise healthy young people, defines the typical coke user; explains why cocaine is so addictive and why addiction is so difficult to overcome; and provides a quiz on some of the myths about cocaine. (58 minutes, color) **Recommended by** *Addiction & Recovery, School Library Journal, and Booklist*

HEROIN

The Opium Poppy The poppy and the juice of its fruit were among the earliest medications for pain; their use as a drug was not far behind. This program looks at opium and its even more active and powerful derivatives, morphine and heroin; presents archival film of an opium smoker of the 1920s; explains the pharmacological effects of morphine, its relationship to the sensation of pain, and its addictiveness; and examines the larger questions of pain, its physiological function, and the role of morphine as a palliative. (26 minutes, color)

Hooked on Heroin: From Hollywood to Main Street This program examines why some of the unlikeliest people have become junkies, like the Boy Scout who (24 years ago) "just wanted to try it," and the housewife who (seven years ago) was "just going to try it one time." It talks to Steve Tyler, lead singer of Aerosmith, who describes what it was like to be down—and to come back up, and recover; to DEA officers who warn of the growing epidemic of heroin addiction; and to a drug dealer who explains the attraction of snorting over shooting up. (52 minutes, color) **Students should see this presentation, not only for the information it offers, but also for the stereotype of the junkie it destroys. It proves that addiction can happen to us all. The video should be part of a high school drug education program."—***School Library Journal*

Female Alcoholism This program examines the changing stereotype of the female alcoholic and analyzed some case histories of alcoholic women. It explains the dangers of drinking during pregnancy, the effect of fetal alcohol syndrome on newborns, and the emotional effect on children of being raised by an alcoholic mother. (19 minutes, color)

Alcohol and the Family: Breaking the Chain This program analyzes the signs of alcoholism and shows how a family member, coworker, or friend can help break the chain; discusses the impact of alcoholism on the children of alcoholics; and evaluates the options and prognosis for alcoholism treatment. (25 minutes, color) **"All viewers, regardless of their circumstances, can gain some knowledge about alcohol abuse from this presentation...Recommended for junior high school through adult audiences.—***Booklist*

Alcohol Addiction Access and attitudes explain why people begin to drink; genetic predisposition may explain why some people cannot stop. At the Rutgers University Alcohol Research Lab, this program explores the nature of alcohol addiction, concluding that addiction is a biochemical disease still best treated by behavioral means. (23 minutes, color) **Recommended by** *School Library Journal*

Adult Children of Alcoholics: A Family Secret In this program, famous adult children of alcoholics speak out about childhood nightmares and adult behavior that continues to reflect the problem of a parent's alcoholism: some chose alcoholic partners, and others developed drug, gambling, or other addictions. All speak of the difficulties of coping with the damage inflicted by an alcohol-centered childhood. (52 minutes, color) **Recommended by *Addiction & Recovery***

Can You Stop People From Drinking? This program looks at how Russia and the U.S. are attacking the seemingly intractable problem of alcohol abuse by means of both old and new weapons—prohibition, hypnotism, imprisonment, surveillance, deception, aversion therapy, and such group therapy as Alcoholics Anonymous. (60 minutes, color) **Recommended by *Booklist* and *Video Rating Guide for Libraries***

Teens and Alcoholism In this timely program, teenagers from varying economic backgrounds—all recovering alcoholics—discuss their drinking histories, tell why and how they began drinking, how the drinking led to eventual alcoholism, and the steps taken to address the problem. Alcohol recovery therapist David Moore discusses the short- and long-term physiological effects of alcohol on younger people, and the overall psychology behind todays's teenage drinking epidemic. (18 minutes, color)

Kids Under the Influence this program looks at alcohol, our number one drug problem among kids. It examines school problems, run-ins with the law, and the long-term physical and psychological disorders caused by alcohol consumption; demonstrates the enormous influence of peer pressure and seductive advertisements; shows the wrenching process of rehabilitation; and explains why alcohol is so easily abused by young people and what can be done about it. (58 minutes, color) Gold **Award, Houston International Film Festival**
Recommended by *Adolescent Counselor, School Library Journal, Booklist, Voice of Youth Advocates,* and *Video Rating Guide for Libraries*

Substance Misuse There is a range of substances which, when used as intended and in the appropriate quantity, are beneficial: when misused, they are often deleterious to health and may be fatal. This program examines the most commonly misused substances, explaining the effects of each and the problems it can cause. The substances covered include: stimulants (amphetamines, caffeine, cocaine, nicotine, MDMA); depressants (alcohol, barbiturates, solvents, benzodiazepines); hallucinogens (cannabis, LSD, "magic" mushrooms); and opiates (morphine, heroin) (30 minutes, color)
Recommended by *School Library Journal*

The Power of Addiction This program covers both chemical and behavioral addiction, describes the sign of compulsive behavior, and analyzes such possible causes of addictive behavior as neurotransmitter imbalance and genetic and environmental factors. It also examines the physiological and psychological mechanisms of cocaine addiction and recovery from it. (19 minutes, color)

The Addicted Brain This documentary takes viewers on a tour of the world's most prolific manufacturer and user of drugs—the human brain. The biochemistry of the brain is responsible for joggers' highs, for the compulsion of some people to seek thrills, for certain kinds of obsessive-compulsive behavior, even for the drive to achieve power and dominance. The program explores developments in the biochemistry of addiction and addictive behavior. (26 minutes, color)

For additional video resource materials, please contact your Allyn & Bacon representative

Nietzel et al., *Abnormal Psychology*, Transparencies

Chapter Thirteen

	Text Figure Number	Text Page Number
71. Criteria for Substance Dependence		446
72. Four Models of How Alcohol Disorders and Other Mental Disorders May Be Related	13.2	452
73. An Expectancy Model of Alcoholism	13.3	456
74. A Spiral Model of the Stages of Change	13.5	468

14 Sexual and Gender Identity Disorders

CHAPTER OUTLINE

I. Human Sexuality (pp. 488-498)
    A. Aspects of Sexuality
        1. Gender identity—person's sense of being male or female
            a. Vast majorities gender identity consistent with biological sex
            b. Very rare case—*cross gender identification*
            c. Extreme—person changes physical appearance, sexual functioning
            d. Gender identity established as early as age two
        2. Gender role—patterns of behaviors expected of males or females in culture
            a. Preindustrial—women gathered food, men hunted game
            b. Contemporary male—assertive behavior aimed at achievement, ascendancy, power
            c. Contemporary female—nurturant behavior aimed at helping others, providing emotional support, preserving relationships
            d. May differ from one culture to another
        3. Sexual orientation—person's preference sexual behavior with male, female
            a. *Homosexual*—sexual activity with member of same sex
            b. *Lesbianism*—homosexual activities by females
            c. *Heterosexual*—sexual activity members of opposite sex
            d. *Bisexual*—sexual activity with members of both sexes
            e. For some, restricted to touching, kissing, genital intercourse
            f. Others, masturbation, oral sex, anal intercourse
            g. Some have only one partner; some have many
    B. Investigating Sexual Behavior
        1. What is *normal*?
            a. For some, acts that guarantee reproduction of the species
            b. For some, defined in terms of moral or religious codes in culture
            c. For some, what is most commonly done
        2. Survey by National Opinion Research Center, University of Chicago called National Health and Social Life Survey, 3000 people aged 18-59
            a. 1.4% of women; 2.8% of men homosexual or bisexual
            b. 60% of men; 40% of women masturbated in the past year
            c. By age 22, 90% of Americans have engaged in intercourse
            d. Only 17% of Americans had more than one sex partner in past year
            e. Only 5% of married admitted to having more than one partner
        3. Study people's sexual fantasies
            a. Mental images they find sexually arousing
            b. Helen Kaplan (1974) "Sex is composed of friction and fantasy."
            c. Brain is body's most important sex organ
            d. Men think sex a lot; ½ say sexual fantasies every day, several times
            e. Women few times a week or few times a month
            f. Reliving prior experience; most conventional; few "forbidden"

C. Biological Influences on Sexual Differentiation
   1. X and Y chromosomes
      a. 46 chromosomes in nucleus of each cell in body
      b. 2 of these, X and Y determine biological sex
      c. Females inherit two X chromosomes; 1 mother's 1 father's
      d. Males inherit one X from mother; one Y from father
   2. Before birth
      a. For first 8-12 weeks development males, females exactly alike
      b. Y chromosome directs cells into testicles, vas deferens, prostate
      c. Testicles then release testosterone (hormone stimulates development of male external sexual organs; substance that suppresses development of a uterus, vagina, other internal organs)
      d. If no Y chromosome, female sexual structures appear
   3. At Puberty
      a. Androgens (including testosterone) called male hormones
      b. Estrogens (estradiol, progesterone) called female hormones
      c. Both men and women produce androgens and estrogens
      d. Labels because men produce more androgens; women estrogens
      e. Androgen stimulates growth underarm and pubic hair in both
      f. Testosterone causes penile growth, muscle mass, beard, deep voice
      g. Estradiol, progesterone begin cycling of menstrual cycle
      h. Ovaries' testosterone stimulates clitoris, breasts, nipples
   4. Congenital adrenal hyperplasis
      a. Inherited disorder; body's adrenal glands produce excess androgen
      b. Masculinizes external genitalia of females in fetal development
      c. Babies born with clitoris so large it is mistaken for penis
      d. Girls demonstrate male gender role behaviors
      e. Gender identity remains female; sexual orientation heterosexual
   5. Testicular feminization
      a. Affects persons with XY chromosome complement typical of males
      b. Defective gene on the Y chromosome; cannot absorb testosterone
      c. Born with female external genitalia, raised as females
      d. Breast development occurs, no uterus or ovaries present
      e. Live lives as well-adjusted females; marry, adopt children
D. Sexual Orientation
   1. Sexual Orientation and Mental Health
      a. Before 1973 homosexuality classified as personality disorder
      b. In 1987 homosexuality left out of DSM-IIIR; not in DSM-IV
      c. Remains at center of moral, political, social controversy
      d. Test show no difference prevalence mental disorders
      e. More depression for homosexuals due to discrimination, rejection
   2. Frequency of Varying Sexual Orientations
      a. 64% non-Western cultures homosexual activities acceptable
      b. Other 36% present but not approved

            c. Strong religious societies—less common or less reported
            d. Kinsey—37% men, 13% women at least 1 homosexual experience
            e. Later reports—2.4% men exclusively homosexual; 2.6% bisexual
        3. Biological Factors in Development of Sexual Orientation
            a. Most homosexuals do not believe they had a choice
            b. Moderate degree of heritability
            c. Genetics play partial, but far from decisive role
            d. Neuroanatomical differences
                (1) Suprachiasmatic nucleus twice as large in homosexuals
                (2) Interstitial nuclei of anterior hypothalamus half the size
                (3) Larger forebrain structure, anterior commisure
        4. Development of Homosexuality: Psychological Factors
            a. Theories applied only to case of male homosexuals
            b. Traditionally believed
                (1) Male growing up with dominant mother who fails to establish healthy boundaries between herself and son
                (2) Fathers in this scenario are weak, passive men who fail to help their sons develop positive gender role identities
            c. Growing up with homosexual parents *does not* make child same

II. Gender Identity Disorders (pp. 498-503)
    A. Confusion about or dissatisfaction with biological gender
        1. Always involve two components
            a. Persistent cross-gender identification
            b. Profound discomfort even disgust with biological sex and organs
            c. Persons sometimes termed *transsexuals*
            d. Important: *not hermaphrodites* (both female and male sex organs)
    B. Prevalence
        1. Uncommon—3% for boys; less than 1% for girls
        2. 1 in 30,000 males; 1 in 100,000 females seek sex reassignment
    C. Gender Identity Disorder in Children
        1. Boys more often described as beautiful or feminine
        2. Not known if attractiveness is cause or effect
        3. Show preference for cross-gender toys, activities age 2 or 3
            a. Boys try to hide penis, tell parents they hope it will go away
            b. Girls wear male clothing, short haircuts, use boyish name
        4. By kindergarten, ostracized, elementary school target of relentless teasing
        5. Behaviors suppressed by negative feedback
        6. In longitudinal study, 80% reported being bisexual or homosexual
    D. Gender Identity Disorder in Adults
        1. Adult transsexuals fall into two major categories
            a. Homosexual (few asexual) experience since childhood
                (1) Seek professional help adopting desired gender
                (2) Sexual gratification limited role in desire
            b. Almost exclusive male; heterosexual in orientation
                (1) Some have married, fathered children

     (2) *Gender dysphoria* (dissatisfaction)
  E. Causes of Gender Identity Disorder
    1. Richard Green—parental indifference key variable
    2. Fathers aloof and uninvolved in upbringing
    3. Girls whose mothers are distant at risk
  F. Treatment of Gender Identity Disorders
    1. Usually first receive professional treatment starting school
     a. Parents worry that in boys may signal homosexuality
     b. Worry that treatment will impair self-esteem, creativity
    2. Critics charge—forces narrow definition of male, female behavior
    3. Psychological Treatments
     a. Goals—maintain self-esteem, teach gender-appropriate behavior
     b. Develop social, academic skills regardless of gender identity
     c. Behavior therapy for child, parent training or both
     d. Restrict time child spends with relatives encourage cross-gender
    4. Sex Reassignment Surgery
     a. Most adult transsexuals believe best intervention for them
     b. Not candidates unless lived for 1 year as member of desired gender
     c. Extensive psychological evaluation conducted to rule out mental disorders that make surgery inappropriate
     d. Female-to-male surgery requires removal of breasts; most do not seek penile surgery due to difficulties in creating functional penis
     e. Male-to-female surgery involves removal of penis, creation of vagina, hormone therapy to promote breast growth, electrolysis
III. Sexual Dysfunctions (pp. 503-516)
  A. The Sexual Response Cycle
    1. Sexual responsiveness 4-stage sequence of psychological changes, physiological reactions
     a. *Desire*—triggered by thoughts, fantasies
      (1) Starts anticipating emotional, physical reactions
      (2) Anticipation intensifies desire
     b. *Excitement*—changes in sexual organs, skin, throughout body
      (1) Increased heart rate, respiration
      (2) *Vasocongestion* (swelling) of penis or clitoris
      (3) Lubrication of vagina, flushing of abdomen, chest, face
      (4) Breast enlargement, erection of nipples
     c. *Orgasmic*—sexual pleasure peaks, involuntary rhythmic contractions
      (1) Males involves ejaculation of semen
      (2) Females contractions of labia minora, vagina, uterus
     d. *Resolution*—disengorgement of blood collected in sexual organs
    2. Sexual dysfunctions: some kind of problem in a phase and/or pain with
  B. Changing Views of Sexual Dysfunctions
    1. Late 19th early 20th centuries
     a. Psychoanalytic—unresolved conflicts from early childhood

                b. Long-term therapy, difficult to treat, outcomes poor
        2. Dramatically changed 1950s; research by William Masters, Virginia Johnson done at Washington University in St. Louis
                a. Laboratory studies with paid volunteers engaging in sex acts
                b. Studies of physiological changes; persons with dysfunctions also
        3. More detailed classification of sexual dysfunctions
                a. Distinguished between lifelong and acquired sexual disorders
                b. Psychological factors can affect sexual dysfunctions
                c. Prior to study only two dysfunctions were impotence, frigidity
        4. William Masters, Virginia Johnson, Helen Kaplan studies basis for sexual dysfunction categories described in the DSM
                a. Periods of stress or sorrow cause temporary disinterest in sex
                b. Host of occupational, familial, social, economic, other stressors
C. Factors Affecting Sexual Responsiveness
        1. Neurological and Vascular Factors
                a. Chronic medical conditions such as diabetes mellitus
                b. Emotional disorders such as clinical depression
                c. Use of certain medications
                d. Men, age-related decrements desire, arousal, activity
                e. Women, decline in estrogen, vaginal lubrication decreases
        2. Attitudes and Beliefs
                a. Religious view extramarital sex forbidden, Hispanic men machismo
                b. Parents punish young child for masturbating
                c. Parents encourage adolescent to carry condoms
                d. Episodes criticism, abuse, coerced sexual activity inhibits
        3. Interpersonal Factors
                a. Emotional closeness between partners enhances sexual behavior
                b. "Desire discrepancy" causes distress
                c. Among all active adults, married couples report highest pleasure
        4. DSM-IV four categories of disorders plus lifelong or acquired
D. Sexual Desire Disorders
        1. Hypoactive Sexual Desire Disorder
                a. Sexual fantasies infrequent, interest in sexual activity nil
                b. One feels distressed, no medical problem or mental disorder
                c. Inhibitions during childhood may carry over into adulthood
                d. Period of active desire stops when intense sexual attraction declines
        2. Sexual Aversion Disorder
                a. One fears or is disgusted by idea of sexual contact
                b. Some experience panic or revulsion of any kind of sexual behavior
        3. Prevalence
                a. Sexual aversion disorder not a common problem
                b. HSDD may affect 15-40% adult men and women in U.S.
                c. One report, 17% men, 39% women lifelong low desire
                d. Among patients seeking therapy, about 65% HSDD

4. Causal Factors
    a. Desire shaped by biological, cognitive, emotional factors
    b. Biological basis may be impaired, sometimes as natural aging
    c. Testosterone levels low, replacement increases desire both sexes
    d. Estrogen in women for comfort and response; not for desire
    e. Androgen and estrogen replacement for women increase desire
    f. Most cases HSDD, clear-cut biological cause not found
    g. Psychological causes more likely, failure to resolve tasks childhood
    h. Concerned with independence, "emotional claustrophobia"
    i. Anxiety, anger squelches desire; depression (prior or current)

E. Sexual Arousal Disorders
  1. Female Sexual Arousal Disorder
      a. Problems attaining, maintaining lubrication, genital swelling
      b. Woman distressed; not caused by medical, mental disorder
      c. History of sexual abuse may be factor
      d. Anxiety about sex major threat to adequate arousal
  2. Male Erectile Disorder
      a. Most common and demoralizing sexual dysfunction
      b. 90% develop after normal functioning; 50% some time in life
      c. 400,000 visits to physicians every year; 10-20 million men in U.S.
      d. Most attributed to medical condition, side effects medication, or other substances (substance-induced sexual dysfunction)
  3. Biological Factors
      a. Endocrine, vascular, neurological systems all contribute to erection
      b. Spontaneous erections diminish with decreases in testosterone
      c. Heart disease, arteriosclerosis (need 3 times more blood erection)
      d. Antihypertension drugs, high doses alcohol, smoking
  4. Psychological Factors
      a. Performance anxiety (Albert Ellis, man was "scared unstiff")
      b. Negative thoughts block out sexual cues
      c. Man becomes *distracted* and misses cues
      d. Myth that men are always ready to engage in sex regardless

F. Orgasmic Disorders
  1. Female Orgasmic Disorder
      a. Women experience normal desire, arousal but cannot have orgasm
      b. 10% of women have never had orgasm
      c. *Pubococcygeus muscle* controls vagina, women once told to exercise; was not answer; tensing and fantasy together work
      d. Excessive alcohol and drug use impairs ability to reach orgasm
      e. Age only psychosocial factor related to orgasmic function
      f. Depression interferes, antidepressant medications diminish
      g. Julia Heiman, sex researcher: sociocultural, interpersonal contexts
  2. Male Orgasmic Disorder and Premature Ejaculation
      a. Male orgasmic disorder
      b. Inability to reach orgasm or inordinately long delay during sex

       c. Still orgasms with ejaculation when masturbate or in "wet dreams"
       d. Some report penises numb after erection, beginning intercourse
       e. Not *retrograde ejaculation* (ejaculate into bladder)
       f. Lack of arousal or conflict with partner possible
       g. Premature ejaculation
       h. Man ejaculates before or immediately after penetration
       i. Occurs before person wants, marked distress, interpersonal problem
       j. Some men simply hypersensitive to sexual stimulation

G. Sexual Pain Disorders
   1. Dyspareunia
       a. Recurring pain before, during, or after sexual intercourse
       b. Both men and women can have, more common in women
       c. Women during intercourse, men during orgasm, ejaculation
       d. Male urinary tract infection; Peyronie's disease (fibrosis of penile connective tissue), prostatitis, gonorrhea, herpes
       e. Females infections of the urinary tract, vagina, cervix, fallopian tubes; scarring following surgery, ovarian cysts, tumors, endometriosis (growth of endometrial tissue occurs in pelvic cavity outside the uterus); decline in estrogen at menopause
       f. Woman associates sex with negative feelings or sexual trauma
   2. Vaginismus
       a. Involuntary spasm of musculature in outer third of vagina
       b. Makes penile penetration impossible
       c. Classical conditioning theory: women whose initial experience with intercourse was painful and aversive
       d. Harsh, demanding behavior by sexual partner

H. Treatment of Sexual Dysfunctions
   1. Masters and Johnson:
       a. Knowledge about sexual functioning; performance anxiety
       b. Teach sensate focus
   2. Treating Disorders of Sexual Desire
       a. Four-phases to become more aware of sexual sensations
       b. Quality of the couple's relationship
       c. Certain antidepressants enhance sexual desire in some
       d. Yohimbine hydrochloride (not an antidepressant) same
       e. Drug to increase heart rate, blood pressure, blood flow to penis
       f. Gonadal hormone therapies
   3. Treating Female Sexual Arousal Disorder
       a. Use of vaginal lubricants
       b. Address relationship problems
   4. Treating Male Erectile Disorder
       a. Reduce performance anxiety; Conflict resolution
       b. Learn to cope with disappointment

            c.   If organic—reduce alcohol use, change medications, correct endocrine imbalances, oral medications, hormone replacement, surgical implants, mechanical erectors
            d.   Penile prosthesis surgery
       5.   Treating Female Orgasmic Disorder
            a.   Dealing with relationship problems
            b.   Cognitive techniques
       6.   Treating Premature Ejaculation
            a.   Squeeze technique; stop-and-start technique
            b.   Medications
       7.   Treating Sexual Pain Disorders
            a.   Teach woman to relax; use sensate focus
            b.   Improve communication; reduce conflicts

IV.   Paraphilias (pp. 516-525)
     A.   Forms of Paraphilia
          1.   Fetishism
          2.   Transvestic Fetishism
          3.   Exhibitionism
          4.   Voyeurism
          5.   Frotteurism
          6.   Sexual Masochism and Sadism
               a.   Sexual sadism: inflicting physical pain or humiliation on partner
               b.   Sexual masochism: receiving painful stimulation; being humiliated
          7.   Sadism and Rape
               a.   Rape motives power, hatred, aggression
               b.   Crime of violence; not paraphilia
          8.   Pedophilia
               a.   Fantasies, behaviors involving sexual activity prepubescent child
               b.   Twice as common toward girls as boys
               c.   Incestuous pedophilia victims are family members
          9.   Prevalence of Paraphilias
               a.   Rough underestimate—80,000 arrests made each year
               b.   500 paraphelic acts per person
          10.   Causes of Paraphelias
               a.   Biological factors
               b.   Psychological factors
          11.   Treatment of Paraphilias
               a.   Behavioral methods
                     (1)   Covert sensitization
                     (2)   Olfactory aversion therapy
                     (3)   Shame aversion therapy
                     (4)   Masturbatory reconditioning
               b.   Multimodal treatment
               c.   Relapse prevention

14 Sexual and Gender Identity Disorders

LECTURE MAKER 14.1

Purpose	To explore possible homophobic attitudes among students. (pp.494-495)
Lecture Introduction	Obsessive hostility and fear toward homosexuals is termed homophobia. To begin the chapter on sexuality, this survey can serve as a "warm-up." Treating homosexuality with sensitivity is a must. Review the DSM-IV *exclusion* of homosexuality as a disorder. Discuss criteria for determining sexual behavior as pathological.
Demonstration	Duplicate the Index of Homophobia as a handout, with scoring. Emphasize that there are no right or wrong answers. This is an attitude survey and indicates only relative comfort or discomfort.
Lecture Capsule	Sexuality is not as "open" a topic in abnormal behavior as others. Students may need a little attitude exploration to be able to approach the concepts and behaviors clinically. This works well as a discussion starter.

LECTURE MAKER 14.2

Purpose	To have students provide their interpretations of normal/abnormal sexual behavior. (pp. 489-492)
Lecture Introduction	Sexuality is a subject that is personal and may be more sensitive than most. Present DSM information regarding abnormal sexual behavior.
Demonstration	Have students define what they believe to be normal sexual behavior. Expect a few giggles and groans. Remind the students that this is simply and exercise in definition building. There will be agreement on some items, and diversity on others. Sensitivity is the watchword.
Lecture Capsule	Students can work in groups in an attempt to solidify a definition of abnormal sexual behavior.

ARE YOU HOMOPHOBIC? 14.1

If you're interested in getting a better sense of whether you're homophobic or not, the Index of Homophobia (IHP) self-administered questionnaire reproduced here can give you an opportunity to find out. This questionnaire is not a test, so there are no right or wrong answers. Answer each item using the following scoring to indicate how you feel: 1 = strongly agree, 2 = agree, 3 = neither agree nor disagree, 4 = disagree, and 5 = strongly disagree.*

1. I would feel comfortable working closely with a male homosexual. _____
2. I would enjoy attending social functions at which homosexuals were present. _____
3. I would feel uncomfortable if I learned that my neighbor was homosexual. _____
4. If a member of my sex made a sexual advance toward me I would feel angry. _____
5. I would feel comfortable knowing that I was attractive to members of my own sex. _____
6. I would feel uncomfortable being seen in a gay bar. _____
7. I would feel comfortable if a member of my sex made an advance toward me. _____
8. I would be comfortable if I found myself attracted to a member of my sex. _____
9. I would feel disappointed if I learned that my child was homosexual. _____
10. I would feel nervous being in a group of homosexuals. _____
11. I would feel comfortable knowing that my clergyman was homosexual. _____
12. I would be upset if I learned that my brother or sister was homosexual. _____
13. I would feel that I had failed as a parent if I learned that my child was gay. _____
14. If I saw two men holding hands in public I would feel disgusted. _____
15. If a member of my sex made an advance toward me I would be offended. _____
16. I would feel comfortable if I learned that my daughter's teacher was a lesbian. _____
17. I would feel uncomfortable if learned that my spouse or partner was attracted to members of his or her own sex. _____
18. I would feel at ease talking with a homosexual person at a party. _____
19. I would feel uncomfortable if I learned that my boss was a homosexual. _____
20. It would not bother me to walk through a predominantly gay section of town. _____
21. It would disturb me to find out that my doctor was homosexual. _____
22. I would feel comfortable if I learned that my best friend of my sex was homosexual. _____
23. If a member of my sex made an advance toward me, I would feel flattered. _____
24. I would feel uncomfortable knowing that son's male teacher was homosexual. _____
25. I would feel comfortable working closely with a female homosexual. _____

*Items 3, 4, 6, 9, 10, 12, 13, 14, 15, 17, 19, 21, and 24 must be reverse scored. Then total your scores for the 25 items. A score of 75 or less indicates no homophobia, 88-99 indicates moderate homophobia, and 100- or more shows a high degree of homophobia.

Questionnaire from "*A Strategy for the Measurement of Homophobia,*" by Hudson and Ricketts, *Journal of Homosexuality* vol.5. pp. 357-372, 1980. Reprinted by permission of The Haworth Press, Inc., Binghamton, New York.

RESOURCES

General AASECT (American Association of Sex Educators, Counselors, and Therapists)
435 North Michigan Avenue, Suite 1717
Chicago, IL 60611
(312) 644-0828
>AASECT publishes the quarterly *Journal of Sex Education & Therapy* as well as a monthly newsletter, *Comtemporary Sexuality*. It will provide a list of certified sex therapists in your locale if you need it.

SIECUS (Sex Information and Education Council of the U.S.)
130 West 42 Street, suite 2500
New York, NY 10036
(212) 819-9770
>SIECUS publishes the bimonthly *SIECUS Report* and maintains an extensive sexuality library at New York University. It provides pre-printed comprehensive bibliographies on many sexual topics and will arrange to do computer searches of its data base on a very reasonable fee-for-service basis.

Society for the Scientific Study of Sex
Box 208
Mount Vernon, IA 52314
>SSSS publishes the bimonthly *Journal of Sex Research*

Kinsey Institute for Research in Sex, Gender, and Reproduction
Morrison Hall
Indiana University
Blooming, IN 47405
(812) 855-7686
>The Kinsey Institute has the most extensive library collection of materials related to sexuality in the United States.

Masters and Johnson Institute
24 South Kings Highway
St. Louis. MO 63108
(314) 361-2377
>While the MJI does not maintain a research library or other materials to assist students conducting research, it does have an active sex therapy program that accepts couples from around the world.

National Gay Task Force: 800-221-7044
Note: Additional listings of national and community-based AIDS organizations can be found in *AIDS Information Sourcebook: Second Edition, 1989-90* (H.R. Malinowsky and G. Perry, eds.) Published by Oryx Press, Phoenix, Arizona (800-457-6799).

Planned Parenthood Federation of America
810 Seventh Avenue
New York, NY 10019
(212) 541-7800

    Planned Parenthood has local clinics in cities throughout the country. (You can usually locate them through your local telephone directory; if not, you can contact the national office.) This organization offers a broad range of information on virtually every aspect of family planning and sex education through a series of pamphlets and classes, as well as providing clinical services such as contraceptive counseling, pregnancy testing, voluntary sterilization, preventive health-care exams (including Pap smears and breast exams), and early abortion services. (In some locations Planned Parenthood also offers confidential testing for HIV.

Population Information Program
Johns Hopkins University
527 St. Paul Place
Baltimore, MD 21202

    This program publishes the highly readable but thoroughly documented Population Reports about various family planning issues on a five times a year basis: back issues are available for many issues. They also run POPLINE, a computerized collection of more than 200,000 citations with abstracts, and will perform searches of this data base for a nominal fee.

Institute for the Protection of Gay and Lesbian Youth
110 East 23 Street
New York, NY 10010
(212) 473-1113

Lambda Legal Defense and Education Fund
132 West 43 Street
New York, NY 10036
(212) 944-9488

National Gay and Lesbian Task Force
1517 U Street NW
Washington, DC 20009
(202) 332-6483

National Lesbian and Gay Health Foundation
P.O. Box 65472
Washington, DC 20035
(202) 797-3708

Hepatitis Hotline: (404) 332-4555

    This service provided by the C.D.C. gives information on modes of transmission, prevention, and statistics related to all forms of viral hepatitis.

Herpes Resource Center: (415) 328-7710
STD National Hotline: (800)227-8922
A service provided by the American Social Health Association, this hotline deals with questions on any STDs.

Archives of Sexual Behavior
Plenum Publishing Company
233 Spring Street
New York, NY 10013

Family Planning Perspectives
Alan Guttmacher Institute
111 Fifth Avenue
New York, NY 10003

Journal of Homosexuality
The Haworth Press
10 Alice Street
Binghamton, NY 13904

Journal of Psychology & Human Sexuality
Haworth Press
10 Alice Street
Binghamton, NY 13904

Journal of Sex Education & Therapy
435 North Michigan Avenue, Suite 1717
Chicago, IL 60611

Journal of Sex & Marital Therapy
Brunner/Mazel, Inc.
19 Union Square West
New York, NY 10003

Journal of Sex Research
P.O. Box 208
Mount Vernon, IA 52314

Medical Aspects of Human Sexuality
Cahners Publishing
249 West 17 Street
New York, NY 10011

Sex Roles
Plenum Publishing Company
233 Spring Street
New York, NY 10013

Sexuality and Disability
Human Sciences Press
233 Spring Street
New York, NY 10013

Siecus Report
130 West 42 Street, Suite 2500
New York, NY 10036

National Center for the Prevention and Control of Rape
National Institutes of Mental Health
5600 Fisher's Lane
Rockville, MD 20857
(301) 433-1910

National Coalition Against Sexual Assault
8787 State Street
East St. Louis, IL 62203
(618) 398-7764

National Self-Help Clearinghouse
33 West 42 Street
New York, NY 10036
(212) 840-1259

If you need help in finding a self-help organization that we haven't listed here this national clearinghouse will help you find it.
Sex Addicts Anonymous
P.O. Box 3038
Minneapolis, MN 55403
(612) 871-1520

Internet

World Wide Web:
URL: **http://www.mit.edu:8001/people/sorokin/women/index.html**

Sexual Assault on Campus
While this list is not exclusively for women, it does concern violence against women on college and university campuses. Learn about anti-rape activist groups and help disseminate information about assaults and methods of reducing sexual assault against women.
Listserv Mailing List:
List Address: **stoprape@brownvm.brown.edu**
Subscription Address:
Listserv@brownvm.brown.edu

Media

In My Country: an International Perspective on Gender. This video is designed to be used as a resource for studying cultural attitudes related to gender. Divided into segments by topic, it covers division of household labor, types of discipline for boys and girls, marriage decisions, control of money, society's view of rape, care for the elderly, and attitudes towards homosexuals. It features interviews with people from Zaire, El Salvador, St. Vincent, England, Taiwan, Sweden, Lebanon, Japan, India, China, the Fiji Islands, and Mexico. (2 volumes, 90 minutes total)

The Sexual Brain. Study of the brain provides some of the answers that separate cultural and social from physiological distinctions between the sexes. This program shows some startling effects of hormone injections on brain structure and raises provocative questions about the sexual and reproductive roots of structural differences between males and females. (28 minutes, color)

Sexually Harassed Children. The bully in the schoolyard has been joined by the sexual harasser; as early as the first grade, a staggeringly large number of children have (or think they have) been sexually harassed by classmates, from getting "looks" to being the butt of jokes to having clothing ripped off or being forced to do something sexual. This specially adapted Phil Donahue show examines whether this is innocent child's play, normal sexual growing up, or burgeoning sexual harassment. (28 minutes, color)

Pedophiles. This program reports on child abusers who, despite repeated convictions and extensive therapy, continue their abusive behavior throughout their lives. The program examines some radical responses to recidivism and stresses the apparent evidence that there is no known effective rehabilitation. (52 minutes, color)

Childhood Sexual Abuse. This program looks at the ways in which adult women learn to work out the problems caused by sexually abusive fathers. Psychiatrists, social workers, and law enforcement officials explain how the pattern of abuse is often spread throughout the family, why children can be manipulated into silent acceptance of abuse, the signs of sexual abuse and how and to whom they should be reported, the reliability of children as witnesses, the teaching of prevention skills to children, and under what circumstances treatment of sex abusers can be effective. (26 minutes, color)

Child Sex Abusers. The typical sex abuse cycle—abused as a child, abuser as adult—is being replaced by an even more frightening scenario: more of today's abusers appear to be children. This specially adapted Phil Donahue program features mothers and their daughters who have been sexually abused by brothers, half-brothers, and neighborhood kids—one of the molesters was 13 and his victim was three. The program also features an expert who deals with abusive children, who counsels what signs to look for and what to do when it comes to abusive kids, and counsels kids who are being abused. (28 minutes, color)

No More Secrets. This program discusses the long-term damage that results from childhood sexual abuse, offers the stories of sexually abused children of adults who were abused as children, and shows how children can be encouraged to share their secret with those who can help put an end to the abuse. (24 minutes, color)

Stop It! Students Speak Out About Sexual Harassment. Students speaking out themselves about inappropriate sexual behavior make this program particularly effective in raising awareness about sexual harassment. The program addresses sexual harassment from the student point of view, form the experiences of those who have perpetrated it and of those who have been victimized by it. It helps students identify different kinds of sexual harassment, and it spells out clearly which behaviors are appropriate and which are not. The program is designed to stimulate discussion among students, faculty, and staff. It details the impact of harassment on victims, and advises students as to what actions they can take to stop harassment when it occurs. (17 minutes, color)

Rape: An Act Of Hate. This program examines the history and mythology of rape, seeks to determine why people rape, and helps people protect themselves against this crime. The program contains interviews with experts in the fields of media, law enforcement, and sociology.

Date Rape. This unique documentary-drama takes us inside the story of a rape, following the investigation as it would be conducted in real life. All of the professionals involved are real, with all the other roles played by actors. The program observes as the police investigate a woman's allegation of rape, friends and witnesses are questioned, forensic evidence is gathered, and the police try to find witnesses to corroborate her story. The man is called in for questioning and relates his version of the night's events. This powerful story demonstrates both the emotional issues of a case of date rape and the process by which police and prosecutors follow-up and prosecute a case. (52 minutes, color)

Men Who Molest: Children Who Survive (FML, 52 minutes, 1985) Four child molesters and their treatment; child victims, their families, and their treatment.

For additional video resource materials, please contact your Allyn & Bacon representative.

Nietzel et al., *Abnormal Psychology,* **Transparencies**

Chapter Fourteen

	Text Figure Number	Text Page Number
75. **DSM-IV Sexual and Gender Identity Disorders**	14.1	489
76. **Criteria for Gender Identity Disorder**		500
77. **The Human Sexual Response Cycle**	14.3	503
78. **Possible Causes of Hypoactive Sexual Desire Disorder**	14.4	507

15 Biological Treatment of Mental Disorders

CHAPTER OUTLINE

I. Psychosurgery (pp. 531-533)
    A. Psychosurgical Procedures
        1. Beginnings
            a. *Trephining*, prehistoric time, middle ages, some cultures today
            b. Holes in skulls of people to "let out the cause" of illness
        2. Later
            a. 1891, Gottlieb Burckhardt, Swiss neurologist destroyed small section of the cerebral cortex
            b. 1935, Antonio de Egas Moniz, Portuguese neurosurgeon introduced *prefrontal leucotomy, or lobotomy*; drill holes, inject alcohol; later injected wire loop and rotated it; made report in 1948
            c. Moniz received Nobel Prize for Medicine in 1949
            d. Americans Walter Freeman and James Watts developed *standard (frontal)* lobotomy, severed connections with rest of brain
            e. 1948, Freeman and Watts introduced *transorbital lobotomy*
            f. In 20 years more than 40,000 mental patients were lobotomized
            g. Popularity declined in 1950s; new information about dangers; introduction of psychoactive drugs capable of controlling disorders
            h. No alternative treatment for severe cases; patients violent, aggressive; surgery conducted in overcrowded mental hospitals
        3. Today
            a. *Cingulatomy*
                (1) Used for intractable cases depression, anxiety disorders
                (2) Lesions in fibers of Papez Circuit
            b. *Stereo-taxic subcaudate tractotomy*
                (1) Used for intractable cases depression, anxiety disorders
                (2) Disconnects portions frontal lobes from limbic system
    B. Outcomes of Psychosurgery
        1. Used for patients not responding to drugs or other treatment
        2. Use of technique highly controversial
        3. Controversy now beyond realm of science and medicine
        4. Ethical question—what should be allowed?

II. Convulsive Therapies (pp. 533-537)
    A. Insulin Coma and Metrazol Therapy
        1. Viennese psychiatrist Manfred Sakel
            a. Accidently gave an insulin overdose
            b. After coma, patient said morphine craving reduced
            c. Attributing her "cure" to coma, used on psychotic patient
            d. Patient's mental state appeared to improve
        2. Hungarian psychiatrist Ladislas von Meduna
            a. Reasoned that seizures and psychosis are incompatible

        b.   If seizure could be induced in schizophrenic, correct it
        c.   Used drug, metrazol to induce seizures
        d.   Although seizures intense, violent; treatment popular
        e.   Serious side effects; now virtual disappearance

B. Electroconvulsive Therapy
   1. Pioneered in Italy by Ugo Cerletti and Lucio Bini
        a.   Replaced insulin and metrazol treatment
        b.   First used 1938 on schizophrenic patient
        c.   Produces full-blown, grand mal epileptic seizure
   2. Modern ECT Procedures
        a.   Bilateral ECT used, but unilateral more common
        b.   Nonlanguage hemisphere selected to receive impulse
        c.   Lowest possible current used to produce seizure
        d.   Patient now given general anesthetic, muscle relaxants
        e.   Patient given supplementary oxygen; EEG used
        f.   Typically 10-12 sessions in 2 to 4 weeks
   3. Side Effects of ECT
        a.   Posttreatment headache, few hours of confusion
        b.   Memory impairment lasting up to 6 months
   4. Applications and Effects of ECT
        a.   1950s, 1960s widely used to treat many disorders
        b.   1970s, popularity reduced by concern, advent of drugs
        c.   1990s, resurgence in use of modern, safer versions
        d.   Now used severe mood, bipolar, major depression, etc
        e.   ECT produces equal or superior benefits to drugs in patients severely disturbed (suicidal, psychotically depressed)
        f.   ECT last resort, only following other unsuccessful treatments
   5. How Does ECT Work?
        a.   Hypothesis—correct imbalances endocrine, neurotransmitter systems
        b.   Affects serotonin, dopamine, norepinephrine, GABA, beta-endorphins
        c.   Not likely benefits due only, primarily to these
        d.   Max Fink—undiscovered substance *antidepressin* stimulated
   6. Current Status of ECT
        a.   Remains controversial therapy
        b.   Uncertainty over mode of action
        c.   Concern over side effects
        d.   Fears that linger from shadowy past
        e.   Proponents including APA see valuable therapeutic tool
        f.   Opponents say ECT cannot be justified under any circumstances
        g.   Topic of occasional court battles
        h.   Regulated by strict ethical and clinical guidelines in U.S.
        i.   Law requires patient's freedom accept, refuse treatment honored
        j.   Benefits and risks must be clearly spelled out

    k. Alternative treatments must be offered
    l. Information repeated before each and every treatment
III. Drug Treatments (pp. 537-554)
  A. Psychopharmacology
    1. Scientific field devoted to study of psychoactive drugs and use of
      a. Drugs called psychoactive or psychotropic
      b. Alter cognitive, emotional, behavioral processes
    2. Not only most common for mental disorders; for all medical treatments
      a. Galen created enormous pharmacopeia of herbal medicines
      b. Johann Weyer recommended cannabis for calming mind
    3. Today psychiatrists prescribe for up to 90% of patients
      a. General practice physicians prescribe them
      b. Late 1970s—8,000 *tons* benzodiazapines prescribed annually
      c. 1980s— 100 *million* prescriptions being written each year
      d. 1995—19 *million* prescriptions for Prozac
      e. Americans currently spend $3 billion a year antidepressants
      f. 1995 Worldwide sales $700 billion in drug therapies
  B. Psychoactive Drugs and How They Work
    1. Mechanisms of Action
      a. Exert effects on thought, mood, behavior
      b. Alter the biochemical environment of nervous system
      c. Modify action, availability of neurotransmitters
      d. Neurotransmitters facilitate, inhibit communication between nerve cells, or neurons, including those in the brain
      e. Altering of processes affect mental, behavioral processes mediated
      f. *Agonists* chemically similar enough to natural, can mimic its effects
      g. *Antagonists* similar, occupy sites but do not stimulate them
      h. Antagonist block action of natural transmitter
      i. Others prolong availability of neurotransmitters in gaps (synapses)
      j. One group antidepressants slows rate serotonin reabsorbed
      k. Blocking reuptake makes serotonin more available to operate
    2. Cautions
      a. Side effects: dry mouth, insomnia, urinary retention
      b. Can be physically, psychologically addictive
  C. Drugs for the Treatment of Mood Disorders
    1. Antidepressants
      a. MAO *monoamine oxidase inhibitors*
        (1) Monoamine oxidase enzyme breaks down serotonin, norepinephrine
        (2) Initially developed for tuberculosis; discovered improved mood
        (3) Create several troublesome side effects
          (a) Eliminate REM sleep
          (b) Combined with tyramine, extreme elevation of blood pressure

- b. *Tricyclic antidepressants* (TCAs) named for 3-ring molecular core
    - (1) Synthesized for treating schizophrenia; more beneficial depression
    - (2) Block reuptake of serotonin, norepinephrine
    - (3) Fewer side effects then MAO, no dietary changes
    - (4) Side effects: dry mouth, sleepiness, constipation, insomnia, blurred vision, decreased sex drive, dizziness, tremulousness, nausea
    - (5) TCAs and alcohol increase effects of both; potentially fatal results
    - (6) Can stimulate mania in persons predisposed to bipolar disorder
- c. *Selective Serotonin Reuptake Inhibitor (SSRI)*
    - (1) Affects serotonin rather than norepinephrine
    - (2) One, *fluoxetine*, marketed as Prozac
    - (3) As effective but has milder side effects than TCAs
    - (4) 1.5 million prescriptions Prozac monthly in U.S.
    - (5) Side effects—insomnia, joint pain, sweating, weight loss, sexual dysfunction, increased nervousness
- d. *Heterocyclic* antidepressants
    - (1) Popular due to relative lack of long-term side effects
    - (2) *Bupropion* (Wellbutrin) blocks reuptake of dopamine
    - (3) Much safer for patients with heart disease
- e. *Nefazodone* (Serzone)
    - (1) Combines mechanisms tricyclics and SSRIs
    - (2) Fewer negative side effects sleep, sexual functioning
- f. Potential dangers increased in elderly
    - (1) Drug metabolism slows with age
    - (2) Drugs do not break downs as readily; doses can accumulate
- g. Taken over long periods can produce dependence
    - (1) Abrupt withdrawal can result in malaise, anxiety, nausea and vomiting, headache, chills, sweating, insomnia
    - (2) Physicians recommend withdraw gradually
- h. Beneficial as long as person takes them
    - (1) 60-70% patient with major depression or dysthymia show improved mood, increased physical activity, increased appetite, beneficial weight gain
    - (2) Feel less hopeless and guilty, get more sleep without early morning awakening
    - (3) Move and think faster
    - (4) Effects do not appear 1 to 2 weeks after treatment begins
    - (5) Effects do not reach maximum for 4 to 6 weeks
    - (6) No type superior
    - (7) None shown effective for severe, psychotic depression
    - (8) Little evidence helpful to depressed children

2. Mood Stabilizers
   a. 1949, Australian psychiatrist, John Cade
      (1) *Llithium*, a mineral salt calmed manic patients
      (2) Now administered as lithium carbonate
      (3) Can prevent recurrence of depression and mania
      (4) Theory: reduces availability of dopamine, norepinephrine
      (5) Differs from antidepressants, alters *secondary messengers*
      (6) May affect electrolyte balances in neurons
      (7) Effective in up to 80% treated bipolar patients
      (8) Often used as *prophylactic* drug
      (9) Must be monitored; can reach toxic levels
      (10) Standard treatment— lithium combined with psychotherapy
   b. Two antiepileptic drugs used as adjunctive
      (1) *Carbamazepine* (Tegratol)
      (2) *Valproic acid* (Depakote or Depakene)

D. Drugs for the Treatment of Anxiety Disorders
   1. The Benzodiazepines
      a. Once known as minor tranquilizers; primarily for relief of anxiety
      b. Discovered in Poland in 1930s
      c. 1950s, scientists Hoffman LaRoche discovered properties Librium
      d. By 1970s Librium, Valium most widely prescribed drugs in N.A.
      e. By 1990, about 60 million prescriptions per year
      f. Developed due to concerns over barbiturates (previous antianxiety)
      g. Barbiturates sold illegally: "goofballs" "downers" "blues" "reds"
      h. Reductions in anxiety short-lived; last only as long as taking med.
      i. Side effects—drowsiness, fatigue, dizziness, clouded thinking
      j. If patient consumes alcohol, problems intensified
      k. Combined effects—severe impairment of motor skills
      l. Can lead to dependence; body develops tolerance; needs more
      m. If discontinued abruptly, panic, anxiety worse than ever
   2. Busiprone
      a. Side effects of benzodiazepine made need for new anxiolytic
      b. Newest nonbenzodiazepine anxiolytic busiprone (BuSpar)
      c. Acts by affecting receptors of serotonin, dopamine
      d. No serious side effects, physical or psychological dependence
      e. Only effects are minor dizziness and headaches
      f. Antianxiety effects for GAD equal to or greater than diazepines
   3. Antidepressants Used to Treat Anxiety Disorders
      a. Monoamine oxidase inhibitors (Nardil)
      b. Tricyclic antidepressants (Tofranil)
      c. Patients experience autonomic arousal, panic never materializes
      d. Specifically affect panic attacks; no relaxation, not agoraphobia
      e. SSRIs shown to have significant antipanic effects
      f. Antidepressant for OCD, *clomipramine* (Anafranil)
      g. Has most bothersome side effects; nausea, fatigue, headache

E. Drugs for Treatment of Schizophrenia and Other Psychoses
1. Drugs called *antipsychotics, major tranquilizers, neuroleptics*
2. Discovered early 1950s; revolutionized treatment severe mental disorders
3. Dramatically reduce hallucinations, delusions, paranoia, incoherence
4. Hospitalized patients no need for straightjackets, padded cells, etc
5. *Chlorpromazine* one of phenothiazines most widely used
6. Seen in U.S. as Thorazine in 1955
7. *Reserpine* (Serpasil) discovered at same time; side effects severe, not used
8. Haloperidol (Haldol) same effect phenothiazines, less sedation

F. Typical Neuroleptics
1. Thioridazine (Mellaril); fluphenazine (Prolixin) trifluoperazine (Stelazine)
2. Benefit thought to be blockage of action of dopamine

G. Side Effects of the Typical Neuroleptics
1. Bothersome effects—dry mouth, blurred vision, constipation, postural hypotension, urinary retention, others
2. More severe side effects—*extrapyramidal symptoms*, Parkinsonism (fine tremor of the hands; a slow, shuffling gait; a blank facial expression; muscular weakness and rigidity; slowed movement) results when dopamine level drops enough to be out of balance with *acetylcholine*. Balance can be restored by administering *anticholinergic drugs* to restore balance
3. Another set side effects called *acute dystonia*: uncontrollable contractions of muscles in head, neck, tongue, back, and eyes; give appearance of seizure
4. Third pattern—*acute akathesia*, patient appears uncontrollably restless and agitated; discomfort if remaining still
5. Most serious movement disorder *tardive dyskinesia* (TD) grotesque spasmodic jerks, tics, twitches of the face, tongue, trunk, limbs. The lips make smacking noises and sucking sounds, the jaw moves laterally, the limbs may writhe uncontrollably, speech is progressively impaired
6. Thankfully rare side effect *neuroleptic malignant syndrome*, potentially fatal disorder involving extremely high fever, muscle rigidity, irregular heartbeat, blood pressure; appears 1% patients within first few days
7. Atypical Neuroleptics
   a. Recent discovery *clozapine* (Clozaril), extremely effective
   b. Reduces positive and negative symptoms schizophrenia
   c. More effective for apathy and withdrawal
   d. Greater effect on D_4 dopamine receptors; weak effect D_2
   e. Potent antagonist serotonin, norepinephrine, histamine,, muscarinic acid (may be rebalances all)
   f. Side effects: dry mouth, sedation, dizziness, constipation, excessive salivation especially when asleep; no extra-pyramidal symptoms
   g. Greatest concern—1-2% develop potentially fatal blood disease (agranulocytosis) loss of white blood cells
   h. Must have blood cell count each week before medication
   i. 1994—*risperidone* (Risperdal) 1996—*olanzapine* (Zyprexia)

H. Drugs for the Treatment of Attention-Deficit/Hyperactive Disorder
1. Most Prevalent, Most Controversial Form of Treatment
   a. By mid-1990s, more than 2 million children in U.S. taking
   b. Psychostimulant most frequently used *methylphenidate* (Ritalin)
   c. Facilitates release of norepinephrine, dopamine; blocks reuptake
   d. *Pemoline* (Cylert) mimics rather than facilitates dopamine
   e. *Dextroamphetamine* (Dexadrine) similar to Ritalin
   f. Decrease disruptive behaviors in school
   g. Decreases in demanding behaviors, increases in "on-task" behavior and greater classroom productivity
   h. Help attention and concentration in most users; not just ADHD
   i. Effects last only while stimulant is in the body
   j. About as many adults as children now taking
   k. Abuse and recreational use now on the rise
2. Side Effects of Psychostimulants
   a. Tend to reduce food intake
   b. Insomnia, abdominal pain, headache, proneness to crying, nervous habits and tic, increased heart rate, blood pressure
   c. Need for *drug holidays* that correspond to school holidays

I. Ethnicity, Gender, and the Psychology of Drug Treatments
1. Vast Majority of Research done on European American males
   a. American population 50% female
   b. Growing proportions of ethnic minorities
   c. Tests done represent only 20% of world's population
   d. Individual differences can affect
      (1) *Pharmacokinetics*: way drugs are metabolized, absorbed, distributed in the body, and excreted
      (2) *Pharmacodynamics*: how drugs interact with receptors; what effects on cognitive, behavioral, emotional processes
2. Ethnicity
   a. Chinese patients in China require only half dose of TCAs
   b. African-Americans accumulate TCAs quicker; more side effects
   c. Chinese, Asians metabolize benzodiazepines more slowly
   d. Asians achieve higher blood concentration of medications
3. Gender
   a. Lower doses of benzodiazepines, neuroleptics needed for females
   b. Females greater side effects, including tardive dyskinesia
   c. Different depending on in menstrual cycle; taking birth control pills
   d. Twice as many females as males receive prescriptions

15 Biological Treatment of Mental Disorders

LECTURE MAKER 15.1

Purpose — To examine rules for safer drug use from a consumer perspective. (pp. 538-540)

Lecture Introduction — Therapists and clients should be medication educated. While it may seem obvious that medications can be dangerous, should be monitored, and need periodic review—it is worth a reevaluation.

Demonstration — Duplicate the Ten Rules For Safer Drug Use and the sample worksheet. Review the rules and the necessity for diligence in monitoring.

Lecture Capsule — Ask your students if they know people, especially elders, who still think it is OK to "share" their medications (an extremely dangerous practice).

LECTURE MAKER 15.2

Purpose — To critically review nine reasons why older adults are more likely to have adverse drug reactions than younger adults. (pp. 552-554)

Lecture Introduction — This exercise can serve as an adjunct to the chapter, integrating medication precautions and disorders related to aging. You might ask student to take a moment to jot down all the medications they have ever taken. That is very illuminating for them.

Demonstration — Duplicate the "Nine Reasons Why Older Adults Are More Likely" information for students. Discuss the implications of this information for therapists, clients, and medical doctors.

Lecture Capsule — Encourage personal responsibility and educated consumer awareness in relation to taking any medications.

TEN RULES FOR SAFER DRUG USE 15.1

Rule 1. **Have a "brown bag" session with your doctor.** Bring in all of your drugs and fill out the drug worksheet with your doctor.

Rule 2. **Find out if you are having any adverse drug reactions.** Obtain a PDR and read the book's descriptions of the drugs you are taking for the adverse reactions they can cause.

Rule 3. **Assume that any new symptom you develop after starting a new drug may be caused by the drug.** If you have a new symptom, report it to your doctor.

Rule 4. **Make sure drug therapy is really needed for your medical condition.** Ask your doctor to explain all the alternatives.

Rule 5. **If drug therapy is indicated, in most cases it is safer to start with a dose which is lower than the usual adult dose.**

Rule 6. **When adding a new drug, see if it is possible to discontinue another drug you are taking.** The fewer medications you take, the better.

Rule 7. **Stopping a drug is as important as starting it.** Do not take a drug any longer than it is necessary.

Rule 8. **Before leaving your doctor's office or pharmacy, make sure the instructions for taking your medicine are clear to you and a family member or friend.**

Rule 9. **Discard all old drugs: Carefully.** Avoid the possibility they might be taken inadvertently.

Rule 10. **Ask your primary care doctor to coordinate your care and drug use.**

Reprinted with permission: *Worst Pills/Best Pills* Sidney M. Wolfe, M.D., et al. Public Citizen Health Research Group. 2000 P Street N.W. Suite 700, Washington, D.C. 20036

SAMPLE PAGE OF DRUG WORKSHEET FOR PATIENT, FAMILY, DOCTOR, AND PHARMACIST 15.1

NAME: Beatrice Jones
PRIMARY DOCTOR'S NAME: Dr. Jackson

PAGE: 1
DOCTOR'S TELEPHONE: 555-1212

	A	B	C		C	D	E	F	G	H	I
Generic name of drug Brand name also	Doctor Date started and changes	Reason why prescribed or changed	Dose? (Each time)	Times per day	What time of day?	How long should you take drug? Days/Weeks/Months	Problems to watch out for which this drug can cause	Interaction of this drug with other drugs or food; diet recommendations	How are you actually taking the drug?	New problems or complaint since drug started? Date it began?	Is drug working?
Example: Hydrochlorothiazide (HydroDIURIL) This is an example only	Dr. Jackson 2/10/88	high blood pressure 180/100	12.5 mg ½ pill	once	morning	at least till next visit in 1 month	muscle weakness cramps from low potassium frequent urination common	1) Eat raisins, bananas, wheat germ, and drink orange juice for potassium	Most days 5-6/week	None	No
	4/8/88	pressure still high 165/100	25 mg 1 pill	once	morning	till next visit in 2 months		2) Avoid salt	stopped 5/1- felt too weak	Feeling tired 4/22/88	No
	5/15/88	pressure 165/95	12.5 mg ½ pill	once	morning	till next visit, 2 months			every day	None	Yes
	Dr. Lewis 10/19/88	pressure 155/87	same	once	same	till next visit 6 months		3) May lower effectiveness of diabetes drugs	every day	None	Yes

Instructions

1) Include all over-the counter drugs you take as well as prescription drugs.
2) When you change doses, draw a single line through the old dose.
3) Bring this with you every time you go to a doctor or pharmacist.
4) Be straightforward with your doctor and yourself about how often you take medicine and why.

Reprinted with permission: *Worst Pills/Best Pills* Sidney M. Wolfe, M.D., et al. Public Citizen Health Research Group. 2000 P Street N.W. Suite 700, Washington, D.C. 20036

NINE REASONS WHY OLDER ADULTS ARE MORE LIKELY TO GET ADVERSE DRUG REACTIONS THAN YOUNGER ADULTS (UNLESS THEY ARE GIVEN FEWER DRUGS AND SMALLER DOSES) 15.3

Some of the changes which eventually lead to more adverse reactions in older adults (in combination with increased drug use(, really begin to occur in the mid-thirties. The definition of older is above 50, younger being below 50.

1. **Smaller Bodies And Different Body Composition**

    Older adults generally weigh less and have a smaller amount of water and a larger proportion of fat than younger adults. Body weight increases from age 40 to 60, mainly due to increased fat, then decreases from 60 to 70 with even sharper declines from 70 on. Therefore, the amount of a drug per pound of body weight or per pound of body water will often be much higher in an older adult than it would be if the same amount of the drug were given to a younger person. In addition, drugs which concentrate in fat tissue may stay in the body longer because there is more fat for them to accumulate in.

2. **Decreased Ability Of The Liver To Process Drugs**

    Because the liver does not work as well in older adults, they are less able than younger people to process certain drugs so that they can be excreted from the body. This has important consequences for a large proportion of the drugs used to treat heart conditions and high blood pressure, as well as many other drugs processed by the liver. The ability to get rid of drugs such as Valium, Librium, and many others is affected by this decrease in liver function.

3. **Decreased Ability Of The Kidneys To Clear Drugs Out Of The Body**

    As people grow older, the ability of their kidneys to clear many drugs out of the body decreases steadily from age 35-40 on. By age 65, the filtering ability of the kidneys has already decreased by 30%. This process keeps getting worse with age, along with other aspects of kidney function. This affects a large number of drugs.

4. **Increased Sensitivity to Many Drugs**

    The problems of decreased body size, altered body composition (more fat, less water), and decreased liver and kidney function cause many drugs to accumulate in older people's bodies at dangerously higher levels and for longer times than in younger people. These age-related problems are further worsened by the fact that even at "normal" blood levels of many drugs, older adults have an increased sensitivity, often resulting in harm, to their effects. This is seen most clearly with drugs that act on the central nervous system such as many sleeping pills, alcohol, tranquilizers, strong painkillers such as morphine or pentazocine (Talwin), and most of the drugs which have "anticholinergic" effects. This latter group includes antidepressants, antipsychotic drugs, antihistamines, drugs which are used to calm the intestinal tract (for treating ulcers or some kinds of colitis) such as Donnatal, atropine, and Librax, antiparkinsonians and other drugs such as Norpace.

5. **Decreased Blood-Pressure-Maintaining Ability**

Because older adults are less able to compensate for some of the effects of drugs, there is yet another reason why they are more vulnerable to adverse effects of drugs and more sensitive to the intended effects.

The most widespread example of older adults' decreased ability to compensate is seen when they git out of bed and/or suddenly rise from a seated position. As you rise, your blood pressure normally falls, decreasing the blood flow to your head, resulting in less blood flow to the brain. Younger people's bodies can compensate for this: Receptors in the neck, sensing that the blood pressure is tending to fall as the person rises, tighten up the blood bessels in other parts of the body, deeping the overall blood pressure high enough. In older adults, these receptors do not work as well. Often, upon standing, older adults feel giddy, lightheaded, and dizzy. They may even faint because the blood pressure in the head fell too rapidly.

The ability to maintain a proper blood pressure is further weakened when you use any of a very long list of drug, the most examples being high blood pressure drugs. Other categories of drugs which cause an exaggerated blood pressure drop include sleeping pills, tranquilizers, antidepressants, antipsychotic drugs, antihistamines, drugs for heart pain (angina) and antiarrhythmia drugs.

This problem of so-called postural hypotension—the sudden fall in blood pressure on standing, brought about by a combination of aging and drugs—can be catastrophic, and the falls which often result can end in hip fractures, a leading cause of death in older adults, or other serious injuries.

6. **Decreased Temperature Compensation**

Younger adults are more easily able than older people to withstand very high or very low temperatures. They sweat and dilate (widen) blood vessels to get rid of excess heat when it is hot, and constrict (narrow) blood vessels to conserve heat when it its cold. Older adult's bodies are less able to do this. As in the case of blood pressure compensation, this "normal" temperature-regulating problem of older adults can be significantly worsened by any of a large number of prescription and over-the-counter drugs, resulting in fatal or life-threatening changes in body temperature. Many older adults' deaths during heat waves or prolonged cold spells can be attributed to drugs which interfere with temperature regulation. Most of these people did not know they were at increased risk. All drugs which contain a warning about anticholinergic effects can have this harmful effect on withstanding heat waves.

7. **More Diseases Which Affect The Response to Drugs**

   Older adults are much more likely than younger adults to have at least one disease—such as liver or kidney damage (not just the decreased function of older age), poor circulation, and other chronic conditions—which alter their response to drugs. Little is known about the influence of multiple diseases on drug effects in the elderly. One well-understood example, however, is the effect of heart failure on the way people can handle drugs. When the heart is not able to pump as much blood as it used to, the change which occurs in heart failure, there is also a decrease in the flow of blood to the kidneys. For the same reasons discussed in point #3, above, the reduced flow of blood to the kidneys harms the kidneys' ability to get rid of drugs from the blood and dump them in the urine.

8. **More Drugs And, Therefore, More Adverse Drug Reactions And Interactions**

   Since older adults use significantly more prescription drugs than younger people, they have greatly increased odds of an adverse drug reaction caused by the dangerous interaction between two drugs. Often, older adults may be taking one or more over-the-counter drugs in addition to their prescription drugs. This further increases the likelihood of adverse drug interactions. One of the more common kinds of adverse drugs interactions is the ability of some drugs to cause a second drug to accumulate to dangerous levels in the body.

9. **Inadequate Testing Of Drugs In Older Adults Before Approval**

   Although older adults use a disproportionate share of prescription drugs, few of theses drugs are adequately tested in older adults before being approved by the Food and Drug Administration (FDA).

   Dr. Peter Lamy of the University of Maryland, School of Pharmacy, has stated that "We test drugs in young people for 3 months; we give them to old people for 15 years."

Reprinted with permission: *Worst Pills/Best Pills* Sidney M. Wolfe, M.D., et al. Public Citizen Health Research Group. 2000 P Street N.W. Suite 700, Washington, D.C. 20036

RESOURCES

Internet The Institute for Safe Medication Practices
A nonprofit organization located in Warminster, Pennsylvania, USA
Voice (215) 956-9181 ▪ Fax (215) 956-9266
E-Mail ismpinfo@ismp.org
ISMP speakers travel extensively throughout the U.S. and internationally to conduct educational programs on adverse drug event prevention. Sponsoring organizations include professional societies, hospitals, professional loability firms, risk management companies, and medical, nursing and pharmacy schools.

Colorful medication safety posters (8.5 x 11 inch) are available from ISMP. The posters stress medication safety themes. Contact ISMP for further information or to obtain posters.

Pharmacology
American Psychological Association, Division of Psychopharmacology and Substance Abuse/galaxy/Medicine/Health-Occupations/Psychopharmacology.data.53012
Organization-HTTP/1.0 200 OK

Department of Defense Psychopharmacology Demonstration Project: Training Military Psychologists to Prescribe
The DoD Psychopharmacology Demonstration Project (PDP) examines the feasibility and desirability of training doctoral-level, licensed psychologists in the uniformed services to prescribe psychotropic medications.

Institute for Human Psychopharmacology
The Institute for Human Psychopharmacology (HIP)—formerly the Institute for Drugs, Safety and Behavior—is an international research centre in the field of human psychopharmacology.

Medical Sciences Bulletin: Psychopharmacologic and Neurologic (CNS) Drug Reviews//galaxy/Medicine/Health-Occupations/Psychopharmacology.data. 54204

CD-ROM **Psychopharmacology on CD-ROM**

CD-ROM, ISBN:0-397-51793-9
Institutional Price: for multiuser and network prices, contact Mike Wisniewski at (215) 238-4389,ISBN:0-397-51793-9
Edited by Floyd E. Bloom, MD, Chairman, Department of Neuropharmacology, The Scripps Research Institute, La Jolla, CA and David J. Kupfer, MD, Chairman, Department of Psychiatry, University of Pittsburgh School of Medicine, Pittsburgh, PA.

Available for the first time on CD-ROM, the gold standard reference, *Psychopharmacology,* brings you the latest advances in the basic and clinical aspects of neuropsychopharmacology. This CD-ROM contains the full text and illustrations from *Psychopharmacology: The Fourth Generation of Progress,* plus access to thousands of citations and abstracts from the world's leading neuroscience and psychiatry journals indexed through MEDLINE.

The user-friendly interface, full range of search capabilities, hypertext links, and state-of-the-art windowing features make Psychopharmacology on CD-ROM an invaluable tool for scientists and clinicians interested in all aspects of neuropsychopharmacology. This CD will run on both Windows and Macintosh platforms

Counseling Services
ASKPHARMACIST.COM
(301) 808-4194
Medication/pharmacy counseling Services
- Medication regimens recommendations, counseling and simplification
- Prescription and non-prescription (medication) product identification, selection or substitution
- Recommendation of dosage adjustments in kidney and liver failure patients.
- Evaluation and appropriate management of medication side effect, adverse drug reactions, drug-drug, food-drug, and drug-lab interactions
- Counseling lactating mothers and pregnant women about their medications

Pharmacotherapy Services:
- Chart reviews for patients, physicians, malpractice attorneys and other relevant health care providers to identify or minimize or eliminate inappropriate therapy
- Drug monitoring for patients on heart, diabetic, cancer, AIDS, asthma and other antibiotics medications
- Pharmacokinetics dosing consults for physicians
- Elimination of unnecessary therapeutic duplications, especially among the elderly
- Assist drug stores respond to audits by reimbursement groups

Media   *Preventing Medication Errors Through Failure Mode and Effects Analysis* (1993). Produced in cooperation with the Center for Proper Medication Use, Philadelphia, PA. (Available from ISMP)

For additional video resource materials, please contact your Allyn & Bacon representative.

16 Psychotherapy

CHAPTER OUTLINE

I. What Is Psychotherapy? (pp. 558-560)
    A. "Treatment of the Psyche"
        1. Treatment of an individual's behavior disorders by a therapist using psychological methods
        2. Therapist helps client change behaviors, thoughts, emotions; client feels and functions better
        3. Therapists can be psychiatrists, psychologists, clinical social workers, pastoral counselors, psychiatric nurses, etc, with training, experience
        4. Must have ability to listen with understanding and sensitivity *without being judgmental*, capacity for warmly supporting clients while challenging them to examine and change behavior
    B. Psychotherapy Clients and Their Problems
        1. People from all walks of life, all age groups, ethnic backgrounds, all social classes, all educational levels can benefit
        2. Women more likely than men to seek; both improve equally well
        3. People of lower socioeconomic class seek less often, stay less time
        4. Those higher levels of education continue in therapy longer
        5. Poor people of ethnic groups least likely to take part
        6. Embodies values usually associated with Western cultures
        7. Essential therapist conduct in culturally sensitive manner
        8. Problems brought to therapy in order of frequency
            a. Anxiety and depression
            b. Interpersonal problems
            c. Marital problems
            d. School difficulties
            e. Physical complaints
            f. Job-related difficulties
            g. Substance abuse
            h. Psychotic conditions
            i. Mental retardation
    C. Therapist Training and Experience
        1. Average psychotherapist sees five to ten clients per day
        2. Some specialize in one or two kinds of problems; some wide range
        3. Researchers claim untrained helpers do just as well as professionals
        4. Nonprofessionals supervised by professional clinicians
        5. Type of training unrelated; psychologists, psychiatrists, social workers all do equally well
        6. Novice therapists do as well as seasoned; lack finesse, make up enthusiasm
        7. Senior therapists better with more seriously disturbed clients
        8. Training, experience not irrelevant; less important than other factors

D. The Psychotherapy Relationship
   1. Single most crucial component of successful psychotherapy
   2. Attempt to build positive relationship (*working alliance*) with client
   3. Carl Rogers, founder client-centered therapy " the process of therapy is...synonymous with the experiential relationship between client and therapist"
   4. Sigmund Freud, therapy relationship primary vehicle for showing clients how early experiences cause current problems
   5. Heinz Kohut uses therapeutic relationship to offer clients new chance at soothing past insecurities and fears
   6. Interpersonal therapists—safe context to try out new ways of interacting
   7. Behavioral, cognitive-behavioral—help encourage clients' cooperation
   8. Therapeutic relationship flourishes when
      a. Client, therapist have strong personal commitment to therapy effort
      b. They communicate clearly with each other
      c. Therapist shows genuine concern for client's well-being
      d. Give clients information early on what to expect from therapy
      e. Tell clients therapist's and client's responsibilities will be
      f. After *therapeutic contract*
         (1) Maintain conditions facilitate relationship
         (2) Keep confidential what clients reveal
         (3) Maintain professional demeanor toward clients
         (4) Do not show sexual attraction, resentment, pity
         (5) Attentive to, supportive of client's attempts to change
         (6) Should not provide outlet for therapists' frustrations, parenting needs, other impulses
         (7) Best relationships when *client's* welfare primary concern

II. Methods of Psychotherapy (pp. 561-574)
   A. Psychoanalysis
      1. Goal—help clients understand *unconscious* reasons they act in maladaptive ways, convince no longer valid, so they can behave more constructively
      2. Involves years of treatment; two types of self-exploration
         a. Clients achieve conscious *insight* long-hidden nature of problem
         b. Now *work through* insights how unconscious conflicts affect now
      3. Free Association
         a. Client says anything comes to mind no restrictions, no censoring
         b. Client lies on couch, analyst sits out of view (reduce distractions)
      4. Dream Interpretation
         a. Freud: "royal road to an understanding of the unconscious mind"
         b. Manifest content less important than *latent content*
      5. Interpretation of Everyday Behavior
         a. Day-to-day behavior reflects unconscious conflicts and defenses
         b. Slips-of-the-tongue; jokes; "accidental" events; forgetfulness

6. Analysis of Resistance
    a. Resistance strategies thought to reveal habitual psychological defenses; major target of interpretations
    b. Clients find ways to resist coming to grips with threatening or conflict-filled material
    c. Resistance appears in intellectualization; substitute logic for the expression of emotion
    d. Unwillingness to talk about certain topics; tardiness; canceling sessions; stating preference not to recline during session
    e. Client develops cough when unconscious material about to emerge
    f. *Acting out*, client behaves in reckless, impulsive ways to escape anxiety bound up with repressed material (substance abuse, spending sprees, other dramatic life changes)
7. Analysis of the Transference
    a. Client begins to unconsciously transfer to analyst characteristics of significant people from the past, usually parent
    b. Client begins to reenact reactions, conflicts, impulses associated with important figures (usually ones at heart of client's difficulties)
    c. Reactions appear as intense hatred or passionate love for therapist
    d. Turns into *transference neurosis*, miniature version client's problem
    e. Transference neurosis becomes focus of treatment
    f. Analysts trained to be keenly alert to their own unconscious feelings toward clients—*countertransference*— so no distortion

B. Variations on Psychoanalysis
    1. Past 25 years, scholars concluded Freud's theory devoid of scientific merit; treatment methods ended up doing more harm than good
    2. Freud's contemporaries revised or replaced principles, techniques
    3. Psychoanalytically Oriented Psychotherapy
        a. Clients sit up and face therapist; 1 or 2 sessions per week, not daily
        b. Conversation about present problems
        c. Does not encourage transference; utilizes empathic relationship
        d. Alexander calls *"corrective emotional experiences"*
        e. Takes less time; 20-30 sessions
    4. Ego Analysis
        a. Heinz Hartman, Erik Erikson, Anna Freud (daughter of Freud)
        b. Freudian analysis too preoccupied with sexual, aggressive
        c. Emphasize importance of ego; ability of people to direct behavior
        d. Focus on ego rather than id
        e. Help clients understand how they relied on defense mechanisms
    5. Adler's Individual Psychology
        a. Alfred Adler most striking contrast to Freud
        b. Individual striving to overcome personal inferiority or weakness most important; *not* sexual and aggressive instincts

    c. Mental disorders seen as consequences of deep-seated *mistaken* beliefs, leading to maladaptive *style of life* aimed at protecting them from *perceiving* their own imperfections and weaknesses
    d. Suggest alternative beliefs, attitudes; encourage client to adopt
   6. Object Relations and Self Therapy
    a. Ronald Fairbairn, Donald Winnicott, Melanie Klein, Otto Kernberg
    b. Heinz Kohut—interactions between caregivers, infants in first 3 years building blocks of adult personality—guide expectations about close relationships for the rest of their lives
    c. Certain personality disorders result inadequate nurturance, empathy
    d. Self-psychology approach—analyst's task to be responsive, empathetic therapist, through transference, allows the client's self to be "completed" by having early unmet needs fulfilled
    e. Three types special transferences essential
     (1) *Mirror transference* early needs to be admired met
     (2) *Idealizing transference* needs protection and soothing met
     (3) *Twinship transference* needs for being close to another person who is like oneself met
     (4) Therapists offer better-late-than-never parenting
 C. Interpersonal Therapies
   1. Harry Stack Sullivan: disturbances in interpersonal relationships, developed out of early interactions between children and their parents and peers
   2. Mental disorders consist of "rigid, constricted and extreme patterns of interpersonal behaviors"
   3. Clients perpetuate maladaptive behaviors by provoking others to behave in ways that reinforce these behaviors
   4. Major goal for therapist to counteract clients' ploys
   5. Help clients understand how they perpetuate conflicts by displaying exaggerated dependence, hostility
   6. Teach style was learned in childhood; now dysfunctional, self-defeating
   7. Teach more flexible, positive ways
   8. Myrna Weissman, Gerald Klerman approach concentrates on developing strategies for coping with
    a. Prolonged grieving over the loss of a loved one
    b. Conflicts between social roles
    c. Difficult transitions between roles
    d. Lack of interpersonal skills
   9. Reduce feelings of dependency and increase self-esteem
 D. Phenomenological/Experiential Therapies
   1. Vary considerably; share five distinguishing features
    a. Meaning of life not intrinsic; constructed by perceiver; came to be known as the *Gestalt* school
    b. Once clients allowed to reach full potentials, find their own solutions; described as *humanistic* therapies

- c. Therapeutic relationship primary vehicle; focus on immediate, moment-to-moment experiences creates positive perception
- d. Clients are regarded as equals; responsible individuals; experts on their own experiences; ultimately can make own decisions
- e. Emphasize importance of experiencing, exploring emotions that are confusing or painful
  - (1) *Empty chair technique* increases awareness of unresolved conflicts and emotions from past
  - (2) Client imagines person from past occupies chair
  - (3) Client expresses, sometimes for first time, feelings about person in chair and events or conflicts in which involved
  - (4) Explore feelings in safe, supported environment
  - (5) Client will take responsibility for and master feelings

2. Client-Centered Therapy
   - a. Pioneered by Carl Rogers
   - b. Self-actualization thwarted by judgments imposed by others
   - c. Judgments create *conditions of worth*
   - d. Therapist must communicate three related attitudes (facilitative conditions)
     - (1) Convey *(unconditional positive regard)*
     - (2) Strive for *empathic understanding*
     - (3) *Genuine* in relating to client; all actions, feelings *congruent*

3. Gestalt Therapy
   - a. Developed by Fritz Perls
   - b. Gaps or distortions in peoples' awareness of their genuine feelings
   - c. Find it difficult to directly experience and express emotions like anger or the need for love
   - d. Develop manipulative social games or phony roles to try to satisfy need indirectly; the more energy, the more unhappy
   - e. Ploys lead people to believe they are not responsible for behavior
   - f. Eventually feel powerless; experience perceived helplessness
   - g. Many want therapist to solve problems for them
   - h. Gestalt therapy focuses on helping clients
     - (1) Become aware of feelings and need that they have disowned
     - (2) Recognize feelings and needs are genuine part of themselves and should be accepted, even celebrated
     - (3) Therapist more active and confrontive than client-centered
     - (4) Talking gets nowhere; they *must reexperience* old hurts, resentments, jealousies, and fears if feelings are ever understood, accepted, and defanged
     - (5) Clients asked to role-play significant people in lives
     - (6) Empty chair dialogues hallmark of Gestalt therapy
     - (7) Client asked to become body part; say what it's expressing
     - (8) Client asked to enact own manipulations
     - (9) Method helps people become aware of genuine feelings

     (10) Reduce emotional upset
     (11) After session; lowered blood pressure, reduced anger
  E. Behavioral Therapies
    1. B.F. Skinner coauthored paper using term
     a. Views disordered behavior as learned
     b. Aimed to literally teach clients to behave more adaptively
    2. Behavior Therapy now includes techniques aimed at
     a. Decrease maladaptive; develop more adaptive behavior
     b. Replace self-defeating thoughts with rational
     c. Control disruptive emotions
     d. Focus on the here and now
     e. Improve social skills, reduce phobias
     f. Practicing self-rewarding thoughts to improve job performance under stress
    3. Systematic Desensitization
     a. Developed by Joseph Wolpe in the 1950s
     b. Relies on principle of *reciprocal inhibition*
     c. Relaxation exercise brings about reduced sympathetic nervous system arousal
     d. Next, client exposed to gradually more anxiety-arousing stimuli
     e. Can be *in vivo* or *imaginal*
     f. Client must be relaxed at one level before attempting next
    4. Exposure Treatments
     a. Direct exposure to frightening stimuli
     b. Anxiety disappears through process called *extinction*
    5. Social Skills Training
     a. Social skills deficits lead person to feel demoralized, anxious, resentful, depressed
     b. *Assertiveness training* express feelings, wants more clearly, effectively
     c. Appropriate expression in way do not infringe on rights of others
     d. Four components
      (1) Distinguishing assertiveness from aggressiveness, submissiveness
      (2) Discussing personal rights and rights of others
      (3) Identifying and eliminating cognitive obstacles
      (4) Practicing assertive behavior
    6. Modeling
     a. Albert Bandura—modeling more efficient than direct reinforcement
     b. Eliminates trial and error; commonly used in fear-reduction therapy
     c. *Coping modeling* model copes with, overcomes fear
     d. Quickly improve competence, increased self-efficacy
    7. Contingency Management
     a. Principles of operant conditioning; reinforcement contingencies
     b. Clients taught to use self-control

                c.   *Contingency contracting* formal agreement client and therapist
                d.   *Token economy*
            8. Biofeedback
                a.   Behaviors to be changed heart rate, blood pressure, brain waves
                b.   Requires special equipment
                c.   Treat high blood pressure, bruxism, seizures, incontinence, migraine
            9. Aversion Therapy
                a.   Use of painful or unpleasant stimuli to decrease unwanted behavior
                b.   Employed as last resort in cases of dangerous behavior
        F. Cognitive Therapies
            1. Alter not only behavior but also maladaptive thoughts and beliefs
            2. Beck's Cognitive Therapy
                a.   Aaron Beck's therapy applied to anxiety, personality disorders, substance abuse problems; most focus on depression
                b.   Therapists teach clients to identify cognitive distortions
                c.   Ask them to examine whether valid evidence for these views
                d.   Clients discover no such evidence exists or they have been exaggerating the importance of negative events or the significance of potential threats (*catastrophizing*)
                e.   Clients helped to develop more realistic thoughts
            3. Ellis's Rational Emotive Therapy
                a.   Albert Ellis core principles simple as ABC
                    (1) Activating events (A) are followed by upsetting emotional consequences (C). A appears to but does not cause (C)
                    (2) Problem in how person *thinks* about activating events; in other words the person's *belief system* (B)
                    (3) Beliefs extreme, irrational, self-defeating
                    (4) RET challenges beliefs, replaces them with logical thoughts
                    (5) Therapists active, challenging, demonstrative, abrasive
III. Evaluating Psychotherapy (pp. 575-584)
    A. Methods of Evaluating Psychotherapy
        1. Experimental Group Designs
            a.   Clients displaying same kinds of disorder randomly assigned to experimental group receives therapy or no-treatment group
            b.   Dependent variables measured in both groups
            c.   Measures repeated at various intervals
            d.   Researchers add groups, conditions (*factorial designs*)
            e.   One group may get *psychological placebo* treatment
        2. Placebo Groups in Psychotherapy Research
            a.   Listening attentively given in placebo is actual therapy
            b.   Carries connotation effects are trivial or short-lived
            c.   Clients in placebo groups show improvement over no-treatment
        3. Within-Subject Designs
            a.   Repeatedly observing dependent variable (fear, depression) before independent variable (treatment) is manipulated

        b.   *Baseline* measures followed by *intervention* phase
        c.   Additional strategies; ABAB design *(reversal)*; multiple baseline
        d.   Sometimes conducted on only one subject (N=1)
              (1)   Offers empirically based look at own effectiveness
              (2)   Allows research on specific techniques
              (3)   Allows clients to see if desired changes are occurring

B.   The Validity of Experiments on Psychotherapy
      1.   Ideal experiment designed for high internal validity
      2.   Allows confidence results due to independent variable
      3.   Try to have high external and statistical validity
      4.   External validity—results can be generalized
      5.   Statistical validity— enough persons to allow statistical analyses
      6.   Analogue research— laboratory approximates of real clinical settings
      7.   *Consumer Reports Survey*, 7000 readers answered questions

C.   Research on the Outcome of Psychotherapy
      1.   Began in 1952 by British psychologist, Hans J. Eysenck
      2.   Reported rate of *spontaneous remission* to be 72%
      3.   Meta-Analysis
          a.   Technique combining results of several studies
          b.   Mary Smith, Gene Glass published *The Benefits of Psychotherapy*
          c.   Results of 475 psychotherapy studies
          d.   *Effect sizes* computed for several dependent variables
          e.   Receiving therapy 2 to 1 chance of doing better
          f.   Type or level of training for therapist did not matter
          g.   Behavioral therapies more effective phobias, panic attacks
      4.   Conclusions About Psychotherapy's Effectiveness
          a.   Is an effective treatment for wide variety of disorders
          b.   *Consumer Reports Survey*
              (1)   90% felt better after treatment
              (2)   No particular approach any better than other
              (3)   Psychologists, psychiatrists, social workers rated higher than family physicians or marriage counselors
              (4)   Gains last as long as 18 months
              (5)   Amount of experience of therapist unrelated to success
              (6)   Benefits appear after 6 to 8 sessions
              (7)   Type of therapy makes little difference to effectiveness
              (8)   Cognitive, behavioral slight advantage over traditional
          c.   Clinical Significance
              (1)   Compare test scores or behavior of treated clients to those of people who do not suffer from disorder under study
              (2)   If treated clients now resemble members of normative group, treatment said to be clinically significant
              (3)   Encouraging to report results of psychotherapy clinically as well as statistically significant

16 Psychotherapy

LECTURE MAKER 16.1

Purpose To examine student's attitudes toward seeking professional psychological help. (pp. 558-559)

Lecture Introduction Many of those who need therapy do not get it for a variety of reasons. Some of those reasons include a negative attitude toward professional therapy. Stereotypes still exist suggesting personal weakness in those who seek help for "personal problems." This exercise highlights some of the stereotypical attitudes.

Demonstration Duplicate the Attitude Toward Seeking Professional Psychological Help scale with scoring and interpretation. If students go into this field, they will surely spend time dealing with these attitudes. It is an excellent illumination device.

Lecture Capsule This is a great starter for the chapter and discussion.

Reference From "Orientations to Seeking Professional Help: Development and Research Utility of an Attitude Scale," by E.H. Fischer and J.L. Turner, 1970 *Journal of Consulting and Clinical Psychology,* 35, pp. 82-83. Copyright 1970 by the American Psychological Association. Reprinted by permission.

LECTURE MAKER 16.2

Purpose To evaluate student ability to elicit self disclosure from others. (p. 560)

Lecture Introduction Techniques can be taught, theories applied, and knowledge amassed. An effective therapist needs the educational foundation and the ability to create a warm and accepting therapeutic atmosphere for disclosure. This exercise is a great opener for a psychotherapy chapter.

Demonstration Duplicate the Opener Scale with scoring and interpretation. Have students complete the scale anonymously. Discuss the implications of high, medium, low scores.

Lecture Capsule Students are often drawn to clinical psychology because other have told them what good listeners they are. This quick inventory can validate that observation. The therapeutic relationship is one of trust, respect, and intimate disclosure. A high score on this test indicates someone who can fairly readily establish an accepting atmosphere. Students enjoy this survey.

ATSPPH SCALE 16.1

Read each statement carefully and indicate your agreement or disagreement, using the scale below. Please express your frank opinion in responding to each statement, answering as you honestly feel or believe.

0 = Disagreement   1 = Probable disagreement   2 = Probable agreement   3 = Agreement

_____ 1. Although there are clinics for people with mental troubles, I would not have much faith in them.
_____ 2. If a good friend asked my advice about a mental health problem, I might recommend that he/she see a psychiatrist.
_____ 3. I would feel uneasy going to a psychiatrist because of what some people think.
_____ 4. A person with a strong character can get over mental conflicts by himself, and would have little need for a psychiatrist.
_____ 5. There are times when I have felt completely lost and would have welcomed professional advice for a personal or emotional problem.
_____ 6. Considering the time and expense involved in psychotherapy, it would have doubtful value for a person like me.
_____ 7. I would willingly confide intimate matters to an appropriate person if I thought it might help me or a member of my family.
_____ 8. I would rather live with certain mental conflicts than go through the ordeal of getting psychiatric treatment.
_____ 9. Emotional difficulties, like many things, tend to work out by themselves.
_____10. There are certain problems that should not be discussed outside of one's immediate family.
_____11. A person with a serious emotional disturbance would probably feel most secure in a good mental hospital.
_____12. If I believed I was having a mental breakdown, my first inclination would be to get professional attention.
_____13. Keeping one's mind on a job is a good solution for avoiding personal worries and concerns.
_____14. Having been a psychiatric patient is a blot on a person's life.
_____15. I would rather be advised by a close friend than by a psychologist, even for an emotional problem.
_____16. A person with an emotional problem is not likely to solve it alone; he or she is likely to solve it with professional help.
_____17. I resent a person—professionally trained or not—who wants to know about my personal difficulties.
_____18. I would want to get psychiatric attention if I was worried or upset for a long period of time.
_____19. The idea of talking about problems with a psychologist strikes me as a poor way to get rid of emotional conflicts.
_____20. Having been mentally ill carries with it a burden of shame.
_____21. There are experiences in my life I would not discuss with anyone.
_____22. It is probably best not to know *everything* about oneself.
_____23. If I were experiencing a serious emotional crisis at this point in my life, I would be confident that I could find relief in psychotherapy.
_____24. There is something admirable in the attitude of a person who is willing to cope with his/her conflicts and fears *without* resorting to professional help.
_____25. At some future time I might want to have psychological counseling.
_____26. A person should work out his/her own problems; getting psychological counseling would be a last resort.
_____27. Had I received treatment in a mental hospital, I would not feel that it had to be "covered up."
_____28. If I thought I needed psychiatric help, I would get it no matter who knew about it.
_____29. It is difficult to talk about personal affairs with highly educated people such as doctors, teachers, and clergymen.

DEMONSTRATION/ACTIVITY: ATTITUDE TOWARD PSYCHOTHERAPY 16.1

Fisher and Turner (1970) developed the Attitudes Toward Seeking Professional Psychological Help (ATSPPH) Scale to assess one's attitude toward professional psychotherapy. Data in the text show that fewer than half of those who need therapy actually get treatment. There are a multitude of reasons for this finding, presumably some of which revolve around stereotypes people hold about therapy, such as the notion that people who are in therapy have personal weaknesses. Negative attitudes about therapy that stop people from seeking help are unfortunate, because potential clients may miss treatment that would be of great benefit to them.

You can use Fischer and Turner's scale to assess students' attitudes toward seeking professional psychological help. The test notes that males are less likely to enter therapy than females. Does your class demonstrate a gender difference in scores on this scale? If not, what other reason(s) might explain the gender difference in seeking therapy?

Scoring of the scale is relatively simple.

Responses on items 1, 3, 4, 6, 8, 9, 10, 13, 14, 15, 17, 19, 20, 21, 22, 24, 26, and 29 must be reversed
(0 = 3, 1 = 2, 2 = 1, 3 = 0).

Add up the responses for all items to find the overall score.

The higher the score, the more positive the attitude toward therapy.

Norms

	Males	*Females*
High score	68+	75+
Medium score	44—67	52—74
Low Score	Below 44	Below 52

Fischer, E.H., & Turner, J.L. (1970). Orientations to seeking professional help: Development and reaearch utility of an attitude scale. *Journal of Consulting and Clinical Psychology, 35, 79-90.*

OPENER SCALE 16.2

For each statement, indicate your degree of agreement or disagreement, using the scale shown below. Record your responses in the spaces on the left.

    4 = strongly agree
    3 = slightly agree
    2 = uncertain
    1 = slightly disagree
    0 = strongly disagree

___ 1. People frequently tell me about themselves.
___ 2. I've been told that I'm a good listener.
___ 3. I'm very accepting of others.
___ 4. People trust me with their secrets.
___ 5. I easily get people to "open up."
___ 6. People feel relaxed around me.
___ 7. I enjoy listening to people.
___ 8. I'm sympathetic to people's problems.
___ 9. I encourage people to tell me how they are feeling.
___ 10. I can keep people talking about themselves.

To score the scale, add up the response numbers for each question.
Miller, Berg, and Archer provided the following norms.

	Females	Males	
High score	35—40	33—40	Easily elicit personal information
Intermediate score information	26—34	23—32	Moderately able to elicit personal
Low score	00—25	00—22	Low degree of personal disclosure elicitation

Miller, L.C., Berg, J.H. & Archer, R.L. (1983) Openers:
 Individuals who elicit intimate self-disclosure
Journal of Personality andSocial Psychology, 44 1234-1244

RESOURCES

General   InterPsych's Scholarly Electronic Conferences

InterPsych's electronic conferences exist to provide a forum for scholarly and clinical discussion of all aspects of psychopathology. Individuals doing research, scholarship, or clinical work (or those who have an interest) in the areas described below are invited to join these e-mail conferences. When you elect to join any of InterPsych's conferences, you will be sent an introduction which elaborates further on the purposes of the conference, lists files in the conference archives, and gives instructions for participating in a conference. Note that InterPsych lists are distributed among several different server computers, each with a different administration and sign on method. These include Netcom, PsyCom, SJU, etc.

The Short List of Email Forums

add_med (substance-related disorders)	SJU
affective-disorders_	netcom
ak-health	APA
anxiety-depression-youth	SJU
anxiety-disorders_	netcom
attach	SJU
assess (assessment-psychometrics)	SJU
behavioral-cardiology	netcom
child-adolescent-psych_	SJU
clinical-psychologists_	NoDak
computers-in-mental-health_	netcom
curent-issues-in-psych	netcom
depression-1	netcom
dissoc (dissociative-disorders)_	SJU
eating-disorders	SJU
emergency-psychiatry	netcom
forensic-psych_	SJU
geriatric-neuro	netcom
group-psychotherapy	APA
helplessness-1	APA
hiv-aids-psycho-social_	netcom
hypnosis-1_	netcom
latin-Psych	SJU
mbhc (managed-behavioral-healthcare)	
mental-health-in-the-media	netcom
neuro-psych_	netcom
personality-disorders_	netcom
psa-public-sphere	Sheffield
psy-language	SJU
psych-admin	netcom

psychiatry-1_	netcom
psych-nurses	netcom
psychiatric-social-workers	netcom
psychiatry-resources	netcom
psycho-analysis	netcom
psychoanalytic-studies	Sheffield
psycho-pharm_	PsyCom
psychotherapy-practice_	PsyCom
psychotherapy-research_	PsyCom
psyphy (clinical-psychophysiology)	APA
research-psychologists	netcom
rural-care	APA
sexual-variants-and-disorders_	netcom
thana-tology_	PsyCom
transcultural-psychology	
traumatic-stress	

The usual method for registering for a forum is via a single piece of e-mail.

SEND E-MAIL TO THE APPROPRIATE SERVER
IN THE BODY OF THE E-MAIL TYPE:
SUBSCIBE name of the forum

For example, here's how Jane Doe subscribes to ASSESS (assessment-psychometrics)

SEND E-MAIL TO:
listserv@sjuvm.stjohns.edu

IN THE BODY OF THE E-MAIL TYPE:
Subscribe ASSESS

Another example, here's how Jane Doe subscribes to affective-disorders

SEND E-MAIL TO:
listserv@netcom.com

IN THE BODY OF THE E-MAIL TYPE
Subscribe affective-disorders

If your web browser supports e-mailing, you can try to subscribe right now. Just click on the server you want to send to, and type in the body of your message.

- =listserv@netcom.com
- =listserv@sjuvm.stjohns.edu
- =listproc@sheffield.ac.uk
- =majordomo@psycom.net

If you are having problems with subscribing or unsubscribing at Netcom, contact the "Vacation Peon" at <u>vacation@netcom.com</u>

For example, here's how Jane Doe sends a message to ASSESS:

SEND E-MAIL TO:
assess@sjuvm.stjohns.edu

IN THE BODY OF THE E-MAIL TYPE
whatever the message is

Another example, here's how Jane Doe sends a message to affective-disorders:

SEND E-MAIL TO
affective-disorder@netcom.com

IN THE BODY OF THE E-MAIL TYPE
whatever the message is

Some forums require user-verification. These are denoted by an asterisk (*) below on the short list of forums.

These other InterPsych forums are limited ofr use to mental health and behavioral science professionals, professional-oriented students, and special others only after user authentication via fax or e-mail.

PSYCHOANALYSIS on mailbase@mailbase.ac.uk

This psychoanalysis mailing list is intended to promote open discussion of psychoanalytic ideas. Discussion of clinical issues, theoretical problems, organizational developments, empirical investigations, applications of psychoanalytic ideas to other disciplines and the history of psychoanalysis. It is open to all those interested in psychoanalysis.

Please remember that material posted on this list is public and may be widely distributed. No clinical material that would not be appropriate for publication in a newspaper should be described here.

To join send the message:

join psychoanalysis firstname lastname

to MAILBASE@MAILBASE.AC.UK

The list's owner is robert Galatzer-Levy, M.D.
psychoanalysis-request@mailbase.ac.uk
or gala@midway.uchicago.edu or Compuserve 72255,1101
181 N. Michigan Ave
Suite 2401
Chicago, IL 60601

American Psychoanalytic Association

Accredited Training Institutes

BALTIMORE-WASHINGTON INSTITUTE FOR PSYCHOANALYSIS, INC
Founded in 1933
14900 Sweitzer Lane, Suite 102, Laurel, MD 20707
Telephone: (410) 792-8060; (301) 470-3635
Fax: (410) 792-4912

BOSTON PSYCHOANALYTIC SOCIETY AND INSTITUE, INC
Founded in 1933
15 Commonwealth Avenue, Boston, MA 02116
Telephone: (617) 266-0953
Fax: (617) 266-3466

CHICAGO INSTITUTE FOR PSYCHOANALYSIS
Founded in 1932
122 South Michigan Avenue, Chicago, IL 60603
Telephone: (312) 922-7474
Fax: (312) 922-5656

COLUMBIA UNIVERSITY CENTER FOR PSYCHOANALYTIC TRAINING AND RESEARCH
Founded in 1944
722 West 168 Street, Box 63, New York, NY 10032
Telephone (212) 927-5000

DENVER INSTITUTE FOR PSYCHOANALYSIS
UNIVERSITY OF COLORADO, SCHOOL OF MEDICINE
Founded in 1969
University of Colorado School of Medicine
4200 East 9 Avenue, C255-64, Denver, CO 80262
Telephone: (303) 270-7776
Fax: (303) 270-7777

FLORIDA PSYCHOANALYTIC INSTITUTE
6701 Sunset Drive, Suite #212A, Miami FL 33143
Telephone: (305) 669-4353

THE INSTITUTE OF THE PHILADELPHIA ASSOCIATION FOR PSYCHOANALYSIS
Founded in 1949
15 St. Asaph's Road, P.O. Box 36, Bala Cynwyd, PA 19004
Telephone: (610) 667-8708; 667-8719
Fax: (610) 667-8719

American Psychoanalytic Association

Affiliate Societies and Study Groups

THE ASSOCIATION FOR PSYCHOANALYTIC MEDICINE (NEW YORK)
c/o Eugene L. Goldberg, M.D. Secretary
903 Park Avenue, New York, NY 10021
Telephone: (212) 879-8850
Fax: (718) 548-8302

ATLANTA PSYCHOANALYTIC SOCIETY
c/o Salley Jessee, M.D. Secretary
5064 Roswell Road, N.E., Suite D-201
Atlanta, GA 30342
Telephone: (404) 252-4525

CHICAGO PSYCHOANALYTIC SOCIETY
122 South Michigan Avenue, Chicago, IL 60603
Telephone: (312)-922-7474
Fax: (312) 922-5656

DALLAS PSYCHOANALYTIC SOCIETY
c/o Fred Griffin, M.D.
8117 Preston Road, Suite 685, Dallas, TX 75225
Telephone: (214)-360-9260

DENVER PSYCHOANALYTIC SOCIETY
4200 East 9 Avenue, C-255-64, Denver, CO 80262
Telephone: (303) 270-7776
Fax: (303) 270-7777

FLORIDA PSYCHOANALYTIC SOCIETY
6701 Sunset Drive, Suite #212A, Miami FL 33143
Telephone: (305) 669-4353

LONG ISLAND PSYCHOANALYTIC SOCIETY
c/o Jerald Steisel, M.D.
11 Flamingo Road North, East Hills, NY 11576
Telephone: (516) 621-8904

LOS ANGELES PSYCHOANALYTIC SOCIETY AND INSTITUTE
2014 Sawtelle Blvd., Los Angeles, CA 90025
Telephone: (310) 478-6541
Fax: (310) 477-5968

NEW YORK PSYCHOANALYTIC SOCIETY
247 East 82 Street, New York, NY 10028
Telephone: (212) 879-6900
Fax: (212) 879-0588

THE PSYCHOANALYTIC ASSOCIATION OF NEW ENGLAND, EAST
c/o Charles Goodstein, M.D.
171 Devon Road, Tenafly, NJ 07670
Telephone: (201) 871-4649

WASHINGTON PSYCHOANALYTIC SOCIETY
4925 MacArthur Blvd. N.W., Washington, DC 20007
Telephone: (202) 338-5453
Fax: (202) 338-1521

WESTERN NEW ENGLAND PSYCHOANALYTIC SOCIETY
225 Bradley Street, New Haven, CT 06510
Telephone: (203) 562-2103

WESTERN NEW YORK PSYCHOANALYTIC SOCIETY
c/o Carol Munschauer-Pearson, Ph.D.
Telephone: (716) 835-8288

STUDY GROUPS

ARIZONA PSYCHOANALYTIC STUDY GROUP
c/o Monique V. King, M.D.
7841 E. Sabino Crest Place, Tucson, AZ 85750
Telephone: (520) 577-3294

MINNESOTA PSYCHOANALYTIC STUDY GROUP
c/o Margaret C. Keenan, M.D.
610 Foshay Tower, 821 Marquette Avenue
Telephone: (612) 339-0736

NASHVILLE PSYCHOANALYTIC STUDY GROUP
c/o Thomas W. Campbell, M.D.
113-30 Avenue N. Nashville, TN 37203
Telephone: (615) 385-9999

PSYCHOANALYTIC STUDY GROUP OF SOUTH CAROLINA
c/o Clyde H. Flanagan, Jr., M.D., Secretary-Treasurer
Department of Neuropsychiatry & Behavioral Science
University of South Carolina School of Medicine
3555 Harden Street Extension, Columbia, SC 29203
Telephone: (803) 434-4250

SOCIETY OF PSYCHOANALYSTS OF PUERTO RICO
c/o Alberto Varela, M.D.
Ave. de Hostos #431, Hato Rey, PR 00918
Telephone: (809) 758-4845

AMERICAN PSYCHOANALYTIC ASSOCIATION
309 East 49 Street
New York, NY 10017
Telephone: (212) 752-0450
Fax: (212) 593-0571
FAX-ON-DEMAND (212) 980-1831

Media **CASSETTES**

Scientific meetings of the American Psychoanalytic Association have been recorded on audio and video cassettes and are available through:

Teach'em Inc.	(312) 467-0424
160 East Illinois Street	(800) 225-3775
Chicago, IL 60601	

Orders for books should be mailed to

The American Psychoanalytic Association
309 East 49 Street
New York, NY 10017
Phone (212) 752-0450
FAX   (212) 593-0571
FAX-ON-DEMAND (212) 980-1831

Approaches to Therapy. In this video, one client is seen in three one-on-one therapy sessions that demonstrate the psychodynamic, humanist, and cognitive-behavioral approaches to therapy. Experts analyze each session, focusing on how the therapist and client interact. They discuss how the three approaches differ and explain the value of eclectic approach. They also offer strategies for finding a good therapist. (30 min, 1990)

Psychotherapy. Part of the series *Discovering Psychology,* this video examines different methods for treating psychological disorders. Featuring demonstrations and interviews with Hans Strupp, Albert Ellis, Rollo May, and Enrico Jones, it profiles the psychodynamic, rational-emotive, humanistic, and behavioral approaches to therapy. (30 min, 1990)

Three Approaches to Counseling. This video teaches how to integrate three models of counseling: psychodynamic dream analysis, humanistic positive reframing, and behavioral assertiveness training. Psychologist Allen Ivey works with a single client using each of the three theoretical perspectives, demonstrating how to apply each approach in a counseling session. (80 min)

Therapy Choices. This program explores three group approaches to therapy: family systems, group, and self-help approaches. Clients are seen in these therapeutic settings and experts discuss each approach. (30 min)

The Clinical Psychologists. This program demonstrates how a clinical psychologist performs an initial assessment, develops a hypothesis that guides initial treatment, and monitors a client's progress. Through the case of an individual recovering from brain damage, it shows how the psychologist assesses emotional, social, and cognitive deficits using both an informal assessment (an interview) and a formal assessment (a battery of psychometric tests). It shows how the psychologist develops a series of coping strategies for a client as well as how he assesses progress.

For additional video resource materials, please contact your Allyn & Bacon representative

Ethnicity and Counseling. Each video in this series contains an introduction to counseling a particular ethnic group, an actual counseling session, interviews with specialists, and a summary of pertinent issues. The videos focus on particular aspects of each culture that may affect a counseling session and show specific strategies for interaction with clients. The individual volumes are *Mexican Clients (43 min), Vietnamese Clients (71 min), African-American Clients (65 min),* and *Native-American Clients (88 min).*

Freud: The Hidden Nature of Man. Using dramatized interviews with Sigmund Freud, this video examines psychoanalysis, the Oedipus complex, the unconscious, infantile sexuality, and the relationship of the id, ego, and superego. It uncovers Freud's ideas in the same way the psychologist himself uncovered them—throught the analysis of dreams. (29 min)

The Talking Cure: A Portrait of Psychoanalysis. This program uses an experimental approach to evoke the experience of psychotherappy. Images of patients' lives are blended with their personal reflections on therapy, helping viewers to understand what happens inside psychoanalysis. Therapists describe traditional psychoanalysis and reveal how patients most commonly respond to the process. (56 min)

Carl Rogers. Carl Rogers compare the humanistic model of personality with other theories. In Part 1, he discusses motivation, perception, and learning, describes his development of client-centered psychotherapy, and points out the pros and cons of encounter groups. In Part 2, Rogers discusses his views on education, student unrest of the 1960s, and issues facing psychologists. (Part 1, 50 min) (Part 2, 50 min)

Title: *Guilt Detection*
Source: Psychology on a Disk
CMS Software
P.O. Box 729
Ellicott City, MD 21043
Type of Software: Simulation
Content: Student go through a free-association task in an interesting exercise in which they simulate guilt in a theft.

Title: *Psychoanalysis of a Dream*
Source: PsychWorld
McGraw-Hill Publishing Company
1221 Avenue of the Americas
New York, NY 10020
Type of Software: Simulation
Content: The student tries to analyze one of Freud's dreams by assessing dream symbols.

Readings AMERICAN PSYCHOANALYTIC ASSOCIATION

PERIODICALS

Journal of the American Psychoanalytic Association (quarterly)

For information regarding subscriptions:

The Analytic Press, Inc.
810 East 10 Street
P.O. Box 1897
Lawrence, KS 66044-1897
(800) 627-0629

Tap-Newsletter Of The American Psychoanalytic Association

For information regarding subscriptions:

The Analytic Press, Inc
Journal Subscription Department
10 Industrial Avenue
Mahwah, NJ 07430-2262
Email The Anayltic Press
(800) 926-6579
Fax: (201) 236-0072

17 Alternatives to Individual Psychotherapy

CHAPTER OUTLINE

I. The Limits of Psychotherapy (pp. 591-592)
   A. Accessibility
      1. Not available to many people who need it
         a. For some, obstacle is financial
         b. In U.S. 30 million people have no health insurance
      2. Even if free some reluctant
         a. Some men feel it is weak or unmanly talking about intense feelings with another person, especially stranger
         b. Family members discourage; think it stigmatizes the family
         c. Cultural expectations influence willingness to enter therapy
         d. Some view as pointless, shameful, or selfish
      3. If everyone wanted it
         a. Never be enough mental health professionals for individual psychotherapy for all those who need it
         b. Psychotherapists concentrated in affluent sections of larger cities, especially along east and west coasts
   B. Focus on Individuals
      1. Assumption something *inside* client needs to change
         a. Way clients think
         b. Emotions they experience
         c. Behaviors they display
      2. Pays too little attention to social aspects of mental disorders
         a. Interventions must address social conditions
         b. Must address environmental stressors
         c. In diathesis-stress model likely to trigger or worsen disorders
   C. Emphasis on Pathology
      1. Critics say individual psychotherapy emphasis on what is *wrong*
      2. Lack of attention to people's competencies
      3. Alternative goal
         a. Maximize positive outcomes by building up strengths
         b. Promote wellness as a goal for *all* people, not just ill
      4. Wellness marked by
         a. Occupational effectiveness
         b. Satisfying interpersonal relationships
         c. Feeling of belongingness, control, self-esteem
      5. *Psychological wellness orientation*
         a. Calls for mental health professionals to be more proactive, less reactive
         b. Design programs that promote wellness from start of life
         c. Not just intervening only after problems identified

II. Alternative Forms of Psychological Treatment (pp. 592-602)
    A. Group Therapy
        1. First practiced by Joseph Pratt, turn of 20th century
        2. Allows several unrelated people to discuss their (usually similar) problems with one another under the guidance and leadership of group therapist
        3. Partial answer to problem— too few professional available to treat flood of mental disorders following World War II
        4. Every major theoretical approach now offered in group format
        5. Popular with nonprofessional, self-help organizations focusing on
            a. Weight loss
            b. Assertiveness
            c. Alcoholism
            d. Recovery from sexual abuse
            e. Any and all problems
        6. Some groups, principles individual psychotherapy employed with many
            a. Treatment methods do not differ substantially from individual
            b. Main special feature is clients can talk to one another, observe
            c. Popular—cognitive-behavioral group for depression, anxiety
        7. Other kinds focus on facilitating group interactions; eight factors
            a. Sharing new information
            b. Consensuality
            c. Instilling hope
            d. Universality
            e. Altruism
            f. Interpersonal learning
            g. Recapitulation of the primary family
            h. Group cohesiveness
        8. Practice of Group Therapy
            a. Usually consist of 6 to 12 people
            b. Some *homogeneous*, members similar in age, gender, problems
            c. Some *heterogeneous*, different types clients and problems
            d. Sessions usually twice as long as individual
            e. Longevity varies—6 sessions to years
            f. Preferred treatment among HMOs
        9. Effectiveness of Group Therapy
            a. Empirical evidence confirms can be effective
            b. Members must clearly understand how group run, what expected
            c. Better outcomes when group is cohesive
            d. No evidence individual treatment superior
    B. Marital Therapy
        1. Statistics
            a. Half of all marriages in U.S. end in divorce
            b. Many that endure racked with conflict, distress
            c. Epidemic of personal unhappiness, millions broken homes

2. Social Problems
   a. Spousal, child abuse
   b. School problems
   c. Conduct disorder
   d. Adolescent suicide
   e. Substance abuse
3. Marital Therapy (Couples Therapy)
   a. *Conjoint* therapy when both members see same therapist in same sessions
   b. Involvement of client's partner recommended when
      (1) Related to depression, alcoholism, severe anxiety disorder
      (2) Effects of partner's alcoholism or depression threaten the integrity of the relationship
      (3) *Separation counseling* to help end marriage or long-term relationship minimum conflict; desirable for child custody
4. The client is the *disturbed relationship*, not the individual
   a. Usually arises from expectations, needs of *couples*
   b. Conflicts, problems
      (1) Sexual satisfaction
      (2) Personal autonomy
      (3) Dominance/submission
      (4) Responsibility for child rearing
      (5) Communication
      (6) Emotional or psychological intimacy
      (7) Money management
      (8) Fidelity
      (9) Expressions of disagreement and hostility
5. Marital Therapy Techniques
   a. Behaviorally oriented approach: communication problems
      (1) Teach to replace hostile, unconstructive criticism with comments to express feelings clearly, requests openly
      (2) *Behavioral exchange* contracts established
   b. *Cognitive-behavioral* approach—change the way they *think*
      (1) Couples become preoccupied with deciding who to blame
      (2) Attribute dishonorable motives to everything said or done
      (3) Therapist may show anger; may reflect anxiety about future of relationship, not necessarily an intention to end it
   c. *Emotionally focused*
      (1) Help partners more comfortable expressing, accepting needs
      (2) Allow partners become aware of and resolve resentment
   d. *Insight-oriented*
      (1) Here, problems may be unconscious
      (2) Unresolved conflicts from family of origin

6. Communication Training
   a. Almost all therapists employ
   b. Theoretical orientation influences
7. Effectiveness of Couples Therapy
   a. As many as half of treated relationships remain distressed
   b. Marital enrichment programs do not produce lasting change
   c. No advantage for different approaches
   d. Behavioral, insight therapies reported improvement
   e. Most of therapy improvements did not last long term
   f. Insight oriented treatment best long term improvement

C. Family Therapy
   1. Change patterns of family interaction to correct family disturbances
   2. Problems seen in individuals have social contexts, consequences
   3. Family dynamics in
      a. Childhood behavior problems
      b. Eating disorders
      c. Schizophrenia
      d. Affective disorder
      e. Various medical conditions
   4. Family environment, parent-child interactions causes maladaptive behavior
   5. Family role shown—schizophrenia or other severe mental disorder patient improves in hospital; relapses when returned to family
   6. Most grounded in *systems theory*; emphasizes three principles
      a. *Circular causality*—behavior of one depends on that of each of others
      b. *Ecology*—understood as integrated patterns; not collection of parts
      c. *Subjectivity*—no objective views; only *subjective perceptions*
   7. Therapy begins by focusing on member having most obvious problem
      a. Person is *identified client*
      b. Family's "ticket of entry" to treatment
   8. Aims at improving communication among family members
      a. Many families methods involve threats or coercive messages
      b. Members give in to coercive demands to avoid more severe conflict
   9. Techniques of Family Therapy
      a. *Behavioral* therapists teach alternative noncoercive communication
         (1) Teach parents to be firm and consistent
         (2) Teach not to blame identified client for all problems
      b. *Strategic or Structural* approach
         (1) Reframe problem as not just identified client; whole family
         (2) Emotional messages disguised or distorted; members talk *at*, not *with* each other; therapist helps communicate clearly
      c. *Paradoxal Directive*
         (1) Therapist asks client to purposely perform, exaggerate, problematic behavior
         (2) Clients learn they control the behavior, *it* does not control

                10. Effectiveness of Family Therapy
                    a. Empirical research shows therapy is an effective treatment
                    b. Behavioral, structural received strongest empirical support
        D. Self-Help Groups
            1. 10 to 15 million people in U.S. and Canada participate
            2. No professionally trained leader
            3. Not a new idea; earlier people turned to relatives, friends, neighbors
            4. Today, people far from families, SHGs provide support, nurturance
            5. Several features common
                a. Members share a well-defined problem
                b. Meetings focus on exchanging information; providing feelings of togetherness, belonging; discussing mutual problems
                c. Social support provided by peers struggling with similar problems
                d. Charge no fees, or low fees; goal to provide mutual aid
                e. Largely member governed; may use professional consultants; rely mainly on group members as primary care givers
            6. Five general types
                a. Habit disturbance
                b. General-purpose
                c. Lifestyle organizations
                d. Significant-other
                e. Physical handicap organizations
            7. Effectiveness of Self-Help Groups
                a. Seldom evaluated empirically
                b. Members convinced groups valuable
III. Psychosocial Rehabilitation (pp. 602-604)
    A. Deinstitutionalization
        1. Effectiveness of antipsychotic medications led to discharge of severely mentally ill people from public mental institutions into community
            a. Mental health center movement of 1960s presented evidence could receive more beneficial, less expensive care as outpatients
            b. Number of patients confined declined from 550,000 to 100,000
        2. What happened to patients released
            a. Very few treated short-term in general, private hospitals
            b. Too few treated in community mental health centers, social agency
            c. Sadly, thousands left to fend for themselves; no treatment
            d. Many have drifted into unemployment, homelessness, responsibility of police, criminal justice systems
            e. Severely mentally ill risks for physical illness, criminal victimization, premature death due to injuries, accidents
            f. Families suffer; overall cost of schizophrenia $19 billion per year in U.S. (Exceeds that of cancer)
            g. Deinstitutionalzation, community-based mental health care failed
        3. Psychosocial rehabilitation
            a. Teaches patients how to cope better with effects of disorders

        b.   Teaches how to prevent or lessen the crises
        c.   Helps normalize their lives, compensate for impairments, achieve highest possible quality of life in the community
        d.   Emerged from cooperative efforts of three groups
            (1)   National Alliance for the Mentally Ill (NAMI)
            (2)   Self-help groups of seriously mentally ill people
            (3)   Community-oriented mental health professionals
            (4)   Efforts recognized in federal legislation mandating that each of them must be represented on mental health planning councils in every state in the United States
        e.   Goal is *empowerment*
            (1)   Teach clients to have mastery, control over own lives
            (2)   Teach basic competencies needed to live independently
            (3)   involve four components
                (a)   Help patients understand their disorder so they can cope with it more effectively
                (b)   Help identify, then learn, skills needed for living in community; especially interacting with other people
                (c)   *Case management*: single staff person assists client in obtaining services related to employment, housing, nutrition, transportation, recreation, medical care, finances
                (d)   Promotes treatment efforts by maintaining a coalition among mental health professionals, family members, and patients
4.   Effectiveness of Psychosocial Rehabilitation
        a.   Research studies show can help administering their own medications, monitoring their own symptoms, engaging in appropriate social conversations, caring for their own safety
        b.   Reduce relapse rates, arrests or imprisonment
        c.   If rehabilitation programs not continued for at least 2 years
            (1)   Clients condition deteriorates
            (2)   Rehospitalization rates increase
            (3)   Overall quality of life declines
        d.   Treatment should be comprehensive and continuous

17 Alternatives to Individual Psychotherapy

LECTURE MAKER 17.1

Purpose   To introduce a useful, pragmatic, approach to crisis intervention and problem solving. (pp. 591-592)

Lecture Introduction   Provide an overview of therapeutic approaches. Regardless of approach, crisis intervention flow-chart can be useful in problem solving. As a crisis develops, tension increases as the person tries old problem solving techniques. Tension spirals as old techniques do not work and emergency measures are taken. With more tension, disorganization follows. Therapies provide ways to assist the individual on his/her return to homeostasis.

Demonstration   Ask students to design a general crisis intervention flow chart.. While stressful events are not as simplistic as a flow chart might suggest, such a model provides a flexible summary for intervention.

Lecture Capsule   Students can be challenged to take one of their own issues and apply the flow-chart approach. Weave this model with other therapeutic approaches.

LECTURE MAKER 17.3

Purpose   To provide an overview of a few support groups. (pp. 594-595)

Lecture Introduction   Review group processes and therapy. Discuss trained leader groups and support groups. Briefly outline a typical support group.

Demonstration   Hand out the basic twelve steps of Alcoholics Anonymous. Many other support groups borrow and re-work the twelve steps for their purposes. Support group literature often includes a series of questions to determine if you "qualify" for membership.

Lecture Capsule   Consider the proliferation of support groups. Is it a passing fad or does it help? Why are groups like these so popular? The discussion relating to support groups will almost always include a member in the midst, or someone who has member in their family.

The Twelve Steps of Alcoholics Anonymous 17.2

1. We admitted we were powerless over alcohol—that our lives had become unmanageable.

2. Came to believe that a Power greater than ourselves could restore us to sanity.

3. Made a decision to turn our will and our lives over to the care of God <u>as we understood Him.</u>

4. Made a searching and fearless moral inventory of ourselves.

5. Admitted to God, to ourselves, and to another human being the exact nature of our wrongs.

6. Were entirely ready to have God remove all these defects of character.

7. Humbly asked Him to remove our shortcomings.

8. Made a list of all persons we had harmed, and became willing to make amends to them all.

9. Made direct amends to such people whenever possible, except when to do so would injure them or others.

10. Continued to take personal inventory and when we were wrong, promptly admitted it.

11. Sought through prayer and meditation to improve our conscious contact with God <u>as we understood Him</u>, praying only for knowledge of His will for us and the power to carry that out.

12. Having had a spiritual awakening as the result of these steps, we tried to carry this message to alcoholics, and to practice these principles in our affairs.

The Twelve Steps are reprinted with permission of Alcoholics Anonymous World Services, Inc. Permission to reprint the Twelve Steps does not mean the A.A. has reviewed or approved the contents of this publication, nor that A.A. agrees with the views expressed herein. A.A. is a program of recovery form alcoholism <u>only</u>—use of the Twelve Steps in connection with programs and activities which are patterned after A.A., but which address other problems, or in any other non-A.A. context does not imply otherwise. Reprinted by permission.

RESOURCES

General

Adult Children of Alcoholics
National Association of Children of Alcoholics (NACoA)
31582 Coast Highway, Suite B
S. Laguna, CA 92677

Adult Children of Alcoholics (ACOA)
Some groups have broadened their focus to be "Adult Children of Alcoholics and Dysfunctional Families" Call NCA

Changes, a magazine published by the U.S. Journal of Drug and Alcohol Dependence, Inc. And Health Communications, Inc.
1721 Blount Rd. Suite One
Pompano Beach, FL 33069
Full of resources, but also illustrates what "big business" the addictions have become.

Creativity and Creative Problem Solving
That problem has really been nagging at you. It sits in the back of your mind taunting you, demanding attention, begging to be dealt with. No ordinary problem solving is going to take care of it. What's the difference between plain old problem solving and creative problem solving? Discover the answer to that question by examining stimulating factors for creativity in product development, strategic issues, and organizational settings.

Listserv Mailing List:
  List Address: **crea-cps@nic.surfnet.nl**
  Subscription Address: **listserv@nic.surfnet.nl**

Family Violence
Home is supposed to be a haven, a place for nurturing and safety. But life doesn't always quite go the way you expect it to and sometimes home is the place you feel the least safe. A networking system has been established to study all aspects of family violence. It is not limited to topics of child-abuse or violence within the family, but serves a wide range of areas covered by the term "intimate violence."

Listserv Mailing List:
  List Address: **intvio-l@uriacc.uri.edu**
  Subscription Address: **listserv@uriacc.uri.edu**

Intimate Violence

Intimate Violence
"Intimate violence" refers to destructive contact in any relationship, whether it is with family members or lover. The *Electronic Journal of Intimate Violence* reports on the latest research and treatment of intimate violence. Some of the topics discussed are physical or sexual child abuse, child neglect, physical or sexual spouse abuse, psychological abuse, elder abuse, and dating violence.

Listserv Mailing List:
  List Address: **ejintvio@uriacc.uri.edu**
  Subscription Address: **listserv@uriacc.uri.edu**

Partnerships Against Violence
Partnerships Against Violence offers information and statistics about violence and youth at risk, including gang problems, drugs, rehabilitation of criminals, programs for violence prevention, including community violence, family violence, substance abuse, and youth violence.

Gopher:
  Name: Department of Housing and Urban Development
  Address: **gopher.hud.gov**
  Choose:
    PAV*NET: Partnerships Against Violence

Title: Goal Setting
Source: Psychology on a Disk
CMS Software
P.O. Box 729
Ellicott City, MD 21043
Type of Software: Simulation
Content: Students have to complete tasks in a situation that is related to how a person's behavior might be shaped.

Media

The Angry Couple: Conflict-Focused Treatment with Dr. Susan Heitler
This program recreates key moments in the six-month course of therapy with a married couple in their early 30s who are locked in conflict. Dr. Heitler demonstrates her approach for helping couples cut through impasses that prolong their conflict and obscure the fundamental issues. The program offers guidance in how to:
- Defuse anger without taking sides.
- Formulate a comprehensive treatment plan.
- Guide resolution of conflicts from initial presentation through exploration of hidden concerns to the final selection of mutually acceptable solutions.
- Build communication skills through specific exercises.
- Resolve underlying family-of-origin issues
- Bring the treatment to a satisfying closure.

*Adult Children of Alcoholics (*MINN, 30 min, 1988). Understanding their problems and typical behaviors (video)

Adult Children of Alcoholics: The Masks of Denial (MINN, 23 Min, 1987) The psychological/emotional problems of growing up with an alcoholic parent. (Film)

Trust in Yourself: Adult Children of Alcoholics (MINN, 25 min, 1988) Deals with the power of denial and confusion =, and the healing potential of forgiveness and group therapy (video)

Groups and Group Dynamics social interaction within and between groups is the subject of this program, which describes different categories of groups and explains how they function, how they differ from other social entities, and how group membership is determined. The video then looks at intra-group relationships, examining conformity and individualism. Finally, the interaction between groups is investigated.

An Approach to Growth: Awareness Training (CRM, 26 min). Filmed at the Lomi School in Kauai, Hawaii, this film shows a variety of exercises and therapies such as Hatha Yoga, bioenergetics, breathing, kinesthetics, dreams, and Gestalt therapy. Subjects are seen talking and acting out their problems in a group.

For additional video resource materials, please contact your Allyn & Bacon representative.

Nietzel et al., *Abnormal Psychology*, Transparencies

Chapter Seventeen

	Text Figure Number	Text Page Number

79. Long-Term Effects of Different Marital Therapies..................................17.1........597

18 Legal and Ethical Issues in Mental Disorders

CHAPTER OUTLINE

I. The Rights of Individuals Versus the Rights of Society (pp. 619-630)
   A. Civil Commitment
      1. Committed to psychiatric hospital against one's will
         a. Done when state believed one required psychiatric treatment
         b. Length of confinement decided by hospital staff
         c. Based on *parens patriae* ("the country as parent")
      2. Changes in 1960s
         a. States began to reform rules for involuntary commitment
         b. New rules allowed patients to resist hospitalization
         c. Allowed protection against *indefinite* commitment
         d. Bias that psychiatrist's lack of success made involuntary hospitalization similar to imprisonment without trial
      3. New laws required the state to prove
         a. Person is mentally ill
         b. Poses imminent threat of danger to self or others
         c. Treatment is available at proposed site
         d. Hospitalization is *least restrictive alternative* for treatment
      4. Public Mental Hospitals and Deinstitutionalization
         a. By end of 1970s, every state and District of Columbia passed laws that some version of these four condition be met
         b. New rules combined with new psychoactive drugs dropped number of hospitalized patients from 550,000 to 100,000 in 1990s
         c. Described as shift from inpatient to outpatient treatment
         d. Appeared promising; combination of myth, missed opportunity
         e. Reasons for disappointing assessment
            (1) Actual number of admissions to *all types* hospitals for mental care increased by 30% from late 1960s to 1980; people now stay shorter periods, admissions, readmissions frequent
            (2) Decreased number in state, Veterans Administration hospitals—much inpatient care now other kinds facilities
                (a) General hospitals now have psychiatric care
                (b) Private, usually for profit, psychiatric hospitals
                (c) Specialized chemical dependency units
                (d) Inpatient facilities run by military
                (e) Indian Health Service
            (3) Overall failure of movement suggested; large percentage severely mentally ill persons drifted into homelessness, wards of criminal justice system
      5. Mental Illness and the Homeless
         a. One million homeless Americans beginning 1990s; estimated one third suffer from severe mental illnesses, schizophrenia, bipolar

- b. About half are also alcohol or drug abusers
- c. Homeless mentally ill disadvantages
  - (1) Disorders impair judgment, ability to comply with treatment
  - (2) Lack adequate shelter, nutrition
  - (3) Suffer serious physical illnesses
  - (4) Seldom employed; if do hold jobs, income $5000 yr. or less
  - (5) Daily rejection; public pities and fears them
- d. The National Institutes of Mental Health Task Force on Homelessness and Severe Mental Illness proposed system of care
  - (1) Assertive outreach orientation with integrated case management
  - (2) Provide adequate housing; they need safe havens until more permanent housing could be found
  - (3) Collection of income support, health care, psychosocial rehabilitation, mental health and substance abuse treatment, education, vocational services ("bundle" psychiatric treatment with food and shelter, because some severely mentally ill persons resist or avoid it)

6. The Mentally Ill in the Criminal Justice System
   - a. Police officers have wide discretion disruptive people who may also be mentally ill
     - (1) Can arrest them or force them into hospital
     - (2) Can do on-the-spot counseling
     - (3) Refer them to mental health agency
     - (4) Return them to friends or family
   - b. Police reluctant to arrest; prefer arrest over hospitalization
     - (1) Aarrest involves less red tape
     - (2) Hospitals often refuse to accept
       - (a) Too dangerous
       - (b) Not dangerous enough
       - (c) Suffer disorder hospital does not treat
     - (3) Homeless mentally ill being "criminalized"
     - (4) Society does not know what else to do with them
   - c. Local jails source of shelter, food, medical treatment, detoxification, remedial education, other services
   - d. State laws changed to include involuntary commitment if people were *gravely disabled*, in danger of *deteriorating* if not hospitalized

7. Types of Commitment in Use Today
   - a. Commitment without a court order
     - (1) Emergency circumstances
     - (2) Patients detained usually from 24 hours to few days; then court hearing must be conducted to determine how long
   - b. Commitment by court order
     - (1) Family member, police officer, petitions court to have person examined by mental health professional
     - (2) Person has right to be presented by attorney

     (3) "Dangerousness"standard; proof "grave disability" criterion that usually determines court's decision
     (4) Judge, jury thinks person in need of care; commitment order Outpatient commitment
     (5) Mandatory treatment in outpatient setting
     (6) Often occur at conditional release from mental hospital
     (7) Oordered to receive treatment, medication
     (8) If person fails to comply; returned to inpatient institution
 B. The Right to Refuse Treatment
   1. Medical patients governed by rules of *informed consent*
   2. Assumed seriously mentally ill incompetent to render decisions
   3. Courts defer to judgment of physicians treating patient
   4. In states that recognize the right to refuse treatment; right is not absolute
   5. Patient is behaving dangerously, medication likely to lessen emergency; patient is judged to be incompetent to make decision; panel substituted
   6. Formal refusals surprisingly infrequent
 C. Other Legal Rights of the Mentally Ill
   1. The Right to Treatment
     a. Committed people have right to *treatment*; not just confinement
     b. 1966 case of *Rouse versus Cameron*
   2. Standards of Treatment
     a. Adequate food, shelter, clothing
     b. Adequate medical care
     c. A safe environment
     d. Freedom from restraint unless necessary to protect patient or others
     e. Such training as may be required to ensure above rights
     f. U.S. Supreme Court held Constitution guarantees above rights
     g. Individual states free to insist on higher standards of care
   3. Rights of Nondangerous Patients
     a. A "state cannot constitutionally confine....a nondangerous individual who is capable of surviving safely in freedom by himself or with the help of willing and responsible family and friends."
     b. Supreme Court tendency to reach conclusions no broader than necessary
   4. Housing Rights
     a. Federal laws: Fair Housing Amendments Act of 1988; Americans with Disabilities Act of 1990 prohibit housing discrimination
     b. Some cities discourage group homes or halfway houses
     c. Supreme Court—cities cannot pass laws requiring special permits for homes for retarded citizens just because community opposes them
   5. Rights of Mentally Ill or Mentally Retarded Criminal Defendants
     a. Poor person who uses insanity as defense must be provided psychiatrist at state expense
     b. Mentally ill convicts granted special protections
     c. U.S. Constitution forbids execution inmate mentally incompetent

II. The Regulation of Mental Health Professionals (pp. 630-638)
- A. Controls Includes Laws
    1. Certification laws restrict use of title to people who have met certain requirements for education, practical training, supervised experience
    2. *Licensure laws* restrict use of title and prohibit unlicensed people from offering traditional services of given profession
    3. Goal to protect public from imposters, unskilled professionals
    4. Regulations give licensed, certified professionals economic edge
- B. Confidentiality
    1. Privilege
        a. Exists between minister and parishioner; husband and wife; lawyer and client; doctor and patient
        b. Most states also between psychotherapist and client
        c. Some courts ruled therapist's obligation to try to protect potential victims of a client's dangerous actions take precedence over obligation to protect that client's privacy
    2. Confidentiality
        a. Not a legal requirement but an *ethical* obligation of therapists
        b. Helps cement bond of trust between client and therapist
        c. 1996 Supreme Court decision
    3. Rights Are Not Absolute; May Be Breached
        a. If therapist believes client needs to be committed to hospital
        b. If client raises mental condition in a trial; therapist called to testify
        c. If client underwent a court-ordered psychological evaluation
        d. If therapist learns from client that client is abusing other people
        e. If client tells therapist of intent to harm another person
    4. The Tarasoff Decision
        a. Prosenjit Poddar was client of psychologist Lawrence Moore
        b. Poddar confided to Moore he would kill Tatiana Tarasoff (she had rebuffed his romantic interest in her)
        c. Moore told his supervisor Dr. Harvey Powelson of threat, wrote campus police, requesting they detain Poddar
        d. They did, but released him on his promise to stay away from her
        e. 2 months after terminating treatment, he killed her
        f. No one had warned Tatiana or her parents of Poddars threats
        g. Dr. Powelson had ordered destruction of all copies of letter, notes
        h. Tarasoffs sued Regents of the University of California
        i. Court said, "The protective privilege ends where the public peril begins." Court decided for the parents.
        j. California therapists required to take "steps to protect"
            (1) Warning victims
            (2) Informing police of danger
            (3) Seeking voluntary or involuntary commitment of client
            (4) Combination of these actions
        k. Accurate prediction dangerousness most difficult challenge

5. The Impact of Tarasoff
   a. Made therapists more alert to potential for dangerous behavior
   b. More anxious about legal liability
   c. Many had been warning before Tarasoff
   d. Now clearer understanding of options

C. Regulation of Treatment Through Malpractice Lawsuits
   1. To Prove Claim of Professional Malpractice
      a. Special professional relationship had to exist
      b. Professional was *negligent* in treating client (standard of care)
      c. Must be shown client suffered *harm*
      d. Therapist's negligence shown to be cause of harm
   2. Psychotherapists Face Malpractice Action
      a. Failing to prevent client from committing suicide
      b. Failing to carry out duty-to-protect obligations
      c. Failing to make proper referral when therapist terminates treatment
      d. Misrepresenting professional qualifications
   3. Malpractice Related to Sexual Contact with Clients
      a. Ethical codes strictly forbid sexual intimacy
      b. 5-8% professionals report having engaged; 4-5 times more men
      c. Intimacy prohibited with *former* patients also
   4. Malpractice Related to Repressed Memory Therapy
      a. Researchers skeptical about accuracy of client's memories
      b. Especially if reports come after contact with aggressive practitioners of memory therapy
      c. Therapists suggest idea of trauma to clients; too uncritical in accepting validity of trauma reports that occur spontaneously
   5. Regulation of Treatment Through Economic Controls
      a. In U.S. psychotherapy often regulated by insurance companies, health maintenance organizations
      b. Third party payers want treatments effective, efficient, necessary
      c. Type and length of treatment controlled by *managed care systems*
         (1) Provide health care to subscribers for fixed, prepaid price
         (2) Case manager who is not therapist makes decisions

D. Regulation Through Ethical Standards
   1. *Ethical Principles of Psychologists and Code of Conduct* issues
      a. Limiting practice to areas of demonstrated competence
      b. Maintaining proper clinical records
      c. Using and interpreting tests properly
      d. Protecting the privacy, confidentiality of clients
      e. Consulting, cooperating with other mental health professionals
      f. Eliminating bias based on cultural, ethnic, religious, or socioeconomic factors
      g. Protection client's welfare
   2. Clinicians who violate ethics can be publicly reprimanded, censured, expelled form organizations; could lose licensure, certification

III. Mental Health Professionals in the Legal System (pp. 638-645)
    A. Provide Legal System with Four Basic Services
        1. Basic scientists
        2. Trial consultants to attorneys
        3. Policy evaluators or researcher
        4. Expert witnesses
    B. The Scope of Expert Testimony
        1. Participate in 8% of all trials held in federal civil courts
        2. Participate in as many as a million cases each year
        3. Three factors responsible
            a. Questions of criminal competence, responsibility
            b. Law permits and encourages it
            c. Can be very lucrative (hourly rates: $100 to $400)
    C. Criminal Competence and Responsibility
        1. Criminal Competence
            a. First decide if competent to stand trial
            b. Considered incompetent if cannot
                (1) Understand nature of trial proceedings
                (2) Participate meaningfully in own defense
                (3) Consult with their attorney
            c. Defendants not competent sent to hospital
        2. The Insanity Defense
            a. Insanity a legal term; not a psychological concept
            b. Definition of insanity known as McNaughton rule
            c. As a result of mental disorder, either do not know what they are doing or do not know their action is wrong
            d. ALI rule
            e. Proving insanity can result in acquittal or protect from punishment
        3. The Insanity Defense Under Fire
            a. Juries reluctant to find violent offenders NGRI
            b. Defendants NGRI kept in hospital until judge deems safe
            c. Insane criminals more dangerous than other ones
    D. Revisions and Reforms in the Insanity Defense
        1. The Guilty But Mentally Ill Verdict
        2. The Insanity Defense Reform Act
            a. Placed burden on defendant to prove insanity
            b. Lack of behavioral control no longer a basis
            c. Prohibited experts from giving *ultimate opinion* testimony
        3. Abolition of Insanity Defense
            a. Idaho and Montana have abolished insanity defense
            b. To be convicted one must have intended the illegal act
            c. States must allow evidence about defendant's *mens rea*
            d. Experts continue to testify effects of mental illness on mens rea
            e. Defendant's mental state can never be eliminated from jurors consideration of guilt

18 Legal and Ethical Issues in Mental Disorders

LECTURE MAKER 18.1

Purpose	To provide a step-wise framework for ethical decision making. (pp.637-638)
Lecture Introduction	Discuss ethical considerations for the therapeutic setting. Practitioners are challenged to assist clients and deal with ambiguity. This can seem an overwhelming task.
Demonstration	Duplicate the "Steps in Making Ethical Decisions" for students. Walk through these steps slowly with students. This is a dynamically useful approach.
Lecture Capsule	It is recommended to follow this exercise with other that evaluate personal values, fears, and biases.

LECTURE MAKER 18.2

Purpose	To self-assess attitudes and beliefs about professional and ethical issues. (pp. 637-638)
Lecture Introduction	This inventory surveys students' thoughts on various professional and ethical issues. It can help solidify personal values and deepen respect for ethical responsibility of therapists.
Demonstration	This is a thought provoker, and there is not necessarily one right answer for each question.
Lecture Capsule	While this is a very long demonstration, it is an advantageous values clarification exercise. It is worth spending the time to explore.

LECTURE MAKER 18.3

Purpose To explore self-doubt, fears and values in the client-therapist setting. (p. 635)

Lecture Introduction Personalizing this chapter often deepens students' comprehension. Approach them as though they are therapists-in-training. First highlight possible sources of fear and self-doubt about being a professional therapist. Review therapist responsibility and influence. Should you impose your values on the clients? What are your most cherished values?

Demonstration This is a long series of exercises. It overs doubts, fears, and values. Every item can lead to an open discussion. Enjoy!

Lecture Capsule Try to convey to the students that the anticipation of a situation is often more distressing to us than is the actual situation itself. It is our interpretation of the event, in this case, the "doing" of what we have only studied that fills us with either anticipation or excitement.

LECTURE MAKER 18.4

Purpose To review National Board for Certified Counselors content areas and work behavioral application. (pp.630-635)

Lecture Introduction Certification for counselors and national examinations are hurdles faced by therapist-interns at the end of their training and education. Review licensure, internships, and state/national standards.

Demonstration This is a comprehensive listing of the topic and work area coverage included in the National Counselor Exam for licensure and certification. Jaws will drop as the list is reviewed.

Lecture Capsule Compare the competency areas with the graduate curriculum in clinical psychology or counseling at your institution.

STEPS IN MAKING ETHICAL DECISIONS 18.1

Some of the following steps, suggested by the creators of various models of ethical decision making, may help you think through ethical problems:

- *Identify the problem or dilemma.* Gather as much information as possible that sheds light on the situation. Clarify whether the conflict is ethical, legal, or moral or a combination of any or all of these. Remember that such dilemmas are complex, so that it is useful to look at the problem from many perspectives and to avoid simplistic solutions. Because ethical dilemmas do not have "right" or "wrong" answers, practitioners are challenged to deal with ambiguity.

- *Identify the potential issues involved.* After the information is collected, list and describe the critical issues and discard the irrelevant ones. Evaluate the rights, responsibilities, and welfare of all those who are affected by the situation. Part of the process of making ethical decisions involves identifying competing moral principles. Consider the basic moral principles of autonomy, beneficence, normaleficence, and justice and apply them to a particular situation. It may help to prioritize these principles and think through ways in which they can suppor a resolution to the dilemma. Good reasons can often be presented to support various sides of a given issue. Different ethical principles may sometimes imply contradictory courses of action.

- *Review the relevant ethical guidelines.* Ask whether the guidelines, standards, or principles of your organization offer a possible solution to the problem. Consider whether your own values and ethics are consistent with or in conflict with the relevant guidelines. If you are in disagreement with a guideline, do you have a rationale to support your position?

- *Obtain consultation.* At this point, it is generally helpful to consult with a colleague or colleagues to obtain a different perspective on the problem. Because of your involvement in the situation, you may have trouble in seeing the forest for the trees. Consultation can help you think about information or circumstances that you may have overlooked. In making ethical decisions, you must justify a course of action based on sound reasoning. Consultation with colleagues provides an opportunity to test your justification.

- *Consider possible and probable courses of action.* Brainstorming is useful at this stage of ethical decision making. By listing a wide variety of courses of action you may come up with a possibility that is unorthodox by useful. Of course, one alternative is that no action is required. In this process of thinking about many different possibilities for action, it is helpful to discuss options with another person.

- *Enumerate the consequences of various decisions.* Ponder the implications of each cours of action for the client, for others who are related to the client and for you as the counselor. You might consider the four fundamental principles (autonomy, beneficence, normaleficence, and justice) as a framework for evaluating the consequences of a given course of action.

- *Decide on what appears to be the best course of action.* In making what you consider to be the best decision, consider carefully the information you have received from various sources. The more obvious the dilemma, the clearer is the course of action; the more subtle the dilemma, the more difficult the decision will be. After deciding, try not to second-guess your course of action. You may realize later that another action might have been more beneficial. But this hindsight does not invalidate the decision you made based on the information you had at the time.

From *Issues and Ethics in the Helping Professions,* by G. Corey, M.S. Corey and P. Callanan Copyright © 1993, 1988, 1984, 1979 Brooks/Cole Publishing Company, Pacific Grove, CA 93950 A division of International Thomson Publishing Inc. Reprinted by permission of the publisher.

Self-Assessment: An Inventory of Your Attitudes and Beliefs about Professional and Ethical Issues 18.2

This is *not* a traditional multiple-choice test in which you must select the "one right answer." Rather, it is a survey of your basic beliefs, attitudes, and values on specific topics related to the practice of therapy. For each question, write in the letter of the response that most clearly reflects your viewpoint at this time. In many cases the answers are not mutually exclusive, and you may choose more than one response if you wish. In addition, a blank line is included for each item. You may want to use this line to provide another response more suited to your thinking or to qualify a chosen response.

___ 1. The personal characteristics of counselors are
   A. Not really relevant to the counseling process.
   B. The most important variable in determining the quality of the counseling process.
   C. Shaped and molded by those who teach counselors.
   D. Not as important as the skills and knowledge the counselors possess.
   E. _____

___ 2. Which of the following do you consider to be the most important personal characteristic of a good counselor?
   A. Willingness to serve as a model for clients.
   B. Courage.
   C. Openness and honesty.
   D. A sense of being "centered" as a person.
   E. _____

___ 3. Concerning counselors' self-disclosure to their clients, I believe that
   A. It is essential for establishing a relationship.
   B. It is inappropriate and merely burdens the client.
   C. It should be done rarely and only when the therapist feels like sharing.
   D. It is useful for counselors to reveal how they feel toward their clients in the context of the therapy session.
   E. _____

___ 4. A client/therapist relationship characterized by warmth, acceptance, caring, empathy, and respect is
   A. A necessary and sufficient condition of positive change in clients.
   B. A necessary but not sufficient condition of positive change in clients.
   C. Neither a necessary nor a sufficient condition of positive change in clients.
   D. _____

___ 5. Of the following factors, which is the most important in determining whether counseling will result in change?
   A. The kind of person the counselor is.
   B. The skills and techniques the counselor uses.
   C. The motivation of the client to change.
   D. The theoretical orientation of the counselor.
   E. _____

___ 6. Of the following, which would you consider to be the most important attribute of an effective therapist?
A. Knowledge of the theory of counseling and behavior.
B. Skill in using techniques appropriately.
C. Genuineness and openness.
D. Ability to specify a treatment plan and evaluate the results.
E. _____

___ 7. I believe that, for those who wish to become therapists, personal psychotherapy
A. Should be required for licensure.
B. Is not an important factor in developing the capacity to work with others.
C. Should be encouraged but not required.
D. Is needed only when the therapist has serious problems.
E. _____

___ 8. I believe that, in order to help a client, a therapist
A. Must like the client personally.
B. Must be free of any personal conflicts in the area in which the client is working.
C. Needs to have experienced the same problem as the client.
D. Needs to have experienced feelings similar to those being experienced by the client
E. _____

___ 9. In regard to the client/therapist relationship, I think that
A. The therapist should remain objective and anonymous.
B. The therapist should be a friend to the client.
C. A personal relationship, but not friendship, is essential.
D. A personal and warm relationship is not essential.
E. _____

___ 10. I should be open, honest, and transparent with my clients
A. When I like and value them.
B. When I have negative feeling toward them.
C. Rarely, if ever, so that I will avoid negatively influencing the client/therapist relationship.
D. Only when it intuitively feels like the right thing to do.
E. _____

___ 11. I expect that I will experience professional burnout if
A. I get involved in too many demanding projects.
B. I must do things in my work that aren't personally meaningful.
C. My personal life is characterized by conflict and struggle.
D. My clients complain a lot and fail to change for the better.
E. _____

___12. I think that professional burnout
   A. Can be avoided if I'm involved in personal therapy while working as a professional.
   B. Is inevitable and that I must learn to live with it.
   C. Can be lessened if I find ways to replenish and nourish myself.
   D. May or may not occur, depending on the type of client I work with.
   E. _____

___13. If I were an intern and were convinced that my supervisor was encouraging trainees to participate in unethical behavior in an agency setting, I would
   A. First discuss the matter with the supervisor.
   B. Report the supervisor to the director of the agency.
   C. Ignore the situation for fear of negative consequences.
   D. Report the situation to the ethics committee of the state professional association.
   E. _____

___14. Practitioners who work with culturally diverse groups without having cross-cultural knowledge and skill
   A. Are violating the civil rights of their clients.
   B. Are probably guilty of unethical behavior.
   C. Should realize the need for specializing training.
   D. Can be said to be practicing ethically.
   E. _____

___15. If I had strong feelings, positive or negative, toward a client, I think that I would most likely
   A. Discuss my feelings with my client.
   B. Keep them to myself and hope they would eventually disappear.
   C. Discuss them with a supervisor or colleague.
   D. Accept them as natural unless they began to interfere with the counseling relationship.
   E. _____

___16. I won't feel ready to counsel others until.
   A. My own life is free of problems.
   B. I've experienced counseling as a client.
   C. I feel very confident and know that I'll be effective.
   D. I've become a self-aware person and developed the ability to continually reexamine my own life and relationships.
   E. _____

___17. If a client evidenced strong feelings of attraction or dislike for me, I think that I would
   A. Help the client work through these feelings and understand them.
   B. Enjoy these feelings if they were positive.
   C. Refer my client to another counselor.
   D. Direct the sessions into less emotional areas.
   E. _____

___18. Practitioners who counsel clients whose sex, race, age, social class, or sexual orientation is different from their own
   A. Will most likely not understand these clients fully.
   B. Need to understand the differences between their clients and themselves.
   C. Can practice unethically if they do not consider cross-cultural factors.
   D. Are probably not going to be effective with such clients because of these differences.
   E. _____

___19. When I consider being involved in the helping professions, I value most
   A. The money I expect to earn.
   B. The security I imagine I will have in the job.
   C. The knowledge that I will be intimately involved with people who are searching for a better life.
   D. The personal growth I expect to experience through my work.
   E. _____

___20. I see counseling as
   A. A process of reeducation for the client.
   B. A process whereby clients are taught new and more appropriate values to live by.
   C. A process that enables clients to make decisions regarding their own lives.
   D. A process of giving advice and setting goals for clients.
   E. _____

___21. With respect to value judgments in counseling, therapists should
   A. Feel free to make value judgments about their client's behavior.
   B. Actively teach their own values when they think that clients need a different set of values.
   C. Remain neutral and keep their values out of the therapeutic process.
   D. Encourage clients to question their own behavior.
   E. _____

___22. Counselors should
   A. Teach desirable behavior and values by modeling them for clients
   B. Encourage clients to look within themselves to discover values that are meaningful to them.
   C. Reinforce the dominant values of society.
   D. Very delicately, if at all, challenge client's value systems.
   E. _____

___23. In terms of appreciating and understanding the value systems of clients who are culturally different from me
   A. I see it as my responsibility to learn about their values and not impose mine on them.
   B. I would encourage them to accept the values of the most dominant culture for survival purposes.
   C. I would attempt to modify my counseling procedures to fit their cultural values.
   D. I think it is imperative that I learn about the specific cultural values my clients hold.
   E. _____

___24. If a client came to me with a problem and I could see that I would not be objective because of my values, I would
   A. Accept the client because of the challenge to become more tolerant of diversity.
   B. Tell the client at the outset about my fears concerning our conflicting values.
   C. Refer the client to someone else.
   D. Attempt to influence the client to adopt my way of thinking.
   E. _____

___25. I believe that the real reason for professional licensing and certification is
   A. To provide information to the public about mental-health services.
   B. To protect the public by setting minimum levels of competence for psychological services.
   C. To upgrade the helping professions by ensuring that the highest standards of excellence are promoted.
   D. To protect the interests of various helping professions and to reduce competitions.
   E. _____

___26. I would tend to refer a client to another therapist
   A. If I had a strong dislike for the client.
   B. If I didn't have much experience working with the kind of problem the client presented.
   C. If I saw my own needs and problems getting in the way of helping the client.
   D. If the client seemed to distrust me.
   E. _____

___27. My ethical position regarding the role of values in therapy is that, as a therapist, I should
   A. Never impose my values on a client.
   B. Expose my values, without imposing them on the client.
   C. Teach my clients what I consider to be proper values.
   D. Keep my values out of the counseling relationship.
   E. _____

___28. If I were to counsel lesbian and gay clients, a major concern of mine would be
   A. Maintaining objectivity.
   B. Not knowing and understanding enough about this lifestyle.
   C. Establishing a positive therapeutic relationship.
   D. Pushing my own values.
   E. _____

___29. Of the following, I consider the unethical form of therapist behavior to be
   A. Promoting dependence in the client.
   B. Becoming sexually involved with clients.
   C. Breaking confidentiality without a good reason to do so.
   D. Accepting a client who has a problem that goes beyond one's competence.
   E. _____

___30. Regarding the issue of counseling friends, I think that
   A. It is seldom wise to accept a friend as a client.
   B. It should be done rarely, and only if it is clear that the friendship will not interfere with the therapeutic relationship.
   C. Friendship and therapy should not be mixed.
   D. It should be done only if it seems appropriate to both the client and the counselor.
   E. _____

___31. Regarding confidentiality, I believe that
   A. It is ethical to break confidence when there is reason to believe that clients may do serious harm to themselves.
   B. It is ethical to break confidence when there is reason to believe that a client will do harm to someone else.
   C. It is ethical to break confidence when the parents of a client ask for certain information.
   D. It is ethical to inform the authorities when a client is breaking the law.
   E. _____

___32. Therapists should terminate therapy with a client when
   A. The client decides to do so and not before.
   B. They judge that it is time to terminate.
   C. It is clear that the client is not benefiting from the therapy.
   D. The client reaches an impasse.
   E. _____

___33. A sexual relationship between a client and therapist is
   A. Ethical if the client initiates it.
   B. Ethical if the therapist decides it is in the best interests of the client.
   C. Ethical only when client and therapist discuss the issue and agree to the relationship.
   D. Is never ethical.
   E. _____

___34. Concerning the issue of physically touching a client, I think that touching
   A. Is unwise, because it could be misinterpreted by the client.
   B. Should be done only when the therapist genuinely feels like doing it.
   C. Is an imortant part of the therapeutic process.
   D. Is ethical when the client requests it.
   E. _____

___35. A clinical supervisor has initiated sexual relationships with former trainees (students). He maintains that, because he no longer has any professional responsibility to them, this practice is acceptable.
In my view, this behavior is
A. Clearly unethical, because he is using his position to initiate contacts with former students.
B. Not unethical, because the professional relationship has ended.
C. Not unethical but is unwise and inappropriate.
D. Somewhat unethical, because the supervisory relationship is similar to the therapeutic relationship.
E. _____

___36. Regarding theories of counseling, I think that therapists should
A. Ignore them, since they have no practical application.
B. Select *one* theory and work within its framework.
C. Select something form most of the theories.
D. Select a theory on the basis of the client's personality and presenting problem.
E. _____

___37. In the practice of marital and family therapy, I think that
A. The therapist's primary responsibility is to the welfare of the family as a unit.
B. The therapist should focus primarily on the needs of individual members of the family.
C. The therapist should attend to the family's need and try to hold the amount of sacrifice by any one member to a minimum.
D. The therapist has an ethical obligation to state his/her bias and approach at the outset.
E. _____

___38. On the matter of developing sexual relationships with *former* clients, my position is that
A. It is strictly up to the people involved to make that decision.
B. It is always unethical.
C. It is an example of taking advantage of a client.
D. It can be either ethical or unethical, depending on the case.
E. _____

___39. Regarding the issue of who should select the goals of counseling, I believe that
A. It is primarily the therapist's responsibility to select goals.
B. It is primarily the client's responsibility to select goals.
C. The responsibility for selecting goals should be shared equally by the client and the therapist.
D. The question of who selects the goals depends on what kind of client is being seen.
E. _____

___40. Concerning the role of diagnosis in counseling, I believe that
   A. Diagnosis is essential for the planning of a treatment program.
   B. Diagnosis is counterproductive for therapy, since it is based on an external view of the client.
   C. Diagnosis is dangerous in that it tends to label people, who then are limited by the label.
   D. Whether to use diagnosis depends on ones's theoretical orientation and the kind of counseling one does.
   E. _____

___41 Concerning the place of testing in counseling, I think that
   A. Tests generally interfere with the counseling process.
   B. Tests can be valuable tools if they are used as adjuncts to counseling.
   C. Tests are essential for people who are seriously disturbed.
   D. Tests can be either used or abused in counseling.
   E. _____

___42. Regarding the issue of psychological risks associated with participation in group therapy, my position is that
   A. Clients should be informed at the outset of possible risks.
   B. These risks should be minimized by careful screening.
   C. This issue is exaggerated, since there are no real risks.
   D. Careful supervision will offset some of these risks.
   E. _____

___43. Concerning the counselor's responsibility to the community, I believe that
   A. The counselor should educate the community concerning the nature of psychological services.
   B. The counselor should attempt to change patterns that need changing.
   C. Community involvement falls outside the proper scope of counseling.
   D. Counselors should become involved in helping clients use the resources available in the community.
   E. _____

___44. My view of personal counseling or psychotherapy for practitioners is that
   A. It is most desirable for beginning counselors.
   B. It is of great value for experienced counselors as well as beginning practitioners.
   C. It should be a strongly recommended component of any counselor-preparation program.
   D. It should not be necessary for most practitioners, unless they are faced with a personal crisis.
   E. _____

___45. As an intern, if I thought my supervision was inadequate, I would
   A. Talk to my supervisor about it.
   B. Continue to work without complaining.
   C. Seek supervision elsewhere.
   D. Feel let down by the agency I worked for.
   E. _____

___46. My view of supervision is that it is
   A. Something that I could use on a permanent basis.
   B. A threat to my status as a professional.
   C. Valuable to have when I reach an impasse with a client.
   D. A way for me to learn about myself and to get insights into how I work with clients.
   E. _____

___47. When it comes to working within institutions, I believe that
   A. I must learn how to survive with dignity within a system.
   B. I must learn how to subvert the system so that I can do what I deeply believe in.
   C. The institution will stifle most of my enthusiasm and block any real change.
   D. I can't blame the institution if I'm unable to succeed in my programs.
   E. _____

___48. If my philosophy were in conflict with that of the institution I worked for, I would
   A. Seriously consider whether I could ethically remain in that position.
   B. Attempt to change the policies of the institution.
   C. Agree to whatever was expected of me in that system.
   D. Quietly do what I wanted to do, even if I had to be devious about it.
   E. _____

___49. In working with clients from different ethnic groups, I think it is most important to
   A. Be aware of the sociopolitical forces that have affected these clients.
   B. Understand how language can act as a barrier to effective cross-counseling.
   C. Refer these clients to some professional who shares their ethnic background.
   D. Help these clients modify their views so that they will be accepted and not have to suffer rejection.
   E. _____

___50. To be effective in counseling clients from a different culture, I think that a counselor must
   A. Possess specific knowledge about the particular group he/she is counseling.
   B. Be able to accurately "read" nonverbal messages.
   C. Have had direct contact with this group.
   D. Treat these clients no differently from the clients from his/her own cultural background.
   E. _____

From *Issues and Ethics in the Helping Professions*, by G. Corey, M.S. Corey and P Callanan. Copyright © 1993, 1988, 1984, 1979 Brooks/Cole Publishing Company, Pacific Grove, CA 93950, A division of International Thomson Publishing Inc. By permission of the publisher.

EXPLORING SELF-DOUBTS AND FEARS 18.3

Students sometimes bring up fears, resistances, perfectionistic strivings, and other personal concerns. Take the time to review the list of statements below to determine if these are things you might say. The questionnaire represents a sampling of the issues faced by those who begin to counsel others. Apply these statements to yourself, and decide to what degree you see them as your concerns. If a statement is more true than false for you, place a "T" in front of it; if it is more false than true for you, place an "F":

_____ I'm afraid I'll make mistakes.
_____ My clients will really suffer because of my blunders and my failure to know what to do.
_____ I have real doubts about my ability to help people in a crisis situation.
_____ I demand perfection of myself, and I constantly feel I should know more than I do.
_____ I would feel threatened by silences in counseling situations.
_____ It's important to me to know that my clients are making steady improvement.
_____ It would be difficult for me to deal with demanding clients.
_____ I expect to have trouble working with clients who are not motivated to change or who are required to come to me for counseling.
_____ I have trouble deciding how much of the responsibility for the direction of a counseling session is mine and how much is my client's.
_____ I think that I should be successful with all my clients.
_____ I expect to have trouble in being myself and trusting my intuition when I'm counseling.
_____ I'm afraid to express feelings of anger to a client.
_____ I worry that my client will see that I'm a beginner and wonder if I'm competent.
_____ I'm concerned about looking and acting like an ethical professional.
_____ Sometimes I'm concerned about how honest I should be with clients.
_____ I'm concerned about how much of my personal reactions and my private life I should reveal in counseling sessions.
_____ I tend to worry about whether I'm making the proper intervention.
_____ I sometimes worry that I may over identify with my client's problems to the extent that they become my problems.
_____ During a counseling session I would frequently find myself wanting to give advice.
_____ I'm afraid that I might say or do something that would greatly disturb a client.
_____ I'm concerned about counseling clients whose values are different from my own.
_____ I would be apprehensive about whether my clients liked and approved of me and whether they would want to come back.
_____ I'm concerned about being mechanical in any counseling, as though I were following a book.

Now go back and select the issues that represent your greatest concerns. You can then begin to challenge some of the assumptions behind these statements.

From *Issues and Ethics in the Helping Professions*, by G.Corey, M.S. Corey and P Callanan. Copyright © 1993, 1988, 1984, 1979 Brooks/Cole Publishing Company, Pacific Grove, CA 93950, A division of International Thomson Publishing Inc. By permission of the publisher.

The following questions may help you to begin thinking about the role of your values in your work with clients:

- Some professional consider it unethical to influence clients in specific value directions. What do you think?
- Do you worry that openly discussing your values with certain clients might unduly influence their decision-making process?
- Is it possible for therapists to interact honestly with their clients without making value judgments? Is it desirable for therapists to avoid making such judgments?
- If you were convinced that your client was making a bad decision, would you want to influence this individual to move in a different direction?
- Do you think that it is the therapist's responsibility to inform clients about a variety of value options?
- Do you have a need to see your clients adopt your beliefs and values?
- Can you remain true to yourself and at the same time allow your clients the freedom to select their own values, even if they differ sharply from yours?
- How do you determine whether a conflict between your values and those of your client necessitates a referral to another professional?
- What specific values do you consider to be essential to the therapeutic process?
- How does honestly exposing your clients to your viewpoint differ from subtly "guiding" the to accept your values?
- To what degree do you need to have had life experiences that are similar to those of your clients? Is it possible that too much similarity in values and life experiences might result in therapy that is not challenging for the client?

Your values will significantly affect your work with clients. It is incumbent on you to clarify them and the ways in which they enter the therapeutic process. Whatever your own values are, there may be many instances in which they present some difficulty for you in your work with clients. Keep the following questions in mind.

- What is my position on this issue?
- Where did I develop my views?
- Are my values open to modification?
- Have I challenged my views, and am I open to being challenged by others?
- Do I insist that the world remain the same as it was earlier in my life?
- Do I feel so deeply committed to any of my values that I'm likely to push my clients to accept them?
- How can I communicate my values to my clients without imposing those values?
- How do my own values and beliefs affect my approach to working with clients?

From *Issues and Ethics in the Helping Professions,* by G.Corey, M.S. Corey and P Callanan. Copyright © 1993, 1988, 1984, 1979 Brooks/Cole Publishing Company, Pacific Grove, CA 93950, A division of International Thomson Publishing Inc. By permission of the publisher.

RELIGION AND HOMOSEXUALITY 18.3

Take a few minutes to assess some of your values involving homosexuality and religion. In the blanks, put an "A" if you agree more than you disagree with the statement, and put a "D" if you disagree more than you agree.

_____ 1. My views on religion would influence my approach in working with clients who have homosexual concerns.

_____ 2. Regardless of what my values relating to homosexuality are, I think it would be important to disclose them to clients with homosexual concerns.

_____ 3. Knowing my own values, I think I'd be inclined to steer my clients in a definite direction rather than encouraging them to choose their own path.

_____ 4. From my viewpoint, I think that homosexuality should be discussed within the framework of religious and moral values.

_____ 5. To be honest, I think that I have some fears of openly discussing the issue of homosexuality with clients.

_____ 6. If a client said he saw himself as a "religious person" and also experienced guilt feelings because of a homosexual orientation, his religious convictions should be challenged in therapy.

_____ 7. I see guilt as a way of controlling people.

_____ 8. If I were working with a client who had decided on a homosexual lifestyle, I'd tend to be supportive of his or her choice.

_____ 9. Ethical practice in counseling with homosexual clients demands that at some point a referral be made to a therapist who is homosexual.

_____ 10. Homosexuals in this society are subjected to unfair discrimination, and they are an oppressed minority.

Look over your responses above, and attempt to clarify your own values pertaining to homosexuality. Do you think you can counsel objectively in this area? Would you be inclined to "push" your own values?

From *Issues and Ethics in the Helping Professions,* by G.Corey, M.S. Corey and P Callanan. Copyright © 1993, 1988, 1984, 1979 Brooks/Cole Publishing Company, Pacific Grove, CA 93950, A division of International Thomson Publishing Inc. By permission of the publisher.

NCC COUNSELOR CERTIFICATION PROCESS 18.4

The NBCC counselor certification process utilizes all facets of the eight content areas of the *Standards*. However, the NCE is generic in nature; it is intended to cover knowledge of counseling information and counseling skills which should be known, at least at minimum levels, by all professional counselors. Accordingly, the section of the *Standards* directly pertinent to the examination is "Section II-B-J: Program Objectives and Curriculum," which delineates eight topic areas that should be covered through various instructional experiences in the generic preparation of all professional counselors. Because it is central to the NBCC examination content (not format), the original CACREP standards merit presentation here:

1. **Human Growth and Development**—studies that provide an understanding of the nature and needs of individuals at all developmental levels.

   Studies in this area include, but are not limited to, the following:

   a. Theories of individual and family development and transitions across the life-span
   b. Theories of learning and personality development
   c. Human behavior including an understanding of developmental crises, disability, addictive behavior, psychopathology, and environmental factors as they affect both normal and abnormal behavior
   d. Strategies for facilitating development over the lifespan; and ethical considerations.

2. **Social and Cultural Foundations**—studies that provide an understanding of issues and trends in a multicultural and diverse society.

   Studies in this area include, but are not limited to, the following:

   a. Multicultural and pluralistic trends including characteristics and concerns of diverse groups
   b. Attitudes and behavior based on such factors as age, race, religious preference, physical disability, sexual orientation, ethnicity and culture, family patterns, gender, socioeconomic status, and intellectual ability
   c. Individual, family, and group strategies with diverse populations
   d. Ethical considerations

3. **Helping Relationships**—studies that provide an understanding of counseling and consultation processes.

   Studies in this area include, but are not limited to, the following:

   a. Counseling and consultation theories including both individual and systems perspectives as well as coverage of relevant research and factors considered in applications
   b. Basic interviewing, assessment, and counseling skills

c. Counselor or consultant characteristics and behaviors that influence helping processes including age, gender and ethnic differences, verbal and nonverbal behaviors and personal characteristics, traits, capabilities, and life circumstances
d. Ethical considerations.

4. **Group Work**—studies that provide an understanding of group development, dynamics, counseling theories, group counseling methods and skills, and other group work approaches.

   Studies in this area include, but are not limited to, the following:

   a. Principles of group dynamics including group process components, developmental stage theories, and group members' roles and behaviors
   b. Group leadership styles and approaches including characteristics of various types of group leaders and leadership styles
   c. Theories of group counseling including commonalities, distinguishing characteristics, and pertinent research and literature
   d. Group counseling methods including group counselor orientations and behaviors, ethical standards, appropriate selection criteria and methods, and methods of evaluation of effectiveness
   e. Approaches used for other types of group work, including task groups, prevention groups, support groups, and therapy groups
   f. Ethical considerations

5. **Career and Lifestyle Development**—studies that provide an understanding of career development and related life factors.

   Studies in this area include, but are not limited to, the following:

   a. Career development theories and decision-making models
   b. Career, avocational, educational, and labor market information resources, visual and print media, and computer-based career information systems
   c. Career development program planning, organization, implementation, administration, and evaluation
   d. Interrelationships among work, family, and other life roles and factors including multicultural and gender issues as related to career development
   e. Career and educational placement, follow-up, and evaluation
   f. Assessment instruments and techniques relevant to career planning and decision-making
   g. Computer based career development applications and strategies, including computer-assisted career guidance systems
   h. Career counseling processes, techniques and resources including those applicable to specific populations
   I. Ethical considerations

6. **Appraisal**—studies that provide an understanding of individual and group approaches to assessment and evaluation.

   Studies in this area include, but are not limited to, the following:

   a. Theoretical and historical bases for assessment techniques
   b. Validity including evidence for establishing content, construct, and empirical validity
   c. Reliability including methods of establishing stability, internal, and equivalence reliability
   d. Appraisal methods including environmental assessment, performance assessment, individual and group test and inventory methods, behavioral observations, and computer-managed and computer-assisted methods
   e. Psychometric statistics including types of assessment scores, measures of central tendency, indices of variability, standard errors, and correlations
   f. Age, gender, ethnicity, language, disability, and culture factors related to assessment and evaluation of individuals and groups
   g. Strategies for selecting, administering, interpreting, and using assessment and evaluation instruments and techniques in counseling
   h. Ethical considerations

7. **Research and Program Evaluation**—studies that provide an understanding of types of research methods, basic statistics, and ethical and legal considerations in research.

   Studies in this area include, but are not limited to, the following:

   a. Basic types of research methods to include qualitative and quantitative research designs
   b. Basic parametric and nonparametric statistics
   c. Principles, practices, and applications of needs assessment and program evaluation
   d. Uses of computers for data management and analysis
   e. Ethical and legal considerations in research

8. **Professional Orientation**—studies that provide an understanding of all aspects of professional functioning including history, roles, organizational structures, ethics, standards, and credentialing.

   Studies in this area include, but are not limited to, the following:

   a. History of the helping professions including significant factors and events
   b. Professional roles and functions including similarities and differences with other types of professionals
   c. Professional organizations, primarily ACA, its divisions, branches, and affiliate, including membership benefits, activities, services to members, and current emphases
   d. Ethical standards of the ACA and related entities, ethical and legal issues, and their applications to various professional activities (e.g., appraisal, group work)

  e. Professional preparation standards, their evolution, and current applications
  f. Professional credentialing including certification, licensure, and accreditation practices and standards, and the effects of public policy on these issues
  g. Public policy processes including the role of the professional counselor in advocating on behalf of the professional and its clientele

These eight core areas, which constitute the eight content domains covered in the National Counselor Examination for Licensure and Certification, serve as the primary theoretical basis for the examination. It is through them that the NCE is linked to accepted professional standards. Each of the eight content domains contains information relevant to the five "Work Behavior Analysis" areas.

Clusters of Work Behaviors

1. Fundamental Counseling Practices
  Counsel clients concerning personal change
  Establish counseling goals
  Assess potential for client to harm self/others
  Evaluate client's movement toward counseling goals
  Evaluate extent of client's psychological dysfunction
  Counsel adults
  Clarify counselor/client roles
  Develop comprehensive treatment plans
  Assist with client's evaluation of counseling
  Reframe client's problem
  Identify source-of-problem alternatives
  Obtain client's informed consent prior to counseling
  Counsel clients concerning life style change
  Inform client about ethical standards and practice
  Clarify client's support systems
  Assess psychosocial needs
  Systematically observe client behaviors
  Evaluate need for client referral
  Evaluate existing (precounseling) client data
  Conduct precounseling diagnostic interview
  Use "active listening" skills
  Maintain case notes, record, and/or files
  Use cognitive-oriented counseling techniques
  Self-evaluate counseling effectiveness
  Inform client about legal aspects of counseling
  Use behavioral-oriented counseling techniques
  Determine DSM-IV classification
  Analyze cost-benefit of treatment alternatives

2. **Counseling for Career Development**
    Assist client in understanding test results
    Facilitate client's development of decision-making skills
    Use test results for client decision-making
    Use interest inventories
    Evaluate client's educational preparation
    Use self-report personality inventories
    Use test/inventory results for intervention selections
    Evaluate client's occupational skills
    Use occupational information in counseling
    Provide career/vocational education
    Facilitate client's development of job search skills
    Use achievement tests
    Provide career counseling for adolescents
    Use print and other media in career counseling
    Select appraisal instruments/techniques for counseling'
    Provide career counseling for adults
    Use nontest appraisal techniques
    Use aptitude tests
    Use career resources library
    Use intelligence tests
    Use computerized career counseling resources
    Provide career counseling for persons with disabilities
    Provide career counseling for older adults
    Provide outplacement counseling
    Use computerized "counseling" software

3. **Counseling Groups**
    Assist with group members' feedback to each other
    Identify harmful group-member behaviors
    Evaluate progress toward group goals
    Resolve conflict among group members
    Self-evaluate group counseling effectiveness
    Determine group counseling termination criteria
    Inform clients of group counseling guidelines and goals
    Systematically observe group members' behavior
    Use "structured" activities during group counseling
    Use group-centered group counseling leadership techniques
    Use leader-centered group counseling leadership techniques

4. **Counseling Families**
   Counsel persons in crisis
   Counsel clients concerning substance use/abuse
   Counsel clients concerning sexual abuse
   Counsel adolescents
   Counsel concerning family member interaction
   Counsel clients concerning personality changes
   Counsel clients concerning physical abuse
   Develop family conflict resolution strategies
   Counsel concerning family change
   Clarify family counseling goals
   Clarify familial behavior norms
   Inform family members of family dynamics/roles
   Inform family members of family counseling guidelines and goals
   Clarify client's moral/spiritual issues
   Counsel concerning divorce
   Counsel children
   Counsel concerning human sexuality
   Counsel concerning divorce-conflict reduction
   Interview client's significant others
   Use behavioral family counseling techniques
   Counsel concerning marriage enrichment
   Use structural family counseling techniques
   Use strategic family counseling techniques
   Use multigenerational family counseling techniques
   Counsel concerning premarriage

5. **Professional Practice**
   Serve as a liaison with other agencies
   Provide consultation service for ethical or legal dilemmas
   Participate in case conferences
   Administer counseling program
   Conduct prevention-oriented developmental activities
   Participate in staffing decision-making processes
   Engage in professional/community public relations
   Participate in continuing education/skill enhancement
   Conduct community outreach
   Correspond orally with others to maintain professional communications
   Evaluate counselors' performance
   Establish programmatic service goals
   Read current professional literature
   Write to other professionals to maintain professional communications
   Participate in professional organization activities
   Assess programmatic needs
   Review legal statutes and regulations

- Supervise staff
- Provide counselor skill-development training
- Review ethical standards
- Provide consultation services for interpersonal skills training
- Provide consultation services for human relationships development
- Provide consultation services for human resource needs evaluation
- Engage in formative evaluation of counseling program
- Engage in summative evaluation of counseling program
- Supervise counselor trainees
- Provide consultation services for professional skill development
- Prepare developmental/preventative media
- Develop program-related reports
- Allocate financial resources for counseling program
- Conduct self-development training for nonclients
- Provide consultation services for organizational development
- Provide multicultural training/education
- Use computer for program data management
- Engage in data analyses
- Write communication for noncounseling, professional activities
- Collaborate in research with other professionals
- Engage in counseling outcome research
- Engage in counseling process research
- Write for publication
- Provide career counseling for children
- Develop appraisal instrument/technique
- Engage in field/observational research
- Evaluate computer software
- Conduct fund-raising activities for program development/maintenance
- Engage in experimental /laboratory research

This Preparation Guide was developed by the National Board for Certified Counselors, Inc. to provide information to professional counselors who plan to participate in the National Counselor Examination for Licensure and Certification. The purpose of this booklet is to assist professional counselors to develop their best respective individual approaches to preparation for taking the NCE. However, enhanced performance on the NCE because of or through the use of this booklet is neither expressed nor implied by NBCC.

Copyright © 1995 by the National Board for Certified Counselors, Inc.

Reprinted by permission

RESOURCES

General

Area Progressive Directory. California Coalition for **Ethical Mental Health Care (CCEMHC)**
--http://www.emf.net/~cheethan/gcare-1.html

Ethical Issues In Mental Health Research With Children and Adolescents
Ethical Issues In Mental Health Research With Children and Adolescents
--http://www.erlbaum.com/1477.htm

Special Issue: *Mental Health in the Age of Managed Care.* Feature Articles. Managed Care in Mental Health: The Ethical Issues
--http://www.projhope.org/HA/archive/fall95.htm

Directory: Psychology and Psychiatry. Discussion Name: CURRENT-ISSUES-IN-PSYCH. Topic: The forum aims to foster discussion of a variety of topics...
--http://www.n2h2.com/KOVACES/CD/2956.html

Ethics. An up-to-date look at the NASW Code of Ethics; a comparison of the Texas CSW Code; the LPC Codes and the AAMCF Code of Ethics.
--http://dali.uta.edu/utaced/humsvcs/ethics.htm

HEALTH CARE. Patient Care
Medical/Ethical Issues. Advising our acute and mental health hospital and nursing home clients on a full range of medical-legal issues.
--http://www.kelleydrye.com/healthpa.htm

Appendix. ETHICAL ISSUES IN CLINICAL RESEARCH: ANSWERS an explanation of the study. The procedures to be followed and their purposes.
--http://nursing.ucalgary.ca/Nursing539/uniteight/appendix.html

Ethics, Malpractice, and Damage Control. This one-day course addresses the multiple legal and ethical issues involved in professional mental health...
--http://dali.uta.edu/utaced/humsvcs/dmgctrl.htm

Media

CENTER FOR HEALTHCARE ETHICS
A Service of St. Joseph Health System
Center For Healthcare Ethics
P.O. Box 14132
Orange, CA 92863-1352
Voice: (714) 997-7690
Fax: (714) 997-7907
E-mail address: ethics@corp.stjoe.org

The center's new video was developed for ethics committees as well as staff throughout the institution. *Improving Communication: Helping Patients Ask Questions* (8 minutes) suggests why ethics committees should—and how they can—help patients become more active and vocal in their own care. Includes suggested educational uses for the video and a sample brochure for patients. $25 ($20 for Center members). CA residents pay 7.25% sales tax. Shipping/handling: $3/one video; $5 two or more videos. Send order to:
Center for Healthcare Ethics
P.O. Box 14132
Orange CA 92863-1532
(714) 997-7690

AIDS and Ethics Committees. A 1991 video in which Judith Wilson Ross, MA discusses the effects of the AIDS crisis on health care and suggests ways in which ethics committees can assist in educating health care professionals about AIDS. (15 minutes) [Item Number V101]

11 Moral Lessons from Oregon for National Health Care $25 A 1995 video in which Leonard Fleck of Michigan State University discusses eleven moral lessons we should learn from Oregon's efforts as we face national health care reform. (19 minutes) [Item Number V107]

Ethical Perceptions of Men and Women: Are They Different? A 1991 video in which John Golenski discusses how gender differences affect communication, interpersonal relationships, and the ethical decision-making process. (11 minutes) [Item Number V108]

Ethics Committee Case Consultation A conversation with Judith Wilson Ross and Corrine Bayley about case consultation by ethics committees. What are the major components of a case consultation? How can the committee assure that these key elements are adequately addressed? What should be avoided? How does this function fit into the larger mission of the committee? (20 minutes) [Item Number V110]

Evaluating Your Ethics Committee Jack Glaser, Center Director, discusses the importance of and methods for evaluating your ethics committee on an ongoing basis. Glaser emphasizes that evaluation should flow from the committee's self-definition. A video worksheet to help define and evaluate the committee is included. (17 minutes) [Item Number V113]

Confidentiality This valuable video was designed to aid therapists in anticipating problems and developing sound judgment concerning the maintenance of confidentiality. Detailing ethical and legal issues, the video presents vignettes of situations in which confidentiality issues may arise. It explains what kinds of responses are appropriate when one's requested to reveal confidential information. (45 minutes)

Ethics and Social Science Professionals This program provides a framework for analyzing the ethical issues commonly faced by social scientists. Among the issues raised are imposing one's values on a client and incorporating professional-client models into one's practice. (30 minutes)

For additional video resource materials, please contact your Allyn & Bacon representative.

Nietzel et al., *Abnormal Psychology*, Transparencies

Chapter Eighteen

	Text Figure Number	Text Page Number
80. An Integrated System of Care for the Mentally Ill Who Are Homeless	18.2	622

NOTES

NOTES

NOTES

NOTES